EVERYBODY'S BUSINESS

By the Same Author

EVERYBODY'S BUSINESS

BY

HARTLEY WITHERS

CITY EDITOR OF 'THE TIMES,' 1906–10;
EDITOR OF THE 'ECONOMIST,' 1916–22

JONATHAN CAPE
THIRTY BEDFORD SQUARE
LONDON

FIRST PUBLISHED 1931

JONATHAN CAPE LTD., 30 BEDFORD SQUARE, LONDON
AND 91 WELLINGTON STREET WEST, TORONTO
JONATHAN CAPE & HARRISON SMITH INC.
139 EAST 46TH STREET, NEW YORK

PRINTED IN GREAT BRITAIN BY J. AND J. GRAY, EDINBURGH
PAPER SUPPLIED BY JOHN DICKINSON AND CO. LTD.
BOUND BY A. W. BAIN AND CO. LTD.

CONTENTS

5

CONTENTS

6

CONTENTS

CONTENTS

8

CONTENTS

9

CONTENTS

PREFACE

One excuse for a preface is that it goes to press last, and so gives the writer a chance of coming up to date, sorely needed in times such as these. This book was finished at the beginning of June and I write this preface, which ought to be called a postscript, at the beginning of August. In the meantime the world's affairs have gone from bad to worse and from worse to so bad that there looks like a chance of improvement.

Political bad temper and the lack of confidence caused by it and the consequent failure of mankind to enjoy a great and increasing store of wealth, are a theme that recurs with 'damnable iteration,' throughout the following pages. In the last two months these influences have worked with terrible effect. From an international capital market dried up by lack of confidence, we have proceeded to a run on Germany, mainly political in origin, in the course of which foreign creditors, by calling in money lent, reduced Germany to the verge of bankruptcy, while the process was assisted by Germans through a flight from the mark.

But there is another side to the picture. On a later page I have suggested that what the nations need is a modern Peter the Hermit to teach them to behave decently to one another. Recent events seem to show that this preacher has been found, and that his name is Fear. Mr. Hoover's proposal, to suspend Governmental debt payments, was a highly courageous action, since it asked American tax-payers, faced by a deficit of £180,000,000, to sacrifice some £50,000,000 of revenue; but he would hardly have called on his countrymen to make this sacrifice for Europe's sake if he had not been convinced that they would suffer much more heavily unless something was done to save Europe from bankruptcy.

It is true that his proposal, though hailed with almost general approval and relief, was so long in being accepted by France, owing to very natural hesitations and objections from her point of view, that much of its first effect was lost, and the run on Germany continued and the London conference merely handed the problem, which is chiefly political, back to the bankers, who were doing more than their best already. But every one knows that much more will have to be done in the direction of political co-operation. Mr. Hoover has sounded a reveille. How will the nations answer his bugle-call?

HARTLEY WITHERS

DANBURY
6th August 1931

CHAPTER I

WHY EVERYBODY'S

The Great Machine in Which we Work – Our Difficulties and Discontents – The Typist's Cup of Tea – How it is produced for Her – The Need for Sense and Good Temper – Our Heritage – Its Possibilities and Dangers – What this Book sets out to show.

IT is everybody's business to know something about how we all get our livings, why certain kinds of work are more highly paid than others, why it is so difficult for many of us to get as good a living as we should like to have, how these difficulties are being removed, and how they might be removed much more quickly, if we all set about their removal more sensibly and with better temper; and how great are the dangers that threaten the smooth working of the whole machine, if we fail to apply this necessary sense and good temper.

Misunderstanding and bad temper, between nations, between classes and between individuals, have made the pace of our material progress much slower than it ought to have been, if we had taken full advantage of all the discoveries that science and invention have made for us; and misunderstanding and bad temper are the chief causes of the crisis – so absurd if it were not so tragical – in which the world is now struggling, because all the things that it wants are too plentiful and cheap. And we all of us make

B

matters worse by thinking more about the things that we should like to have, than about the immense range of comforts that the poorest of us enjoy, and the marvels of the machine of world trade that turns out these comforts for us from its farms and mines and factories and shops.

When a typist goes into a shop for a cup of tea she draws, with her two pennies, on the work of this great machine; and it, with the help of several continents and climates and most of the sciences, industries and ingenuities that man has devised through many centuries, delivers her cup of tea.

If she is gifted with a roving fancy she may sometimes think of the tea gardens in India and China and of the coolies who have sweated to clear the ground and plant the trees and pluck the leaves, and perhaps also of the ship that has brought the tea to her own country. But she cannot be aware of a tithe of the processes and activities that had to be set to work before her want could be satisfied. But it is owing to these activities and the work of hundreds of people who are beyond her ken that her standard of comfort – in this matter of cheap and easy tea-drinking – is higher than that of an eighteenth-century duchess.

For her behoof Puffing Billy was started puffing, railways were built, with the labour and inventive power of all who have given us iron and steel, out of the capital of all the stockholders who found, out of the proceeds of many different kinds of work, the money for laying the lines and building the rolling stock and setting the engineers to plan and survey; forests were felled to provide wood for sleepers and coal mines had to find the fuel; and companies had to be formed and stocks dealt in and newspapers had to be created to chronicle their movements. And a much longer tale of skill and daring and bitter combat against storm and sea had to be told before the ship could be built that brought her tea ashore. Thousands of sailors had to be wrecked and drowned in the course of the battle with Nature that sea-borne trade involves. Iron and steel and coal and wood were needed again, and the compass and the boilers, and the steering gear and the skipper and the engineers and the stokers and the fo'c'sle hands and the man who invented the foghorn and the Lloyds underwriters and their clerks who insured the ship and the shareholders and managers and clerks and workers of the company that built her, and a fresh set of active members of the company that owned her, and for each company a multitude of investors who found the capital.

There had to be docks and harbours and engineers to plan and build them, and dredgers to keep them clear and pilots and port officers and stevedores and dock workers and (until tea was put on the free list) customs officials to see that the duty was paid so that a fraction of our typist's payment should be used to pay for the country's government and defence, or to provide unemployment pay for those who are unlucky enough to be out of a job.

And when the tea had come to port, there had to be merchants and their clerks to deal in it and a warehouse to stow it in and carriers to take it (probably in a lorry needing petrol, from America or Venezuela or Persia) to the shop where it is treated with water boiled, perhaps, by means of electrically generated heat, to create which another army of inventors and workers and managers and investors has had to be busy. And when the tea was made, there had to be a host of nimble damsels ready to distribute it to the shop's customers.

Besides all these people who had to work before the tea could be grown and carried and put into the cup (we must not forget all the invention and science and labour needed for the making of the teapot and the cup) there are also hosts who had to think and plan and invent and work so that the milk and sugar should be handy.

And even if we had enough knowledge and imagination to think of all the work that has been necessary before the ingredients of a cup of tea can be assembled and put before the customer, we still have to remember that all these movements of production and trade have to be financed. Besides all the investors who have supplied capital for the many companies that have been concerned in this job (including, probably, one that owns the teashop itself), the shipment of the tea from grower to consumer has been covered by mysterious things like letters of credit granted by banks, which also had to be organized and managed by busy officials and clerks, and bills of exchange discounted by bill-brokers. The whole monetary machine, itself a monument of ingenuity that keeps a horde of workers and critics busy, had to help. And when it is added that the tea would certainly not have been so cheap, if it had arrived at all, without armies and navies and police to provide security and peace, and keep the sea clear of pirates, we open up another immense horizon of work that had to be done for the refreshment of this fortunate lady.

It is very likely that she may not see that she is fortunate at all. She may retort that in spite of all these wonders that have been done for her, she finds life in many ways a dreary business. She does not see why she should not be as well off as the people whom she sees portrayed in the newspapers as being presented at Court or enjoying themselves at race meetings and garden parties. She may think that getting a living is cruelly difficult nowadays and that most of the people who somehow succeed in doing so, do not get nearly as much fun out of life as they might if things were better arranged.

In fact, according to the calculations of that great statistician Sir Josiah Stamp, we are all just about four times as well off as were our forefathers and foremothers a hundred years ago.[1] Unfortunately we most of us know nothing about how they lived and we know all about how we live. And so we look at the evils and injustices of to-day instead of thinking of the immense improvements that science and enterprise have wrought in providing us with material comforts.

In the example of the typist and her cup of tea we saw a worker exchanging a fraction of her weekly earnings into a grateful stimulant, to produce which and put it into her cup hundreds and perhaps thousands of people had worked in the remote and recent past. To the extent of her twopence she was the heiress of the ages that have built up the world as farm, mine.

---

[1] *Wealth and Taxable Capacity*, by Sir J. Stamp, p. 94.

21

factory and shop. We all share this mighty heritage to the extent of the income that we enjoy by our own or somebody else's exertions. Some are born with silver spoons in their mouths and inherit large incomes made by work of some kind done, or service of some kind rendered, by some ancestor or benefactor who has left it to them. Boys and girls who are not old enough to work for themselves are supplied with a living by their parents or by somebody else who works for them or has inherited the fruits of somebody's work. Some of us have left off working and are living on pensions paid to us by the firm or company that employed us or annuities bought out of our own savings from an insurance company. And others who have not been able to find or keep a job that will give them a living, are provided with one by the State out of taxes that it collects from other people, who provide it out of the proceeds of work. In whatever way the living is got, it is finally a question of the exchange of one kind of work for another.

At present, owing to the violent jolts that have lately been inflicted on this system of work and exchange of work, most of our livings are a good deal less certain than they used to be. Those that come by inheritance are criticized by some reforming spirits as an injustice and are subjected in England to taxation so severe that the business of leaving a great accumulation of wealth to one's descendants is now a most expensive luxury. Those that come by work done to-day are threatened by the miracles of mechanical invention that are always harnessing more machines to do things that used to be done by human effort – not only such machines as work in fields and factories and have displaced the old spinners and weavers and hay-makers, but also those amazing devices that can add up and calculate and play music and sing and talk to us and teach us when once a voice has been put into them. Such inventions ought to make life easier for most of us, and will do so, when once things have been better arranged. At present they make it more difficult for many of us to earn a living.

And even when we have done our life's job and earned or saved our pension we are not as secure as we may be inclined to think. We are sure to receive so much money, but if there is a great rise in the price of the things that we want to buy, the real value of the pension may be halved or even wiped out alto-gether. This actually happened in Germany, Russia and other countries after the war; and even in America and England the rise in the cost of living since the war has made a great difference to those who have to live on fixed incomes.

These things happen when a great deal of new money is created, because Governments want money and do not want to impose more taxes, and so get banks to print notes for them; or, as has sometimes happened in the past, because great masses of gold are discovered underground. If a great deal of new money is created or found, and there is no corresponding increase in the amount of things to be bought, it takes more money to buy goods and prices rise. This danger hits, besides the pensioner, the owner of inherited wealth if, as is likely, the amount of his income is a fixed sum. In Russia and Austria and Germany the

23

rentier class, living on fixed money incomes from Government securities and other kinds of debts, was wiped out because the money due to them was made worthless by this process which is now commonly called 'inflation,' when their Governments worked the printing press too hard.

By the energy and enterprise of our forebears, working the discoveries of science, the world has been harnessed to provide us with an ever-growing flood of material comforts. And yet most of us are more than ever dissatisfied, chiefly because we think more about what others have and we have not, than about what we have; and so we find life hard because we make it so by thinking about it in the wrong way.

To get out of this bad habit, it may help us if we get a clearer notion as to:

(1) why some people get big rewards for doing jobs that look easy to those who have not tried them, or for doing nothing at all;

(2) whether the big rewards that some people get do the rest of us any harm;

(3) how the nations work and trade together to provide us with goods and comforts; and

(4) what are the difficulties that obstruct, and have lately obstructed with special violence, the effectiveness of this working and trading.

To give clearer notions on these points, to those who are not accustomed to thinking about them, is the object of this book.

CHAPTER II

WORK AND REWARD

What is Meant by Work? – Should we Avoid it as far as Possible? –
Most of it Pleasant – In Itself or by Producing Companionship –
Difficulties of Leisure – Anomalies of Reward – Why they Exist –
The Price of Responsibility – Their Tendency to Diminish.

WORK is defined by the *Concise Oxford Dictionary* as
'expenditure of energy, striving, application of effort
to some purpose.' In this wide sense the word would
evidently cover such amusements and pleasures as
swinging oneself in a hammock or chewing one's
dinner; and the distinction between work and play is
often a very dim and wavy line. In the Oxonian sense
all play is work; and to those happy people who love
their work and would rather do it than anything else,
all work is play.

For our present purpose it is necessary to get a
narrower definition. We come close to what is generally
meant by work when we say that it is what one does
in order to earn money. This definition is unsatis-
factory because it leaves out the immense amount of
unpaid effort that is contributed for the common good
by public-spirited folk who sit on Committees and
do other kinds of dreary jobs from a sense of duty;
and also it omits the still more important tasks – perhaps the most important of all that are done in the

world – of millions of women who manage our households and see that our food is good and our houses are clean and bright, and do all these difficult and harassing things just because they are wives and mothers – or sometimes sisters or daughters – and not for any salary or wage that is paid them as such.

Nevertheless this definition is the nearest we can get for our present purpose, which is to trace the connection between what we put into the common pool and what we take out of it. We put into the pool by helping to grow or make something, or to render some service, that others want, and we take out of it when we spend the money that we get for doing this job.

It is generally supposed that when we approach this question of working for our livings we should aim at doing as little work as possible for the largest possible reward; and that this is what most of us do. In his *Elementary Political Economy*, for example, Professor Cannan tells us that 'every nation, as well as every individual, should endeavour to attain wealth with as little labour as possible.' This doctrine, of course, is perfectly true, if labour – or work as I prefer to call it, because labour is now often used of manual work only – is a tiresome nuisance that everybody wants to avoid. But in fact some kind of activity or effort or motion is necessary for most of us, if we want to escape being hopelessly bored. Very few people really like sitting still and doing nothing; and it is a pathetic fact that a very large number of us find it extremely difficult to amuse our leisure in the intervals of work.

I have already referred to those happy people who love their work and would rather do it than anything

else; and when you think the matter out you will
see that there are far more of these than would generally be supposed. Artists using every possible moment
in designing, painting, drawing or carving, and
musicians never really happy unless they are studying
or producing harmonious (or perhaps discordant)
noises, are obvious examples of those to whom the
work is the joy of life and the reward, if it comes, is a
minor detail, welcome only as a sign that the work
has been liked by others. But a great many other kinds
of work convey this sort of satisfaction to those who
carry them out. Could any joy be more thrilling than
that of the great Dumas when he was creating Chicot
and the Three Musketeers, and covering his pages
with their bold devices and glorious actions? And
even those writers who devote themselves to the darker
and more sordid aspects of life may probably get a
great deal of pleasure from showing us what a nasty
set of creatures we all are.

And besides these creative artists, the recorders and
interpreters of history and thought must find extraordinary joy in their work. Macaulay must have
chuckled over some particularly well-balanced sentence in every page of his history and essays; and how
serene was the satisfaction of Mr. Lytton Strachey,
when he put the Eminent Victorians in what he
thought was their right place!

That men of science love their work is as well known
as their general indifference to the extent of its reward
in money or even in fame and reputation; and even
men of business, who are usually supposed to be so
sordid in outlook, are often far more interested in their

jobs than in anything else. They, it is true, usually want all the reward that they can get, but that is chiefly because the money earned is the tangible sign of success; as is well known, they often lead extremely simple lives in the matter of personal enjoyment, and are rather bored than thrilled by all the lavish display in which the successful business man is expected to indulge.

To all these folk work is not a tiresome nuisance to be avoided as far as possible, but the chief salt of life; and those who enjoy it are often tempted to devote themselves to it to the neglect of other interests and of other activities.

But, it may quite rightly be objected, these examples have all been chosen from the head and brain workers and from the successful among those. Is work also the salt of life to those on the lower rungs of the ladder who spend all their working lives on uninteresting drudgery, professional or manual?

To such as these it would be absurd to contend that their work brings anything like the same thrill as it does to those who succeed. Nevertheless even to the humbler members of the professions – doctors going their daily round with the cheery word that really does the healing, teachers putting a sense of the 'decent thing to do' into ever fresh generations of boys and girls, lawyers keeping their clients out of the law courts – the feeling of a useful job done as well as they can do it is often the best thing that they get out of life.

When we come to the salaried and wage-earning classes it would seem at first sight that to most of them, especially in these days of specialization and mechanization, the daily task must be a dreary business. There are, of course, exceptions, namely, those who are still craftsmen, such as carpenters, gardeners, farm workers and the host of mechanics who still do varied work such as the repairing jobs in garages. I know a carpenter who goes on carpentering at his home in the evenings because he had much rather carpenter than do anything else. And in all our country villages we see cottage gardens ablaze with flowers grown, in their leisure, by gardeners and farm workers just because making things grow is what interests them most.

But even occupations that do not appear to be attractive in themselves seem to exercise some sort of fascination over those who practise them – witness the preference of miners for their job and the persistence with which their sons follow their fathers underground. A bank clerk in a quite subordinate position lately told me that he was not at all looking forward to the day, then approaching, when he would be due to retire from what looked like a purely mechanical and un-interesting job. He had, he told me, come to look on the bank as a club, where he spent the pleasantest part of his life.

This is probably the reason why so many people like work that looks dull and uninteresting. It is not the work that they like, but the fact that the work brings them companionship. We are so gregarious and sociable that we are happier when we are crowded with a number of others into a big office or factory, to check passbooks, type letters or mind looms, than when we are told that we may stay at home and amuse ourselves. 'Sunday is a difficult day,' said a friend of mine many years ago. 'I'm always glad to be off to the office on Mondays.' At the office he did a very small business as a half-commission stockbroker, and in his home he lived apparently quite happily with a very pleasant wife. But the office, with all the gossip and cheery banter that enlivens stock exchange society even in the gloomiest times, was where he fain would be. But this was long ago, before motor cars were cheap or the wireless miracle had relieved the dullest homes from their deadliest monotony. The problem of spending leisure has been greatly simplified since then.

It still remains, however, and, as we shall see, it might, if the problem of work were more sensibly and good temperedly dealt with, be the most important problem of the future. We have yet to learn to 'fleet the time carelessly as they did in the golden world.' In the meantime, there are these two facts which make us accept with caution the doctrine that work is a thing to be avoided as far as possible:

(1) that a very large number of people like their work, and a still very much larger number like the companionship and society and friendships that work brings with it; and

(2) that the use of leisure is difficult, because a pathetically small number of us have the knack of amusing ourselves, and the amusements provided for us by others, though much cheaper and more plentiful than they used to be, cost something, and are not so satisfying as those that we make for ourselves.

When we come to the reward of work we are faced, at first sight, by a tissue of anomalies and absurdities. All the nice, pleasant, clean and apparently easy jobs are rewarded with high fees or salaries, while those who do the dull, dirty and laborious work take, as a general rule, the smallest shares out of the common pool. Moreover, a certain number of people take enormous shares out of the pool, and, apparently, put nothing into it. All that they have done, as Beaumarchais said of the French marquis, is to 'take the trouble of being born' in a position from which they are relieved from all need to do anything, except enjoy the fruits of other people's work, which they command by means of huge inherited incomes. These are not the kind of arrangements that many of us would have made, if we had been planning an ideal commonwealth.

But we live, not in an ideal commonwealth but in a workaday world. For its efficient working and steady improvement it is essential to secure the services of people who have certain qualities which most of us lack, and, as things are, such people have to be paid well for providing them. As a general rule those who have the well-paid jobs possess driving power, a faculty of decision and readiness to take responsibility. Their work, which looks so pleasant and easy to those who have never tried it, involves harassing anxieties which are avoided by those who do the more mechanical jobs. And the decisions that they have to take in their stride as they bustle over their daily hurdle race involve qualities of confidence and courage that are comparatively rare. I have been told that those who decide about the promotions in the big business organizations, which in these days have so many responsible jobs to fill, are often surprised by the lack of ambition shown by many members of the rank and file of their staffs. Up to a certain point promotion is competed for eagerly, but when real responsibility and decision are called for, there are many, otherwise apparently qualified, who lack the necessary stiff upper lip and prefer moderate pay and position and an easy mind free of anxiety.

As to the big prizes of business enterprise, it is true that many of them are due to flukes and that luck is as evident in their distribution as in the other fields in which fickle Fortune amuses herself with her freaks and caprices; but we shall see that they have, under present conditions, this all-important justification, that they are the carrot that is dangled before the donkey who keeps all the wheels of the big machine running. The organizer, enterpriser, undertaker or adventurer is the one person in the whole community who can least be spared, because, as things are, progress in business matters depends on him. He takes the big responsibilities and runs the big risks. We must be very careful how we cut down the size of the carrot, enormous though it sometimes is, that makes this patient animal plod through his life of anxiety and stress. And there is less need to try to diminish the dimensions of the carrot, because we shall see later that the patient animal cannot munch more than a small part of it itself, but has to pass most of it on to the rest of us, in return for services rendered. This being so, the best way to deal with the anomalies in our system of rewards is to raise those given to the

32

toilers who do the dull and tedious work. And this is happening. The big difference in extent between the rewards of the drudgery jobs and of those that look pleasanter and easier has lately been greatly reduced and seems likely to be reduced still further. Already in the United States the income of a mechanic is sometimes above that of a fairly successful professional worker. During the war all our old ideas about the value and scarcity of certain kinds of work were very violently shaken. Moreover, modern business, organizing itself on a great scale, has to find a public that can and will buy, on an equally great scale, a mass of cheaply produced articles.

Consequently, it suits Big Business better that there should be a great crowd of folk with a reasonable amount to spend on the general necessaries and comforts of life than that there should be a small number of well-to-do people who buy, fastidiously and expensively, artistically fashioned articles. This prospect may shock those who think that beauty and good taste are the most precious things in life, and matter much more than widely diffused comfort enjoyed by an undiscriminating public. And there might be good reason for the judicious to grieve if it seemed at all likely that mass production was going to drive all other forms of production off the field. But there is good reason to hope that along with mass production, turning out standardized articles, cheap and plentiful, for those who want them, there may also be ample scope for the artistic worker and a growing number of customers for his products.

For the moment, however, the point that concerns

us is that employers, at least in America, have at last recognized that a high level of wages and salaries, giving plentiful buying power to an immense multitude, is essential to the profitable conduct of industry on a great scale. For eight years before the collapse of 1929 America showed the world the unique spectacle of a country in which high wages, high salaries, big profits, low costs of production and low prices of commodities were all enjoyed together in a whirlwind of prosperity. The whirlwind had an unhappy ending; but the prosperity had surely taught industrialists of all countries a lesson. And while enlightened self-interest is thus awakening to the fact that high pay for those who do the dull and mechanical work is conducive to high profits for employers and shareholders, at the same time the wider spread of education is diminishing the scarcity value of a tutored brain. Already in Germany, America and England and other countries that are setting the pace in the matter of teaching their citizens, it is nearly true to say that no one need lack education who shows any power of being able to make good use of it.

Graduated taxation, designed to make those who get most out of society pay a larger proportion of their receipts towards the expenses of government, is now generally recognised as fair and is being applied to an increasing extent – an extent which, as we shall see, carries certain dangers with it. It, however, by falling chiefly on those who have an income that gives them a surplus above what is required to buy the necessaries and decencies of life, also tends to reduce the net reward of those whose reward is on the higher scale.

So we see the enlightened employer, the teacher and the tax-gatherer all working to help the earners of wages and salaries to achieve their claim for a larger relative share out of the common pool. That this result should be secured is evidently desirable on every ground, national and human. It may still be true that no levelling up of incomes will ever secure anything like real equality of standard, because it is at least as important to know how to use money as to get it. But a great increase of wealth, better diffused among all classes, giving a chance of life and leisure to those who, so far, have enjoyed little of either, will give us more profitable trade and a more stable society and wipe out much of the bitterness that makes so many reformers churn the milk of human kindness into venom.

It will also be much pleasanter for the members of those classes that are at present comparatively comfortable. All of us who have seldom known what it is to want a good meal will surely be able to enjoy the good fortune that is ours much better, if we are no longer haunted by the knowledge that millions of people have never had a chance of a hearty pull at life's beaker. As things are, it is only those who are either ignorant or selfish that can find much satisfaction in the way in which work and its rewards are arranged.

Of the extent to which it is influenced by flukes and accidents anyone who has seen much of it must be well aware. We choose our job, or are shoved into it by somebody else, generally at a time of life when it is much too soon to know what sort of work we are good

35

for; and if we happen to draw a lucky number and succeed in life, it is likely that the smile of fortune has had
a good deal to do with our success. And even if we
have forced our way through by sheer determination
and ability, it is important to remember that we could
not have done it if the rest of the community had not
been there to provide us with the opportunity and the
material to work on. The old charge brought against
landlords, that they get rents out of their tenants
merely because an increasing number of people want
ground to build houses and offices and factories on,
applies, in a modified degree, to all the earners of big
rewards. The King's Counsel could not earn his
thousands a year unless the public wanted to settle
their disputes in the courts; the fashionable doctor
would cultivate a bedside manner in vain if there were
no patients to beguile, and even captains of industry
would find it difficult to produce a good profit and loss
account after a year spent in solitude on a desert island.

'That may be so,' the successful ones will probably
observe, 'but all those other fellows whom we have
left behind were surrounded by the same opportunities
and had the same materials to work on.' But this is
not quite true, because we do not all start even. It is
much easier for those who have been born in the right
sort of position and been to the right sort of school to
win through to success.

Moreover, though no one wants to belittle the effort
of ability and energy, the finest ability and the most
tireless energy could take nothing out of the common
pool if the pool were not there to be divided. Like the
typist in the teashop they have the energy of all the

working world to draw on to the extent of the contribution that they make. Their contribution may be Titanic, but it would not have produced much result if the great machine had not been working for them and with them.

From which it follows that even those whose success seems to be most entirely personal and individual are deeply concerned with the whole world's progress towards increasing the common store of good things and pleasant enjoyments out of which we are all supplied. Our work may be the chief means of earning material reward for ourselves, but the second and immensely important means is the furtherance of the common welfare. If our work is to be well rewarded, a great growth is needed in the fund of goods and services out of which all reward has to come; and we have none of us done our best for ourselves if we have neglected any opportunity of oiling the great machine at which all the rest of the world is working.

At the same time those eager reformers who want to take short cuts to a better world in which reward is more evenly distributed, will do well to beware lest the experiments that they propose might not seriously lessen the growth of the common fund. If more evenness meant all-round diminution, it would not make for general comfort, and the pleasanter life for all that we want to secure.

CHAPTER III

THE WAGE-EARNERS

Increasing Numbers, Decreasing Demand against Them – For
them, Growth of Trade, Organization in Unions, Political Power –
Mass Production needs High Wages to Secure Mass Consumption –
Adam Smith on Employers – Mr. Ford on High Wages – Strikes
and Strife – Early Factory Conditions – High Wages and British
Industry – The Employers' Difficulties – The Wage-earners' Case
– Lord Weir's Evidence – England's Handicap – High Wages for
Good Work – Improvement Secured.

THIS problem of the reward of those who do the manual,
mechanical and uninteresting work is evidently the
door through which, if it can be successfully thrown
wide open, mankind will win its way to that Greatest
Happiness of the Greatest Number that most of us
want to achieve – in so far as happiness can be got
through a better share of the world's wealth. Work
for everybody at a good reward that will rise as the
world's productive power grows, and plenty of leisure
that will increase as machinery continues to relieve
human effort by doing jobs that used to need brawn
and muscle and sweat – if we can secure these things,
which we can do if we set the machine to work in the
right way, we shall have gone far to wipe out most
of the worst blots on our material civilization.

By saying that 'labour is the real measure of the
exchangeable value of all commodities,' Adam Smith

38

unwittingly set in train a process of mistaken argument and false conclusion that has wrought untold mischief. It has been assumed that when he spoke of labour he meant manual labour only, and his words have been twisted into a theory that the only thing which gives value to an article of commerce is the amount of manual labour that has been put into it, and that consequently the manual worker was the only party that had any just claim to any part of the product, or of the money fetched by the sale of it. Whereas in fact, misdirected labour, as has been shown by countless examples, may easily be devoted to the production of articles for which there is no demand; and such articles, from the business point of view, have no value whatever. The directing mind, which thinks and plans and dares and guides the efforts of the rank and file into making things that will find a market because they will be wanted by the buying public, is essential to the production of valuable articles; and another essential is the equipment in the shape of tools and machinery that are provided by those who lend money to enterprise and are called capitalists.

Ricardo was another great economist who left us a legacy of muddle, because his readers have misunderstood what he meant by labour, when he said that 'the value of a commodity . . . depends on the relative quantity of labour which is necessary for its production.' But the muddle has been to a certain extent corrected by a very earnest Socialist, who is now (in 1931) Prime Minister of England in a Labour Government.

'The Ricardian dictum,' says Mr. Ramsay Mac-Donald in his book on *The Socialist Movement*, 'that all wealth is created by labour is not exactly true. It carries one much further than the statement which is true – that no wealth can be created without the service of labour. But there is much wealth which labour cannot create without the aid of capital. A man can go into the forest and tear boughs off trees with his hands for his fires, but he cannot fell trees without an axe of some kind, which is capital.'

Nowadays the manual worker works less and less with his or her hands and muscles and is more and more a machine minder. Out of their ranks there is a constant movement, owing to the progress of education, into those of the clerkly workers, who keep books and type letters and so on, and the shop assistants. There is still some outward distinction between those who work in overalls and those who dress neatly for their jobs; but all these folk who carry out orders and are not expected to exercise judgment or discrimination have interests more or less in common.

According to the 'law of supply and demand' which tells us that what is more plentiful and less wanted tends to be cheap, their relative claim to a share in the pool might be expected to diminish, because they increase in numbers more quickly than other classes, while the development of machinery continually reduces the need for the purely manual workers in factories and on the farms; and even those qualified for clerkly work find that mechanical inventions such as typewriters, dictaphones and calculating machines reduce the need for human effort in this field. Moreover, the 'rationalization' process in industry and commerce tends to enlarge the companies that do the work of making and carrying and selling by the concentration of small units into huge organizations; and so it reduces the need for clerical workers by eliminating a number of small businesses, each employing its own staff for correspondence and book-keeping, and joining them into one great whole which does a larger trade with a smaller number of hands.

These influences make it difficult for the rank and file to improve or maintain their standard, but there are other ones which work vigorously on their side. The most sound and satisfactory of these is, or ought to be, the growth of trade and production and the consequent expanding need for rank and file work, a need that should be urgent enough to absorb those whom the improvement of machinery and the progress of rationalization sets free to look for new jobs. When machinery was first introduced and the manual workers displaced by it rather naturally expressed their feelings about it by smashing it when they got a chance, they were lectured, by comfortable folk who had not quite the same point of view, for lack of foresight and intelligence; they were told that the machines that they wanted to smash would bring with them such a growth of production and wealth that all those displaced by them, and a great many more, would soon find fresh work to do and be paid a good deal better for it.

In the broad sense of this prophecy it came true, though some of those who had special manual skill must have gone through hard times before they could adapt themselves to the new conditions; and it is possible that the same optimistic assurance might be equally correct to-day if trade and production were given free elbow-room for expansion. Unfortunately the world's business arrangements have got into an uncomfortable tangle and the demand for more hands, through expansion of industries and the creation of new ones, is no longer nearly as effective as it was.

It seems to have worked quite adequately in America in the years of prosperity that culminated in 1929. But unfortunately America, though most lavish and thorough in giving us the figures and records of most of the aspects of her business activity, has hitherto told us nothing about this matter of unemployment because there were practically no official records. So far she has not found it necessary to make provision for it out of the federal taxes and so definite light on this most important matter fails us from the country which gives us more statistical information than any other. Fortunately, America is now working hard to find out the facts about the unemployed in her own area, who were estimated to number approximately eight million in February 1931, according to the New York correspondent of the *Economist*.[1]

In England, as we all know, the process of reabsorption has failed to the extent of leaving us with more than two and a half millions of unemployed. This may be partly due to the check to emigration. The United States Department of Commerce, in an industrial, commercial and financial handbook entitled *The United Kingdom*, compiled by Mr. Hugh Butler and others, points out that 'if the rate of emigration shown in 1912 and 1913 had been maintained during the decade

[1] *Economist*, 11th April 1931, p. 783.

42

from 1919 to 1928, the population of the country would be lower by about 1,360,000 persons.' It may therefore be argued that a large part of the recent unemployment is solely due to the fact that too many of us have stayed at home instead of seeking our fortunes abroad. But this contention is not altogether satisfying, for the mere existence of all these additional bodies needing to be fed and kept ought, if the world's trade had been running on an even keel and our own business arrangements had been on a sound basis, to have enabled us to set them, or some of them at least, to work to provide the goods needed for their food and keep, or to be exchanged for them if they had to be imported. But this question of the unemployed comes later. At present we are dealing with the reward of the working rank and file and the influences which tend to its maintenance in spite of growing numbers and reduced demand. When business expansion fails to absorb their greater numbers their earning power is supported by the organization which has been established by their unions, their political power which secures for them the support of Governments, and human sympathy which is freely given to them both by their employers and by the general public.

By means of the trade unions the wage - earner organized a bargaining power which put him in a position to deal on something like even terms with those who employed him, and had the advantage of accumulated capital and profits behind them. A single workman with a family to keep and with little or no store of saved money, and in the days when the only refuge of the unemployed was charity or poor law relief, was helpless when his employer told him that his wage must be reduced and that, if he did not like to take a lower wage, he must seek another job. Combined in a union, with a practised spokesman to represent him and with the funds of the union, provided by the contributions of the members, to fall back on, he could argue the question of wages with much greater force and confidence.

Politically, the rank and file obviously have an enormous pull in all countries in which the franchise is widely extended and where the popular vote is really effective. Their numbers make them a mass whose voting power gives their side of the case a more than respectful hearing. As to the employer, his outlook concerning the wages of the rank and file worker has been revolutionized in America by mass production, which needs mass consumption to keep the plant at work, and so requires a mass of well-paid buyers to do the consuming. And in England also it is beginning to be recognized that good wages are good for trade. 'I am not,' said the Chairman of the Amalgamated Anthracite Collieries at its meeting in March 1930, 'a believer in reducing the earnings of any section of the working population, because that is not the short way to national prosperity.'[1] But in old days it was another matter. Adam Smith, who wrote at the end of the eighteenth century when the Industrial Revolution had hardly begun, tells us that the 'masters are always and everywhere in a sort of tacit but constant and uniform combination, not to raise the wages of labour above their actual rate. To violate this com-

[1] *The Times*, 24th March 1930.

bination is everywhere a most unpopular action, and a sort of reproach to a master among his neighbours and equals. We seldom, indeed, hear of this combination, because it is the usual, and one may say, the natural state of things which nobody ever hears of. Masters too sometimes enter into particular combinations to sink the wages of labour even below this rate. They are always conducted with the utmost silence and secrecy till the moment of execution, and when the workmen yield, as they sometimes do, without resistance, though severely felt by them, they are never heard of by other people.'[1]

From this picture of the employers, 'always and everywhere' combined to keep wages from rising and often combining 'with the utmost silence and secrecy' to put them lower, it is a far cry to the portrait of the enlightened employer of to-day drawn for us by one of them who speaks from his own experience, Mr. Henry Ford. He tells us in his book, *To-day and To-morrow*, that 'an underpaid man is a customer reduced in purchasing power. He cannot buy. Business depression is caused by weakened purchasing power. Purchasing power is weakened by uncertainty or insufficiency of income. The cure of business depression is through purchasing power, and the source of purchasing power is wages. . . . The effect of wages is the continuity of work. Reduce wages and you reduce work because you reduce the demand upon which work depends. Wages is more of a question for business than it is for labour. It is more important to business than it is to labour, low wages will break business far

[1] *Wealth of Nations*, Book I, Chapter VIII.

45

more quickly than it will labour. . . . If you cut wages, you just cut the number of your own customers. If an employer does not share prosperity with those who make him prosperous, then pretty soon there will be no prosperity to share. That is why we think it is good business always to raise wages and never to lower them. We like to have plenty of customers. . . . Many a manufacturer sincerely believes that he is paying the highest wages his business will stand. Perhaps he is. But no one knows what he can afford to pay until he tries. In 1915 we raised our wage from an average of two dollars and forty cents to a minimum of five dollars[1] a day. Then we really started our business, for on that day we first created a lot of customers for our cars, and second, began to find so many ways to save, that soon we were able to start our programme of price reduction. If you set yourself a task, it is really remarkable how many other things grow out of doing that task. You simply cannot make a thing cheaply and well with cheap men.'

Between these two employers – one always and everywhere combined to keep wages down and the other seeing that, as a matter of cold calculating business, high wages pay him best – there has been a century and a half of strikes and strife and bitterness. Concerning the loss inflicted by strikes on industry, and the community in general, and especially on the wage-earners themselves, plenty has been said in late years and said truly. With Adam Smith's testimony before us reinforced by Mr. Baldwin's recent statement that 'had the employers of past generations all of them

[1] Rather more than £1.

dealt fairly with their men, there would have been no unions,'[1] it is evidently absurd to lay all the blame for this loss at the door of the trade unions, as comfortable old boys in arm-chairs at clubs are apt to do.

But we may go further and suggest that the mistakes made on both sides were largely due to ignorance on the part of men who were groping their way among new and puzzling conditions. The wage-earners and their unions were working for a better standard, and it is now acknowledged that it pays everybody for them to have it, if it can possibly be granted in the teeth of competition with foreign industries that are not yet awake to the benefits of high wages. If they were sometimes in too much of a hurry, it was a fault on the right side and was generally committed owing to well-founded belief that their claims, whether reasonable or not, would be resisted by the employers.

As to the employers, they knew that it was their job to make their business pay, because if it did not pay it would die, and if that happened they themselves would be bankrupt and all their wage-earners would be thrown out of work. Wages were generally the biggest item in their expenses and resistance to their increase was a natural instinct, especially in the early days of large-scale industry, when many employers had risen from the ranks and did not see why their workers should get more than they had received themselves.

It is true that in those early days when work in factories was superseding work at home, some employers committed, in the treatment of their wage-

[1] *The Times*, 15th January 1931.

earners, what we now see to have been horrible crimes. Karl Marx spent many years of his life accumulating in the British Museum the materials for his indictment of capitalism from blue books and newspaper files; and he sets out a terrible list of these crimes in the pages of his book, *Capital, an Analysis of Capitalistic Production*. We read, on the authority of a county magistrate, of privation and suffering in the Nottingham lace trade 'unknown in other parts of the kingdom . . . – children of nine or ten years are dragged from their squalid beds at two, three or four o'clock in the morning and compelled to work for a bare subsistence until ten, eleven or twelve at night, their limbs wearing away, their frames dwindling, their faces whitening and their humanity absolutely sinking into a stone-like torpor, utterly horrible to contemplate.'[1] Mr. Bertrand Russell, quoting this and other horrors in his *Roads to Freedom*, says that page after page and chapter after chapter of facts of this nature 'cannot but stir into fury any passionate working-class reader, and into unbearable shame any possessor of capital in whom generosity and justice are not wholly extinct.'

Fury and shame are both very much to the point. But the fury should be visited less on the individual employer who was mostly what his conditions and chances had made him, than on the ignorance and callousness and stupidity and cruelty that made such things possible in an apparently civilized country in the 1860th year of the so-called Christian era; and as a general rule the children employed in factories do not

[1] Karl Marx, *Capital*, Part III, Chapter X, Sec. 3, p. 227.

seem to have been worse off than those employed at home. The factories produced a long overdue reform. Mr. J. R. M. Butler in his *History of England, 1815-1918*, says that 'to the squalor and discomfort of slum life the factories added monotony, rigid discipline, and new fears of accident and disease, but they did not necessarily lower the standard of living. Conditions in the early textile mills were often scandalous, but so were the conditions in the domestic handicrafts they supplanted, and the exploitation of child labour was nothing new. It should be remembered also that not for several decades after 1815 did the factories include more than a small minority of the wage-earning population, and that by the time factory work became common factory regulation had become usual too. It was the novelty of "these dark Satanic mills" and the comparative ease of supervising them which most fortunately for the nation exposed them to denunciation and reform.'

And if some of those old employers may seem to us now to have been devils, others took the lead in reform. The first true Factory Act, as Mr. Butler tells us, was due to the initiative of two enlightened employers, Sir Robert Peel, the elder, and Robert Owen. This Act of 1819 prohibited the labour of children under nine in cotton mills, but in them only. 'Children from five to six years old were at this time greatly in request as "piecers" in the steam mills established in populous districts, and they frequently worked fifteen or sixteen hours a day.' And the provision under the Act of 1833 of Government inspectors of factories, which was 'suggested by certain mill-owners and scorned by the operatives, has in fact proved the key to the success of the British system of factory legislation, which the world has copied.'[1]

But these horrors belong to a long ago past, and only had to be mentioned because they must have branded into the minds of those who suffered from them, thoughts and beliefs about the relations of employers and wage-earners which have left their mark until to-day in the minds of their descendants. They must not be forgotten by those who are inclined to be critical about labour's claims and labour leaders' ways of trying to enforce them.

What we are concerned with at present is the question, How far has the American doctrine of high wages, as best in the interests of industry, penetrated other countries? and the further question, How far is it possible for countries like England, which has to face fierce foreign competition, to carry out this doctrine in advance of its foreign competitors which provide a lower standard of reward to their wage-earners?

America stands in a class by herself, with her immense area, wealth and population, which make her export trade a matter of minor importance in her business life. She could, if she chose, make laws unto herself, regardless of what is happening in the Eastern hemisphere, loaded with burdens of debt inherited from centuries of war and preparations for war and other results of bad temper and governmental bungling.

But England has to buy from abroad hundreds of millions' worth of food and raw materials to feed her population and keep her industry at work. In order to

---

[1] J. R. M. Butler, *History of England, 1815-1918*, Chapter III, p. 55.

do this she has to sell abroad in competition with the industries of keen and hard-working rivals less rich than she is, and all the more formidable for that reason, because they are less exacting in the matter of profits, wages and scale of rewards in general.

If England fails in this competition the only prospect for her industry and her inhabitants, when they have consumed the stock of accumulated fat acquired in the last century, before competition was so keen, is gradual or rapid decline, as industry dwindles and the food supply, bought with the proceeds of its exports, is cut down.

Looking, then, at this problem of the reward of the wage-earners in the light of our necessity for export, we have to consider whether the American doctrine of high wages can be adopted in this country without a careful eye on the standards of our neighbours and rivals.

In England, the advantage of high wages is not so direct and evident as in America, owing to the much greater dependence of British industry on export trade. Mr. Henry Ford found when he raised wages that he had created a large number of customers for his cars. A Lancashire mill-owner, by raising wages at home, would not thereby stimulate a keener demand for his cotton goods in India, China, South America and other countries where he finds most of his market. The average British employer of to-day does not want to underpay those who work for him. But he knows that he is highly taxed as compared with his rivals, that he already pays higher wages than Continental employers, that he is vexed by much official control and regulation on the one hand and by trade union interference on the other, that the countries to which he tries to sell put obstacles in his way in the shape of high tariffs, while his home market is open to the goods of all the world; and he asks how it is possible for him to improve or even maintain the already relatively high standard of those who work for him. To which the wage-earners retort that it is not high wages that make profits difficult to earn, but antiquated machinery and methods, faulty organization and management, bad salesmanship, too many intermediaries taking toll of the product and so on; and they tell the employers and the public that before there is any question of lower wages, industry had better bring itself up to date.

This contention is based on a view – that British industry needs vigorous overhauling – that can be plentifully supported by the criticisms of it that have been uttered by leading industrialists. For some years it has been a common cry that there is urgent need for reconstruction and 'rationalization' – this new word meaning nothing but the application of common sense to business – in Great Britain, especially in view of the more up-to-date equipment and methods of other countries.

America, with the accumulated wealth of the Old World poured into her pocket by the war and with her passion for novelty and ingenuity in new devices, had all the capital and instinct and spirit needed to keep her industrial equipment in tune with, or ahead of, the latest developments.

France and Belgium, having seen their industrial

areas laid waste by the war, had to have a brand new outfit out of reparation funds when the war was over.

In Germany the same result was produced by bad money. The printing press turned out money so fast that it lost value so quickly that every one who received money made haste to turn it into something else; and German industry turned its bad marks into new machinery and plant.

In England, industry was left with enormous and largely useless plants constructed at the urgent instance of the Government for war production, and faced by a rate of taxation such as would have been scouted as impossible five years earlier. This high taxation was necessary because England had not, like America, made big profits on balance out of the war, and had not, like Germany, France and other countries, wiped out or greatly reduced her war debts, and pre-war debts, by printing money till it was worthless, or worth one-fifth of its value when the debts were contracted. Capital was scarce and timid, industrial strife was chronic, culminating in the General Strike and coal stoppage of 1926; and other causes, which will appear as we go on, made the position of British industry especially difficult in the after-war period, and tended to postpone the effort of reconstruction which was generally admitted to be necessary.

With this admission constantly dinned into their ears, it was natural that labour leaders should resist wage reductions, arguing that reconstruction should first be tried. And it is not only labour leaders who have said that the wage level in England is not in need of readjustment. Lord Weir, a distinguished and highly successful industrialist, in a letter to *The Times* published on 1st January 1929, urged the rejuvenation of our basic industries and stated that there were few things being produced in the United States which we could not produce at least as economically and as efficiently, if we organized ourselves to do it. 'An analysis,' he wrote, 'of United States costs of production' – he had just returned from a round Atlantic voyage – 'seems to me to prove conclusively that, with similar production facilities and methods, with British geographical freight advantages, with British labour even at remuneration in excess of existing rates, British costs can be economic and command the world's markets.'

In the opinion of this distinguished employer, it thus appears that British labour might be given a still higher standard, if British industry were 'rejuvenated'; but it should be added that he also advocated, with regard to iron and steel, the 'immediate granting by the Government of as complete and sensible a degree of safeguarding as is required to ensure that our entire iron and steel requirements will be provided for by home production'; and so he may be assumed to be in favour of Protection,[1] stiff enough to be prohibitive of all imports, for all industries to which the home market is important.

Here, then, we have a great industrialist maintaining that the British level of wages or even a higher one need not prevent British industry, if properly organized, from commanding the world's markets, if the home market is secured to it.

But a Memorandum on *The Industrial Situation*, issued

[1] See below, Chapters XIV and XV.

in February 1931 by the National Confederation of Employers' Organizations, says that 'disparities between ourselves and our competitors permeate the whole of our industrial and social life, and this may be illustrated by the following comparisons:

(*a*) *National Taxation.* – The disparity in national taxation per head of the population is approximately as follows (*Hansard*, 4th November 1930):

Great Britain	100
France	64
Germany	50
Belgium	38
Italy	30

(*b*) *Wage Levels.* – The disparity in the level of real wages, *i.e.* money wages expressed in terms of food-purchasing power, is approximately as follows (*Ministry of Labour Gazette*, 1929-30):

Great Britain	100
Germany	74
France	59
Belgium	50
Italy	45

(*c*) *Social Services.* – The disparity in the cost per head of the population for the five Social Services of Unemployment, Health, Workmen's Compensation, Old Age Pensions and Poor Law Relief, was in 1924 approximately as follows (*Report of Royal Commission on Health Insurance*, 1926):

Great Britain	100
Germany	48
France	17
Belgium	7
Italy	4

Taking account of the developments in the various countries since 1924, including the addition of Widows' and Orphans' Pensions in Great Britain, the above figures still represent the approximate comparative position to-day, except in the case of Germany, which within recent years added considerably to its Social Service expenditure, but has within recent months taken steps to restrict it.

Any comparison between our standards and those in the United States must take account of the fact that the United States, with its great natural resources, is self-supporting and does not depend upon its export trade for its existence. Its real wage level stands at 188 but its taxation level is little more than a third of ours and as it has not adopted the policy of providing these Social Services for its workers other than Workmen's Compensation, its expenditure per head on these Services is negligible.

It is idle to think that a country like ours, which depends upon its export trade for its existence, can, in the industrial world of to-day, continue to set up and maintain standards of living and public expenditure regardless of those of its competitors without paying the price of unemployment.

It is through continuing to pursue that policy during the past ten years that the present grave situation has arisen.

The superiority of British standards dates from a time when the other nations, which are now our industrial competitors, were in the early stages of their industrial development and when we could therefore afford to pursue our own standards regardless of what they did.

That superiority has been enjoyed for so long that it has come to be taken for granted as a national prescriptive right and that traditional attitude has persisted even when our competitors with their lower standards have been steadily overhauling us in the race for world trade.

Indeed, but for that deep-rooted tradition it is inconceivable that this country, with its heavy share of the war burdens, would have pursued during the past ten years the policy of increasing its standards regardless of its competitors, and heedless of the constant warnings in its unemployment figures of the inevitable end of such a policy.'

And a recent utterance by an Italian paper, the *Popolo d'Italia*, on the subject of English industry and wage-earners tells us that the mines are still working, in an age of electricity, with steam plant, that nearly all machinery, especially in the cotton trade, is of old nineteenth-century pattern and that the workers, although they may belong to the Labour Party, 'want to do little work and to receive Imperial wages which the Continental worker does not claim.'[1]

More power to the British workman, most of us will say, in trying to get the best reward he can for his work and showing the way to his Continental neighbours

[1] Quoted by *The Times*, 9th August 1930.

towards a better standard. But at the same time there evidently must be limits to the extent to which he can march in advance of those who work for British industry's competitors. England has immense advantages of position and her workers are unrivalled in skill and intelligence. Let us go back to Lord Weir's letter of 1st January 1929, quoted a few pages ago. As you will remember, he had, when he wrote, just been visiting America, and he says: 'As regards operative labour, anyone who has experience of the degree of intelligence of average American labour appreciates the much higher value of our British worker. Then as regards foremen and assistant managers, it is no secret that America is always ready to offer them good jobs on account of their intelligence and general ability.'

These advantages enjoyed by British industry go far, but is the energy in work of the British workers as good as their intelligence and ability?

Trade union organization, as we have seen, has given them the strength of collective bargaining. United, they have secured the chance of a fair deal with those who employ them. But collective bargaining implies, to some extent, working to a common standard; which means to say that, except when work is paid for by the piece, the pace and vigour of the best workers are apt to be kept down to the standard of the least effective.

Another influence that tends to produce the same result is the belief that there is never more than a certain amount of work to be done, and that if it is done too quickly there will be so much less demand for the labour of the wage-earners. In these times of generally prevalent unemployment there is a good deal of excuse for this belief; but those who act on it help to produce the limitation of demand for their work that they are trying to avoid; because by working at a slow stroke they raise the cost of production and so make it difficult for those who employ them to compete, or for those who buy the article to afford it.

If a job that might have been done in a week takes a fortnight the wages bill and the overhead charges – rent, rates, light, management expenses, and so on – are doubled; and this extra charge either has to be added to the price of the thing or things produced, or come out of the profits of the employing company or firm.

If it is added to the price at which the goods are sold, fewer people will be able to afford them and there will be less likelihood that another lot will be wanted.

If competition, whether by home or foreign makers, prevents this addition to the price, then the profits of the employing manufacturer will be curtailed and perhaps turned into a loss. In either case there will be less chance of expansion in the business and of maintained or increased demand for the work of the wage-earners.

Just as it is to the interest of employers that wages should be high, so that there may be a big public with plenty of money in its pocket to buy the products of industry: so it is to the interest of the wage-earners that the things which they turn out should be cheap, so that a growing demand for them may keep the firms that make them busy, and ready to pay good wages for good work.

The example taken – a fortnight for a week's job – may seem to be impossibly exaggerated. It may be, but in the first place exaggerated examples may make things clear more easily; and in the second, one hears quite amazing statements about the relative slowness of British workers when they first go to America, and the ease with which they catch up and pass their colleagues when they start to do so. A big American employer told a friend of mine lately that in normal times he always gets a few new hands from England every year, that the Englishman, when he begins, works at about one-fifth of the pace shown by other workers in the factory, that in a few months' time he is level with the average, and that in two years' time he is generally in one of the leading and best-paid jobs.

Touching this allegation of deliberately restricted output, the wage-earners can retort that the employers do exactly the same thing when they form combines and make working agreements with the object of restraining competition and maintaining prices. As for us, the poor consuming public – 'the hungry sheep look up and are not fed,' and the net result is bad for all parties to the bargain.

As to the resistance of the wage-earners to the full use of machinery, we have lately had an example in the cotton trade lock-out in Lancashire owing to the operatives' opposition to the 'more looms to a weaver' system. This dispute is estimated to have cost the industry between six and seven million pounds. 'If,' said the *Economist* of 21st February 1931, in commenting on it, 'rationalization on these lines is to be opposed with such intransigence by Labour, the outlook is dark.' In America, where the organization of Labour in trade unions has not gone nearly so far as in England, the speed expected in return for high wages is readily given. The final report of the Balfour Committee, appointed in 1924 to inquire into the conditions and prospects of British industry, tells us on page 151 that 'the characteristic feature of the economy of the great industrial establishments of the United States is not merely the high wages which prevail, but the combination of high wages and low labour costs per unit of output, and this combination depends on the power of making the freest use of mechanical aids to productivity, and of applying the services of all grades of workers in the manner most conducive to output without any hindrance from trade customs or restrictions.'

By working on these lines the American wage-earners provided great prosperity for themselves and for the rest of the community, until all the world's prosperity was bowled over in 1929 by causes which are discussed in Chapters XVII to XXI.

It thus seems to be clear that the trade unions, while doing a great work in improving the standard of the wage-earners, have, at the same time, by a mistaken sense of their interests, produced results which have increased the difficulties of British industry, and so tended to defeat the objects for which the unions were working. The efforts made by the late Lord Melchett and Mr. Ben Turner to bring about closer co-operation between employers and employed should help to reduce causes of friction, and the present spell of adversity is a hard master that is teaching all parties in industry lessons that will, we may hope, be helpful when the adversities have passed away.

As to the progress of the wage-earner towards a better standard, anyone who has been alive for a few decades has seen it, visible and obvious. And we can cite evidence on the point from a veteran trade union leader, Mr. Ben Turner. In an interview with a representative of *The Times*, published in its issue of 1st September 1928, Mr. Turner said that 'the great changes of the past forty years in the industrial and social life of our country must be pleasing for every Englishman to look back upon. The advancement in the homes of the workers from bare sanded floors to carpets and rugs, from grocers' almanacs on the wall to oil-paintings and water-colour drawings, to pianos and wireless, to electric light and other domestic amenities, had added much to the value of life.'

'That is only one side of it,' he continued. 'The change in the dress of the woman worker from the old canvas apron to the dress of the period, which is light and attractive and healthy, is another vast change for the better. In those early days of mine the young man's dress used to be confined to one suit for Sundays, and he always used to wear his working-clothes at night. Then, it was also clogs and shawls for women and clogs and smocks for men. Thus there has been a vast change for the better in personal attire and amenities.'

Speaking of the changes in the wage outlook, Mr. Turner said that 'while big changes had taken place since the war there had been at least 30 per cent. improvement in wages between 1890 and 1910.

Another big change in industry had been the reduction in the hours of labour, which had been applied to practically every industry. Forty years ago the working week was fifty-eight hours, then it was lowered to fifty-five, and was now forty-eight hours.'

In the Balfour Committee's final report, page 152, we find that 'such figures as are available indicate that over a period of forty years (1888-1928) the weekly rates of money wages for similar grades of work have advanced by about 120 per cent., and the cost of living by about 90 per cent., showing an advance in "real" weekly wages of about 16 per cent. The average rise in the level of "real" earnings, taking into account such considerations as the changes in the proportion of different grades of workers, would probably be considerably in excess of this percentage. A similar comparison with the period immediately before the war shows that the average increase in weekly money rates of wages for similar grades of work since that time has not been much greater than that in the cost of living, so that the average level of "real" wages is at present only slightly higher than it was just before the war. But it is important to note that the rates of wages of unskilled labourers, *i.e.* of the classes nearest to "subsistence level," are those which have risen in the greatest proportion, with the result that the average "real" wages of unskilled labour are now 10 per cent. or more above the level of 1913.'

(Real wages are money wages related to buying power. If wages are doubled and prices likewise, real wages are unchanged.)

The improvement shown is certainly striking, and

it does not tell nearly all the story; for while this growth in the wage-earners' receipts has happened, there has been at the same time an enormous increase in the amount spent by the public authorities on social services – health, education, old-age pensions, widows' pensions, sickness and unemployment insurance – all of which is spent for the benefit of the wage-earners.

'Social Services,' said Sir Robert Horne in a recent speech, 'which are met partly out of taxes, partly out of rates, and partly from compulsory contributions by industry, to-day cost £366,000,000 as against £63,000,000 in 1911.'[1]

Thus, in a period in which a terrific cataclysm shook civilization to its base, the wage-earners, and especially the least well paid, have achieved a considerable improvement in their standard, and a still greater relative improvement owing to the high taxation which has cut off half the incomes of the very rich.

It makes one's mouth water to think how much greater the improvement might be in the next forty years if we have peace abroad and good temper and sweet reasonableness at home, and machinery is given a fair chance to work for us. It may be that our wage-earners have tried to go too far in their demands and that it is not possible for them to force the pace, while their Continental brethren lag behind, as is shown by the table given on page 55. Even on the Continent, however, there has been a considerable improvement in the lot of the wage-earner.

Mr. H. B. Butler, of the International Labour Office, in an address given to the Manchester Statistical

[1] *The Times*, 28th January 1931.

Society on 12th March 1930, said that 'whether one considers hours, the conditions of employment of women and children, or the protection of workers against social risks, it is impossible to avoid the conclusion that during this period an immense advance has been made in the general well-being of the industrial population of the Continent. This progress has not been confined to a few of the richer and larger countries, but is virtually universal in its scope. As a result, even where their real wages have not been increased, and in spite of the depression which has marked many of the post-war years in nearly every European country, millions of workers throughout Europe are considerably better off than they were before the war. Their hours of leisure are longer, their conditions of employment better, and they have an increased measure of protection against the misfortunes of life.'[1]

[1] Quoted by Mr. George Peel, in his interesting book on *The Economic War*.

CHAPTER IV

THE LEARNED PROFESSIONS

Their Comparatively Poor Reward – Their Indirect Contribution to Comfort – Brainy People apt to be Dismal – And Unpractical – Education and Respectability – The Professor and his Standard – Intellect as an Asset.

APART from the manual workers, it is only possible to make guesses concerning the rewards granted to other classes of those gainfully employed. 'Dim glimpses into the obvious' are all that we can get. But it is probably true that in most countries members of the learned professions, though they do work that is of enormous importance to the community, do not, by and large, get so big a share out of the common pool as those who are commonly described as business men. A few of them make huge sums, as fashionable physicians, leading lawyers or popular novelists or artists. Some of them, such as scientists, inventors and engineers, who are employed by companies engaged in production, are amphibious figures, half professional and half business, and it is significant that these are more likely to be amply rewarded than those who have stuck to purely professional work.

Here, perhaps, we see the reason for the comparatively poor reward that goes to the professions. Business is business; and it is concerned with increasing the world's material wealth; and so the world's wealth tends to gravitate towards the pockets of those who 'deliver the goods' and give the consuming public what it wants in comforts and amusements. What the general public wants is to be comfortable and happy, and it rewards those who will help it to this very sensible ideal. Some day it may want to be intellectual and then it may provide larger rewards for those who can develop its brains and explore the marvels of Nature and the riddle of the universe for it. At present it has much more admiration for the athlete and the man of action than for the sage; and it is worth noting that in this respect it is following the example of the Greeks, the most intellectual and intelligent people who have lived in the pages of history.

Comfort and amusement are not directly provided by the professions. Scientists with their researches have immensely and incalculably furthered the command of men over the forces of Nature, and so have made possible a mighty growth in population living in much greater comfort than their forebears; but the researches of the scientist could not have had these marvellous effects if they had not been applied by enterprising business men with capitalists and manual workers behind them to provide the plant and handle it. Doctors can tell us how to keep our homes and bodies wholesome; but we cannot do what they tell us to do unless we have been provided by business enterprise with houses, drain-pipes, clothes, food, warmth, light and other essentials.

Teachers are, or ought to be, able to tell us how to use our brains and cultivate our taste to enjoy the finer emotions – the rarest, finest and most precious gift that man or woman can possess, says the sage. But the man in the street doubts. Brainy people, he thinks, are not happier and jollier than the common herd; on the contrary they are generally rather dismal. And this is on the whole true, because being happy and jolly is usually a matter of behaving pleasantly and kindly to others and living among folk who behave pleasantly and kindly to oneself. And development of the brain very often neglects this most important matter, especially if it tends, as is likely, to a sedentary habit of body and lack of exercise; because pleasant and kindly behaviour comes more naturally to those who are active and healthy and sweat their gross humours out through wholesome exertion. Moreover, a finely developed intellect often seems actually to impede the exercise of that quick decision which is needed for practical success. Macaulay says of the great Lord Halifax that 'in wit and eloquence, in amplitude of comprehension and subtlety of dis-quisition, he had no equal among the statesmen of his time. But that very fertility, that very acuteness, which gave a singular charm to his conversation, to his oratory, and to his writings, unfitted him for the work of promptly deciding practical questions. He was slow from very quickness. For he saw so many arguments for and against every possible course that he was longer in making up his mind than a dull man would have been.'[1]

If Hamlet had spent less time in sharpening his intellect at the University of Wittenberg, he would

[1] *History of England*, Chapter XI.

have wasted less time in talking about killing his
wicked uncle. Instead of allowing his 'native resolu-
tion' to be 'sicklied o'er with the pale cast of thought,'
he would have spoilt the play by running the bad
King through the body in the first act.

It is a question of degree. Those who develop their
intellect at the expense of their intelligence and decision
and human sympathies are not likely to succeed in
business, which is an intensely human affair. Short
of that, a well-trained intellect is useful anywhere;
and now that a certain amount of brain development
is beginning to be thought necessary to business
success, the teacher may have a better chance of
reward, as long as he confines himself to teaching
what is 'practical' – modern languages, 'stinks' and a
smattering of economics. But so far the world has
treated him shabbily, and with some justice from the
business point of view, because his work has hitherto
done little, on the material side, for his pupils.

In fact, those who teach the elements of education
appear to have rather diminished their earning power,
at least in America, by increasing the number of
'white collar workers.' Mr. Stuart Chase in his sceptical
analysis of American prosperity asks: 'How many
thousands of women have scrimped and saved and
worked their fingers to the bone in order that the boys
might have advantages which their fathers never had?
And how much of that devoted toil, under 1929 conditions, is love's labour lost? In many cities to-day a
bank clerk earns about \$30[1] a week. A plumber is
getting \$46.[2] Perhaps one in a thousand tellers will

[1] £6.   [2] £9, 4s.

some day become a bank president. Plumbers have become bank directors; frequently they rise to the ownership of their own business.' And he goes on to quote Professor H. D. Kitson of Columbia University, who says that 'the white collar ideal is one of the most vicious things in our civilization. . . . If youth were informed concerning the disparity in the economic possibilities of jobs, they would cease to flood the white-collar fields. So far as actual opportunity for advancement goes, the man doing manual labour is much better off.'[1]

Such is the effect on earning power, in the country whose earning has been most successfully developed, of learning the elements of education. Its pupils, obsessed by a craving for what is thought to be respectability, turn to the clerkly career in which their chance of reward is less, from the manual jobs in which they had better opportunities of rising to increased comfort.

As to the University professor, it takes him, if he is lucky, says Mr. Stuart Chase, about fourteen years to become an associate professor at $4000 or £800 a year, which sum is also quoted as about the income of the American engine-driver; in another eleven years he may become a full professor at $7000 – £1400. This in the land of big rewards. 'One-third,' continues our authority, 'of the faculty of the University of California are now working throughout their summer vacations in order to balance their slender budgets. Many able scholars and scientists find it impossible to balance their budgets at all. They leave the university

[1] *Prosperity, Fact, or Myth*, by Stuart Chase (C. Boni, New York).

for business, and become corporation research men, technical advisers, higher executives. They gain in income; business gains in profits, but the nation loses able and impartial scientists, and so one of its most priceless assets.' But does the nation lose them altogether?

'To make matters worse,' Mr. Stuart Chase goes on, 'the professor, together with all the upper ranks of the middle class, is expected to keep his white collar spotlessly clean. He cannot stoop to celluloid; he has a position to maintain. The new standard of living addresses itself to him remorselessly. The car, home furnishings, the arts, clothing for the family, the proper neighbourhood, the country club, entertaining – all must keep abreast of the Joneses. For this reason, James Truslow Adams believes that the professional man is *worse* off than he used to be. His income has not increased as fast as the new demands upon it – leaving a more slender margin than a generation ago, or even than a decade ago. He calls it "prosperity without peace of mind." '

Here we have an apt example of the tendency which defeats the efforts of the producer to make us comfortable. He provides the comforts and we turn them into a nuisance by misusing them. Just as the manual worker increases his respectability but reduces his reward by being turned, thanks to his mother's mistaken self-sacrifice, into a white-collar employee, so the professor loses his peace of mind because he is foolish enough to aim at a standard that he cannot afford and 'keep abreast of the Joneses.' He is enjoying much more comfort and even luxury than his predecessors, but he does not really enjoy them because he is having more than he can quite afford.

Mr. Stuart Chase seems to imply that the professor is helpless in the iron grip of some inexorable fate. But it may be suggested that he has only himself – or more probably his womenkind – to thank for submitting to this social snobbery which robs him of his right to live his own life on his own lines, and let the Joneses go to Davy Jones's locker. He has much less excuse than the manual worker's mother, in being thus misled by 'respectability.' She knew no better. He does, or ought to. In fact it is the educated classes with a fund of mental wealth behind them – the power to appreciate beauty in all its forms – who ought to be leading the van in the army of protest against the tyranny of the advertiser and the booster, who now lay down laws as to how mankind is to live. Instead of which, according to this sympathetic but perhaps rather acrid, American authority, they are driven like sheep with the rest of the flock. This matter is of quite dreadful importance; for America has shown the world how to get wealth, and if she is also going to show the world how to misuse it, there are plenty to follow her example on this side of the Atlantic.

In England teaching has never been a well-paid profession, and the comparatively few schoolmasters who have earned large incomes have done so not as teachers, but as hotel-keepers – by being housemasters at public schools and making profits out of boarding and lodging their charges. And in these days, the high rate of income tax, which they and other middle class earners have to pay, probably in most cases leaves them actually worse off than they used to be. Not only, as in America, have they to 'keep abreast of the Joneses' but the abhorred shears of the tax-gatherer cut a big slice out of their incomes, to pay interest on war debt and to provide the millions that are spent on social services for the benefit of those on the lower rungs of the ladder.

With civil servants it is the same story, but they have the advantage of coming into contact with the business leaders, and the latter are beginning to appreciate the services of keen brains and to know where to look for them in Whitehall.

Lawyers are another class that must have gone back, relatively, in net reward in recent years, at any rate in England, owing again to the high income tax. The solicitors, who make our wills and see that the business is all shipshape when we buy houses, jog along pretty steadily year in and year out. Those whose business was more concerned with litigation have been hard hit lately, because trade depression has taught us to avoid the law courts as too expensive a luxury in these hard times. And this abstinence has told with terrible severity on the barristers, always ill-paid on the whole in spite of the huge incomes that used to be earned by the star performers. But then the Bar used to be looked on as a door into the higher ranks of politics.

Doctors, again, are another class in which a few fashionable leaders make mouth-watering fees, but by and large the profession works terribly hard for a poor living in view of the immensely valuable work that it does. Much of their work is done for nothing and nowadays not even a 'Thank you.' A friend of mine, a country doctor who is unfortunate enough to live on a main road, was hastily summoned on a Sunday evening lately because some reckless young folk on motor bicycles had come tearing round a corner on a greasy surface and collapsed in a heap in a general skid and collision. Nobody was much hurt, and when he had sorted them out and put them on their legs again and seen that no serious damage was done, the local policeman suggested that some of them might properly be asked for a fee. 'Oh,' said my friend, 'I've long given up expecting that for a job like this, but I should like to suggest to you young people that you've called me out on a wet night and not one of you has had the grace to give me even a word of thanks.'

We see, then, that the professions as compared with business are on the whole ill paid, and have lost ground, in this respect, relatively in the midst of the general progress. It is not pleasant to see a class to which the community owes so much in the matter of refinement and culture and thinking power, going behind in the race, but there are consolations.

One result of it is that good and well-educated brains go more and more into business, which has need of them, to cope with the big problems that face it. Moreover, the possession of refinement and culture and thinking faculty is a priceless reward in itself, if those who own it would be satisfied with it, and not always strive to be 'abreast of the Joneses.' It gives to those who own it the shortest of all cuts to real wealth, which is the faculty of living very easily and contentedly on very little. Those who enjoy good literature and good music and appreciate the beauties of Nature and art are possessed of an asset that no money can buy. 'Millionaires can buy pictures,' said an artist friend of mine, 'but they can't buy an eye to see them with.'

CHAPTER V

THE BANKERS

Create Money and Credit and, to some extent, regulate their Amount – Importance of their Task – Limits on their Power – Supposed Easiness of their Work – Suggestions for its Nationalization – Objections to this Proposal – Messrs. Baldwin, Snowden and Russell on Weaknesses of Politicians.

Now we are coming to people who draw, with large and powerful hands, out of the common pool; because, as things are, without their work the pool could never be kept full, to say nothing of its being filled fuller and fuller, for the rest of us to draw on.

The same thing might undoubtedly be said, and often is said, and quite truly, of the manual worker and the clerk. But there is this enormous difference between the work of the leading banker and that of the rank and file. The former has to make decisions, and sometimes make them very quickly, involving enormous responsibility and risk to himself and to other people. The rank and file do the much simpler and easier and less nerve-racking job of carrying out the orders, filtered down to them through what may be called the non-commissioned officers of the business army, that arise from the decisions of the responsible leaders. Responsibility and decision and courage, backed by intelligence and judgment, are the gifts for which the business world is ready to pay highly if it can find them. Sometimes it pays highly for a tinkling cymbal of a man who does not possess them. This happens either because someone, or more probably a Committee, has made a mistake about choosing the right man – itself one of the most difficult and responsible jobs that can be undertaken – or because there has been favouritism somewhere. But in these days of keen rivalry, when all the responsible folk are being keyed up to concert pitch, soft jobs for sons and nephews are not so easy to come by as they used to be. It is still a great help to be connected with the great ones of the business world, but it only gives a lad a better chance of a favourable start. He has to 'make good' or he does not go very far.

By bankers, I mean the people who create money, and, within limits that will be evident as we go on, control its supply. Without money we should be back at the stage of barter, unable to exchange what we make for what we want until we have found someone who not only makes what we want but wants what we make. Endless delays and difficulties would follow; and without money as a medium of exchange, the business of providing for our wants, on our present scale, could not begin to be done.

In most countries that can be called civilized, from the business point of view, the money that does the big work consists of pieces of paper that we accept in payment for our work because we know that everybody else will accept it from us when we want to buy things. That, at least, is the reason which we should probably give ourselves if we stopped to wonder why we take money in payment. Actually we take it because taking and spending it is part of our lives and always has been, and we do not think about it or question it.

Pieces of paper, bank notes or cheques, do the big work of settling the large transactions; but for pocket money when we pay for cheap articles at shops or eating-houses or railway booking-offices, we use coins made of silver or nickel or bronze, minted and issued by the Government in response to the demands of the bankers. Some of us remember the days when in England we had neat little silver sovereign purses attached to our watch-chains and always carried a few jolly-looking gold pieces. Those days are gone and the British sovereign has been replaced by the Bank of England one-pound note.

When we look at all this money, whether made of paper or of metal, the first thing we notice about it is that it is no use to us until we pass it on to somebody else. A store of it, up the chimney or in a bank, gives us a comfortable feeling of safety because we know that there it is if we want it on a 'rainy day,' and the bank will perhaps give us a small payment for its use if we promise to leave it for a certain time. But the money only does its real work if we hand it on to someone else and take something that we want, or think that we want, in return for it.

We can postpone this use of the money and increase it in the meantime by investing it, as will be shown later; but we do that, if we are prudent and thrifty-minded folk, so as to have a larger amount to be spent, or reinvested, some day, by ourselves or our heirs.

Since money is thus only wanted in order to be spent – to give us the right to draw on the common pool of good things that we want – the most important quality that we need from it is steadiness in value. When we receive so many pounds or dollars or francs, or whatever it may be, we want to be sure that when we spend them to-morrow or next week or next year or ten years hence, they will give us as good a right to draw on the pool of goods as if we spent them at once. We do not want to be startled and disgusted by finding that, between receiving the money and spending it, a rise in the prices of the things that we want to buy has made the money go not nearly so far as we expected in supplying our needs.

It suits us much better if prices fall and the money goes further. But when this happens, it is likely, as will be shown later, that trade is bad and money is not so easy to earn.

When these uncomfortable things happen, and prices go up and our money loses value, or prices go down and money is less easy to earn, we do not naturally suppose that they happen because there is anything wrong with our money. We think it is because things are scarce or plentiful, or somebody is charging too much or somebody has got goods on his hands that he wants to get rid of or something of that sort.

And it is often the fact that influences like these are at work and pushing prices up or down. But sometimes it is the money that is causing the mischief, by being too plentiful or too scarce. In the middle of the nineteenth century, the discovery of new goldfields increased the quantity of money much faster than the quantity of goods was growing, and so, according to what economists call the Quantity Theory of Money, prices went up. This theory tells us that the general level of prices – the average price of all the goods that come to market – will be steady if the quantity of money increases in step with the increase in the output of goods; if money increases faster than goods prices go up, and we get what is called inflation, because there is more money handy to buy each article; and, contrariwise, if money does not keep pace with goods, prices will go down, and deflation sets in.

An extreme example shows the working of this puzzling business. If you woke up to-morrow and found that some good fairy had doubled the amount of money in your pockets, or your handbag, or your bank balance, you would almost certainly spend more; or if you were very thrifty you would invest more, which means that you would hand more over to somebody else to spend. But if the same thing happened to all the rest of us, we should all be spending more; and as it would not be possible to increase the output of goods all in a moment, the shopkeepers and the merchants and all the other people who had stocks of goods would put the prices up with a rush as they saw their stocks being devoured up by this sudden crowd of buyers. In the same way, if everybody's money were suddenly halved, those who have goods to sell would be forced to take lower prices for them because there would not be enough money to pay for them unless they did so.

What the gold discoveries of last century did for prices has been done during and since the war by Governments turning out enormous amounts of paper money, either printing it themselves or making banks print it; so much so that in some countries, such as Germany and Russia, the money became quite worthless and a fresh start had to be made. Then there came another turn of the wheel and money became relatively scarce again and some very high authorities tell us that the present trade depression and terrible unemployment in America, England, Germany and many other countries, can be largely if not wholly explained by the failure of the supply of money to keep pace with the supply of goods, and by the consequent fall in prices.

Leaving this question, like so many other things, for discussion on a later page, we have seen enough of this matter to make us recognize how immensely important and responsible is the work of those who create money for us and regulate the amount of it. This job is done by the bankers though their powers are, to a certain extent, controlled by the laws of the country in which they work and also by the demands, or lack of demands, upon them by the public which they serve.

In all the leading countries there is a roughly similar system, though the manner and spirit in which the system is worked varies considerably.

Gold, though seldom seen circulating as coin – practically never now in England – is still the basis of the system. The chief regulator of the system is a central bank; the Bank of England here, the twelve Federal Reserve banks in America – it had to have twelve because of the vast area of the country and for other reasons – the Bank of France across the Channel, and so on. Generally the central bank does little or no business with the general public, but acts as banker to the Government and to the other banks of the country, usually spoken of as the commercial banks, which keep the balances of the business community and of every one else that has a banking account, taking care of their money for them and lending them money when they need it. By lending the money they create the currency with which the business world does its work, because the loans made by the banks become bank deposits against which business men draw the cheques in which all the big payments are made. Gold is the basis of the matter in this wise and to this extent. The central banks all keep a stock of gold as backing for the notes that they issue and the credits that they create, by lending to the Government and to the commercial banks. The gold is wanted because it is still, owing to the many centuries in which it has been taken by mankind as a form of payment, universally accepted as such in all civilized countries; and a stock of it has to be held by central banks, for use when other forms of international payment are lacking.

With the support of this gold backing the central banks issue notes and create credits to an extent which is usually regulated by law – that is to say, the central banks have to keep a certain proportion of gold to their notes and deposits.

Most of the principal central banks, however, keep so much more gold than the law obliges them to have, that in normal times their gold holdings depend more on their own judgment and policy than on legal enactment.

Now let us see how they create currency and credit. The currency part is clear, for currency only means money, and notes are money, and so the notes issued by central banks are evidently a creation of currency. The creation of credit is shown by the deposits that the central banks include among their liabilities. These deposits consist chiefly of the balances held with the central banks by the Government and the other banks – the commercial banks of the country.

If the Government needs temporary accommodation at a time when revenue is coming in slowly it borrows from the central bank, which so creates a deposit for it, which is passed on to the commercial banks, as the Government pays out the money.

If the commercial banks want credit from the central bank, they can get it by discounting bills, which means selling bills to the central bank or borrowing from them on the security of bills, or of any kind of security that the central bank may take.

Bills are promises to pay issued by banks, Governments, traders and others. They are due to be paid at an early date – three months is, in these days, the longest life of those usually issued by banks and traders, though Governments sometimes put out bills that run for a year. Anyone who wants to know more about them, and all this puzzling business of money creating, than is necessary for our present purpose, can turn to my book on the *Meaning of Money*.

We can illustrate the matter by a simplified central

bank balance sheet showing its assets on the right side and its liabilities on the left.

Capital	Gold
Government deposits	Bills of Exchange
Bankers' deposits	Securities
Notes in Circulation	Advances

The assets are what the central bank has got. The liabilities are what it owes. It owes its capital to its shareholders, its deposits to its customers, and its notes to those who hold them.

The central banks, however, can also increase the amount of credit in the hands of the commercial banks on their own initiative. Besides buying bills that are brought to them for discount, they can, and do if they think fit, buy bills in the open market and the sums that they pay for them are added to the balances of the commercial banks. It is also usual for the central banks of most countries to hold a certain amount of the Government debt among their assets; and some of them, like the Bank of England, can hold any invest-ments that they choose without any legal or other restriction. When central banks buy securities, they pay for them by giving a credit in their books which is added either to the deposits of the commercial banks or to those of the Government if the securities are bought direct from it. In either case this addition means an increase in the volume of credit outstanding. And contrariwise, if the central banks think that the amount of outstanding credit is too big they can sell securities or borrow on them. By so doing they cancel a certain amount of credit because the buyers or lenders pay with a draft on one or other of the commercial banks, whose balance at the central bank is thereby reduced.

Such in rough outline is the system by which the central banks of the chief countries provide and regulate the note issue and the credit on which the commercial banks work – we shall see how in a minute. But before we leave the subject of the central banks it is better to note – in order to prevent misunderstanding – that the Bank of England is not legally obliged to have a certain proportion of gold to note issue, but is forbidden to issue notes at all above a certain limit – now £260,000,000 – except against gold; on the other hand it may create credit by discounting, lending and buying securities to any extent that it thinks fit.

These technical divergences, however, make no difference to the main principle on which the functions and duties of the central banks are based. It is their business to provide the commercial community, through the commercial banks, with notes and credit, and at the same time to keep the reserve of gold that is required from time to time when a country has been buying from other countries more goods and services than it has been selling, or lending abroad so freely that the balance of payments is against it, and gold has to be sent out in order to settle the difference. All which will be made clearer when we come to discuss the matter of international trade and payments.[1]

Now we have to see what the commercial banks do with the notes issued and the credit created by the

[1] See Chapter XIII, p. 220, and Chapter XVIII, p. 294.

central banks. They, it will be remembered, are the banks which deal with the general public, keeping your balance and mine if we have got one, and lending us money if we can show a reasonable certainty of being able to pay it back.

As to the notes, they pass them on to their customers when the latter want them for pocket money, and keep a certain amount in their tills for the purpose of meeting the public's demands for currency. These notes that they have in hand and their balance at the central bank form their cash reserves, just as gold forms the cash reserves of the central banks for international purposes. On these reserves the commercial banks create credit for manufacturers, traders, and all the rest of us and so provide the money, in the form of cheques, with which all the large and most of the small transactions are settled. Their balance sheets would show, among the resources or assets – the things which they hold to meet demands from them and to earn profits for their shareholders – such items as:

Cash in hand, meaning notes and coins.
Balance at central bank.
Bills.
Investments.
Loans and advances.

And on the other side, which shows the liabilities – the sums that they have to account for to shareholders or pay back on demand to customers – there will be one principal item which will be by far the largest, the deposits owed to the general public.

Just as the central banks, on the foundation of a stock of gold, issue notes and create credit for the commercial banks by discounting, lending and investing, so the latter on the foundation of cash in hand and a balance at the central bank – which can be turned into cash at any moment – create credit for their customers by buying bills and securities from them and making loans and advances to them. There is this small difference, that when a central bank buys bills or lends money the credit that it creates is generally left with it as a deposit; but the commercial banks create credit that is left as a deposit either with the bank that creates the credit or with one of its rivals. They create deposits for themselves and one another.

These deposits give their customers the right to draw cheques which are the money of commerce in countries which enjoy the benefit of a highly developed banking system. Bank deposits are thus potential currency, and become currency as they are passed from hand to hand in the form of cheques. The extent to which the commercial banks can create this currency is in some countries regulated by law, but in England is left to the prudence of the bankers. In those countries in which the law imposes a legal proportion between a bank's stock of cash and its deposits, the commercial banks usually have a considerable margin of cash above the legal limit, and so, in this case again, banking practice is generally the real influence which determines the policy of the banks.

The immense importance of their work is already plain and will be still more so when we discuss in more detail the effects on trade of the supply of money. But a word of warning may be put in here against a tendency, rather common to-day, of crediting the bankers with more power than they really possess. Some people assume that the banks can contract and expand the supply of credit to any extent that they choose, contracting it by calling in loans and selling securities, and expanding it by lending freely and cheaply and buying securities. In fact their powers in both directions are severely limited.

They cannot call in loans except to a moderate extent and with a very gentle hand on the curb; because if they did it roughly and ruthlessly they would cause a panic and ruin some of their customers; and in the case of the commercial banks, competition obliges them to meet the needs of solvent customers for fear of losing them; and selling securities is also a measure that has to be carried out with a cautious hand, lest trouble should be caused and more harm done than good. What the banks can do is to raise the price that borrowers have to pay. This is done by a rise in bank rate – the price charged for discounts and loans by the central bank which regulates, roughly and more or less, the charges made by the commercial banks. This movement is commonly accepted by the business world as a danger signal, intimating that it is not wise to have too much sail spread, and in normal times is usually effective, at least to the extent of preventing a further expansion in credit.

When it is a question of expanding credit, the power of the banks in increasing loans and advances is limited by the demands of their customers. It takes two to make a bargain. If the business world does not want to borrow, the banks cannot make them. Here again something can be done by lowering the price of loans, by a reduction in bank rate followed by the charges of the commercial banks. But if the business world is in one of its dismal moods and cannot see any result but loss from any expansion of business, it will not want to borrow even if it is offered money for nothing. By buying securities the banks can do something to expand credit, but here again their power is limited, for a holding of securities, beyond a certain amount, is not a good banking asset.

Nevertheless, when all these cautions have been entered against the common tendency to regard the bankers as all-powerful autocrats who can restrict and swell credit, and therefore trade, as they please, the fact remains that they have great powers and enormous responsibility, which fully justify the big rewards that go to those who wield the power and face the responsibility.

There is another common delusion about them, which is that their job is quite easy and simple and could be carried out very well by Government officials if the banks were nationalized; and the earnest reformers who advocate this measure generally go on to argue that under a nationalized banking system, credit, which is a national asset which the bankers have managed to monopolize for their own profit, could and would be used for purposes that are nationally and socially desirable, instead of being supplied to business men in search of profit that is often acquired by questionable and anti-social methods.

As to the ease and simplicity of banking, anybody of

course can accept deposits that are paid in, take care of customers' securities and collect their dividends and do all the simple services of this kind; but even in the matter of honouring customers' cheques, the question of a doubtful signature sometimes has to be decided with more promptitude than is usual in Government Departments. But it is in deciding about loans that the difficulty of the bankers' problem is greatest. Should Smith, who wants an advance of £10,000 or £1,000,000 have it or not? On the promptitude and skill with which this question is answered, the course of the country's trade depends. If Smith ought to have the loan and does not get it, trade is hampered. If he ought not to have the loan and gets it, bad trade is done, Smith gets deeper into difficulties, and the bank has a bad debt to write off.

Mr. Bernard Shaw in the stimulating pages of his *Intelligent Woman's Guide to Socialism and Capitalism* refers to the retail hiring of money to 'ordinary tradesmen and men of business' as if it were a minor detail of banking that anyone could do. It would be interesting to put Mr. Shaw in charge of a bank branch, with a connection among ordinary tradesmen and business men, for a week, and see how much money and how many customers he would lose for the bank.

It is certainly true that many Government officials would have made excellent bankers if they had been caught young and trained to the business: for they are a highly educated and very intelligent set of people who work very hard at their job. But if banking were nationalized it would have to be worked on official lines. There would be forms to be filled in, memoranda to be circulated all round the office before an answer could be given, and so on. All the promptitude and elasticity with which banking is now worked would be lost. 'When the Bank becomes the State,' says Mr. O. R. Hobson,[1] 'the conditions of accommodation must inevitably become stereotyped; they must be reduced to rules and regulations which can be printed in White Papers. The man who can show a balance sheet up to a certain standard will obtain a certain quantum of credit; the man whose balance sheet falls short of the prescribed specification in any particular will not get it – how otherwise will the Minister of Banking be able to justify himself in replying to questions in Parliament? For let there be no mistake about it, under the socialized system there will be no keeping such questions out of the political arena. Credit policy will become a matter of wire-pulling and lobbying. The member for one constituency will want to know why A Ltd., employing five thousand of his constituents, was refused accommodation and was compelled, therefore, to resort to short time, while B Ltd., in the neighbouring division, got the credit it needed. Elections will be fought on the cry, "More credit for the cotton trade or the coal mines or the steel industry!" "Larger loans for brewers" will be the modern version of "Hands off the poor man's beer!" '

This danger of the intrusion of politics into banking, with very bad effect on banking, is serious. Mr. Baldwin has stated his opinion in a public speech, that there was no Government on earth that he would

---

[1] *The Case Against Nationalising the Banks*, by O. R. Hobson, published by the National Association of Merchants and Manufacturers.

trust to manage a currency, and that the outstanding advantage, to his mind, of a gold currency was that, as far as anything in the world could be, a gold currency was 'knave-proof.' This is an unkind reflection on politicians from such a genial authority, but who knows what bitter experience was behind it?

And if Mr. Baldwin's evidence is rejected, as it may reasonably be by Socialists, on the ground that he is a Tory and a capitalist, we can cite Mr. Snowden, himself an ardent Socialist, as a witness on the same side. Speaking at a Labour Party Conference at Birmingham in October 1928 he associated himself heartily with the remark made by his leader, Mr. Ramsay MacDonald, on the previous day, that the control of currency and credit must be kept free from political influences. When asked 'Why?' by an interrupting delegate, he said bluntly that Parliament is not a competent body to deal with the administration of such highly delicate and intricate matters. He, he said, knew something of the dangers of the control of credit and the means of starting an inflation policy. That power might be in the hands of a Government who wished to use it in order to serve some purpose or to gain popular support. 'He was not prepared to put that control in the hands of any Government.'[1]

So Mr. Snowden, almost echoing Mr. Baldwin's words. As was to be expected, his statement did not meet with unanimous approval from his hearers. Miss Ellen Wilkinson, M.P., said that politicians had been referred to as if they were a race of fearsome insects

[1] *The Times*, 5th October 1928.

preying on the body politic. It seemed to be forgotten that politicians were the elected representatives of the people.

Now we all know that many politicians are very earnest, high-minded men doing tiresome and exasperating work with no thought of reward except such as comes from trying to serve their country. Why should a Conservative Prime Minister and a Socialist Chancellor of the Exchequer agree in damning them so heartily?

A philosophic explanation of the weaknesses of politicians is provided for us by that very advanced and learned thinker – so advanced that perhaps he should be described as a Communist – Mr. Bertrand Russell. 'Let us,' he writes in his book, *Roads to Freedom*, 'dismiss from our minds such criticisms of parliamentary government as are bound up with the present system of private property and consider only those that would remain true in a collectivist community. Certain defects seem inherent in the very nature of representative institutions. There is a sense of self-importance, inseparable from success in a contest for popular favour. There is an all but unavoidable habit of hypocrisy, since experience shows that the democracy does not detect insincerity in an orator, and will, on the other hand, be shocked by things which even the most sincere men may think necessary. Hence arises a tone of cynicism among elected representatives, and a feeling that no man can retain his position in politics without deceit. This is as much the fault of the democracy as of the representatives, but it seems unavoidable so long as the main thing that all bodies of men demand of their champions is flattery.'

Many people may think that Mr. Russell in this passage has slandered both democracy and its representatives. Perhaps he has. But such weaknesses, even if described in somewhat exaggerated terms, are a more than sufficient explanation of Messrs. Baldwin and Snowden's refusal to trust Governments with the business of working the machine of currency and credit.

Mr. G. D. H. Cole, though in favour of a socialized banking service, says that it 'will have, at the cost of incurring an additional risk, to pay more regard to the merits of the enterprise and less to the question of security'; and he admits that 'State banking will not be quite so safe as joint stock banking has become.'[1] He thinks that there is plenty of margin within which extra risks can be incurred. Most of us will think that safety in banking is a first essential.

In fact, the danger of allowing not only banking, but industry in general, to be controlled by Government is now admitted by a large number of advanced Socialists. Mr. Cole himself has lately said, in an article published in *Everyman* on 6th February 1930, that 'it is plainly undesirable to "politicalize" however necessary it may be to "socialize" the management of industry both because Parliament is already overburdened with work, and because the Civil Service method of administration is too rigid and slow in its working to fit the needs of a big modern business.'

[1] *Next Ten Years in British Social and Economic Policy*, by G. D. H. Cole (Macmillan), p. 245.

How far it is possible to socialize the management of industry without at the same time politicalizing it, is a matter about which one may feel a certain doubt. Enough has been said to show that bankers and banking are the linchpins of a wheel on the machine that keeps us all supplied with food and goods, and that if they were nationalized and made into a Government Department, there is serious danger that the wheel might not spin nearly as easily and smoothly as it does now. For this reason banking seems to be the last of our business activities that judicious reformers should want to nationalize instead of being put down among the first to be so treated. If they began with other industries and proved that they could work when nationalized, and if at last the nation were being supplied with all its needs – or all the needs that the Government thought fit to satisfy – then, when all production and consumption had been controlled and rationed, credit might very well be rationed also by nationalized banks, dealing it out according to rule, as decided by the Government. But as long as there is competition and risk and the public is allowed a say concerning the things that it would like to enjoy, banking will have to share the risks, providing credit to those whom it thinks likely to satisfy the public's changing moods, for only by doing this directly or indirectly can profits be earned and credit be made effective and repaid. Such is the interesting and anxious life of the banking leaders, taking quick decisions of the greatest importance to trade, and earning their reward as the linchpin in a wheel of the great machine. This machine puts the work of all of us into the hopper and turns out, for the use of all of us, the work of all the rest of the world. It would be very awkward if its wheels got out of gear.

As to the contention that if the banks were nationalized the credits that they make could be used for finer purposes, before accepting this doctrine one wants to know who is to make the decisions touching the purposes to which credit is to be put. Presumably this task would fall to some kind of a Committee. If it were wise and practical it might do splendid work. If it were foolish and fanciful its decisions might have disastrous results.

As it is, the banks grant credits to customers who may fairly be expected to make a profitable use of the money so that they can pay it back to the banks. These customers can only make profits by increasing the wealth of the world and producing something that you and I want, or think that we want. Our wants may often be foolish, but it is pleasant to have them satisfied.

CHAPTER VI

FINANCIERS AND SPECULATORS

Financiers collect Money from Investors to be lent to Borrowers –
Public Loans – Company Promoters and Directors – The Function of Companies – Stockbrokers and Stock Markets – Investment and Speculation – The Utility of Speculation.

BY financiers I mean all those who deal and traffic
in the money that is created by bankers, as we saw
in the last chapter, with the co-operation of their
customers. Financiers thus include loan-mongers,
company promoters and directors, bill brokers, exchange dealers, stockbrokers and Stock Exchange
dealers, and perhaps we ought to include speculators,
as useful camp followers who hang on to the outskirts
of the monetary army.

It is a motley herd, including the best and worst of the
workers in business. When they do their work well all
of them are useful and some indispensable, but it is
from this quarter of the business world that the worst
and most sensational scandals generally proceed, and it
is here that the critics of the capitalist system, when
they are wanting to prove that it is a noisome sink of
iniquity, find their most striking examples.

This quarter is like one of those streets to be found
in most big cities, which at one end is lined by fine
houses dwelt in by nice clean people, but gradually

degenerates as one walks through it, till at the other end it is a foul slum full of folk who earn a precarious living out of the vices of the public. It is easy, and quite true, to say that such an ending to such a street is a disgrace to our civilization.

It is also easy to say that such a slum should be cleared out. But such slums and their inhabitants will never really be abolished until the public cleans itself of the vices on which the slum dwellers fatten. As long as there is a greedy and ignorant public hoping to get rich quick by buying gold bricks, gold bricks will be forthcoming; and if instead of curing the public of its greed and ignorance, we try to make the penalties of selling gold bricks severe enough to stop the sellers, we run a serious risk of frightening away the sellers of real gold, and cramping genuine business. The need for reform is urgent and imperative; but the reform has to be done sensibly and at both ends of the problem.

In general the work done by all these financier folk is putting money that its owners do not want to spend into the hands of those who need it and will pay for its use, either in interest or dividends or the promise or hope of dividends.

Dealers in exchange hardly come under this description, for they do the incalculably useful work of making international business possible by turning, so to speak, different monies into one another – dollars into pounds, francs, marks, rupees and all the currencies of the civilized and half-civilized world. Much of this work is done by bankers, but the dealers create a specialized market which is one of the speediest and most efficient wheels in the machine which puts all the products of the world at our disposal. They are included here because they traffic in money and so their work is essential to the conduct of international finance ; but their work is equally essential to the conduct of international trade, travel, and intercourse.

Bill brokers borrow money from bankers and others who want to find a temporary use for it, and use it in dealing in the bills which we found among the assets of the bankers. These bills are promises to pay, generally secured on materials and goods moving from seller to buyer. The loan granted through the bills covers the period of movement and manufacture of the goods, enabling the seller to get his money at once and giving the buyer time to work the goods up for the final purchaser. A specialized market in them is a great advantage to trade and to the smooth working of a money market. But an exploration of the beauties and uses of the bill is too technical a matter for our present purpose, and may be found in the pages of the *Meaning of Money* and many other works.

It is when we come to the loan issuers, company promoters and stockbrokers that we see the importance of this financial group to the public, both that which has money to lend and that which has money to spend. You will remember, when we considered the example of the young lady and her cup of tea, how many companies we found to have been brought into being before the spending of her twopence could provide it for her.

It is, of course, quite possible to imagine that the trade of the world might have been organized on different lines which would have worked equally well.

or better. All that we are concerned with here is the fact that the immense increase in our command over the good things of life, enjoyed by a greatly increased population, has in fact been achieved, first, by the efforts of private owners or private firms and partnerships, and afterwards, especially during the last half-century, by the working of joint-stock companies. In these companies the public invests money that it does not spend in immediate wants. By so investing, it spends the money on promoting enterprise that will supply its wants, and, if successful, will provide it with an income and enable it to get back the money invested, possibly increased in amount, if ever it wants to turn its investment into cash. If the enterprise does not succeed, the money invested in it is lost, wholly or in part.

But we had better begin the investment subject with loans, because those who handle them are highly important members of the financial world – so much so that one of them, the firm of Baring Brothers, still a great leader among them, was described in 1819 by the Duc de Richelieu as one of the six Great Powers, the others being England, France, Russia, Austria and Prussia.[1]

Loans are generally issued to provide money that is needed by Governments, states, municipalities and other public bodies, which promise to pay interest on them and (probably) to repay the loan some day, out of the revenues that they raise from the taxpayers or ratepayers in their area.

Governments want more money than they can, or

[1] Ellis Powell, *Evolution of the Money Market*, p. 340.

think they can, collect by taxing their citizens, most certainly and urgently when they are at war. Practically the whole of the loans which compose the huge British debt have been raised for this purpose. Macaulay in his *History of England* relates how, at the end of every one of her great wars, from that with Louis Quatorze to that with Napoleon, England has been told by scandalized observers of the growth of the debt, that the burden was greater than she could possibly bear and how, on every occasion, she has proceeded to bear it and to thrive in spite of it. The historian concludes by observing that 'a long experience justifies us in believing that England may in the twentieth century be better able to bear a debt of £1,600,000,000 than she is at the present time, to bear her present load.'[1] He was well within the mark. The debt is now £7,000,000,000 odd and the old country staggers along under it, with the general standard of comfort enjoyed by her citizens higher than it has ever been before. She has found out that the payment of interest on a debt that is almost entirely owed by all the citizens as taxpayers, to some of the citizens as debt-holders, does not diminish the wealth of the country as a whole, though by diverting to debt-holders wealth which has to be provided by industry, it may have a cramping effect on industry and so check the growth of wealth.

When the debt is held abroad it is another matter, for then the payment of interest and what is called a sinking fund, by means of which a sum is paid each year towards the extinction of the debt, is a drain

[1] Macaulay, *History of England*, Chapter XIX.

from the debtor country into the pockets of the foreign creditor. England, as every one knows, has lent in the past immense sums to the Governments of her own Dominions and of countries such as Japan, China, Argentina, Brazil and the new States of Europe. And so these countries have to pay to the British bondholders who subscribed to, or have since bought, the securities representing these loans, so much a year in interest, and probably so much a year in sinking fund, which is either used to pay off a fraction of the loan year by year or is accumulated by the issuing house to pay off the whole loan when it falls due. This loan charge thus reduces the income of the Argentine citizens, or whoever it may be who have to pay taxes to provide it, and added to that of Englishmen in the form of interest received or debt paid off. The payment has to be made, unless it is met by fresh borrowing, which often happens, by the export from the debtor country of goods or services, and by the import of goods or services into the country of the creditor bondholders. The export and import need not be direct from one to the other – Brazil, for instance, owes most of her foreign debt to English investors, but she sells her coffee, her chief item of export, mostly to the United States and the Continent of Europe; that part of the proceeds of her coffee which is needed to meet the charge on the debt to English investors finds its way to England by devious courses through the never-resting mechanism worked by the dealers in exchange – the international money-changers who swop claims on one country against claims on another.

All this will be made clearer, I hope, when we come

to consider the trade balances of the nations. For the moment we are concerned with Government and public loans; and we have seen that when they are held internally, like the English debt, they affect the distribution but not the total of the nation's income; but when they are held abroad the annual charge diminishes the nation's income because it has to be sent abroad in goods for which no payment is received, because they are themselves a form of payment.

But this yearly drain is met, in return for the benefit conferred on the borrowing country by the loan, which has, or ought to have, furnished it with equipment in the form of railways, harbours, roads, clearances and other kinds of development, which have enabled it to meet the drain and keep a handsome margin for itself in its improved capacity for growing and making things. If the money raised by the loan has been wastefully spent on building railways designed to 'placate' political supporters or on armies and navies that were only required by national vanity, backed by designing armament-makers abroad, or on paying governmental expenses which ought to have been met out of taxation, then the drain involved by its annual charge is a serious drag on the borrowing country's progress.

Here we begin to see the very heavy responsibility shouldered by the loan-issuing houses, whether banks which handle this business in many countries, or private firms which do most of it in England. It is their first business to make sure that any loan which they offer to the public is being raised by them on behalf of a solvent borrower who may confidently be expected to meet the annual charge on it; and, further, as long as any of the loan is still outstanding and unredeemed, to watch over the interests of the bond-holders, and, if default or postponement of sinking fund is necessary, to see that the terms of any composition made are fair to both parties. But it is their second and at least equally important business to see that the proceeds of the loan are spent on works that will improve the borrowing country's power to produce and handle the goods that will pay for the loan. If they neglect this duty there is likely to be disaster ahead both for borrower and lender. Such disasters have been only too common in the bad and early days when the loan-issuing business was sowing its nasty crop of wild oats and before it had been concentrated in a few strong and responsible hands with prestige, tradition and experience behind them. But when loans are made on the sound lines indicated above, they are of immense benefit to the borrower, as shown above, and likewise to the country that lends the money, because, not only do its investing citizens get a good security and a satisfactory rate of interest, but its producing citizens, manufacturers and carriers, get a demand for the goods and services that they have to sell.

Here again I am anticipating the subject of the trade balance, but for the moment I may be allowed to assert that just as the borrowing country has to send goods or sell services abroad in order to meet the annual charge of the debt, so the lending country has to send goods or sell services abroad to the net amount of the loan (after deducting all expenses of issue) when or soon after the loan is issued. Dr. Stephen Leacock, head of the Department of Economics at McGill University, Montreal, and well known as author of *Arcadian Adventures among the Idle Rich* and other delightful works, put this matter clearly in a few sentences of his latest book, *Economic Prosperity in the British Empire*. 'The adoption of limited liability (1858),' he writes, 'made it possible for millions of shareholders to enter the field. But long before this the London money market and the London financial houses were well started on their way. What they seemed to do was to make loans out of funds gathered in London. What they really did was to help spread all over the world British goods from British ships.'

This, then, is what the loan issuers do for the world when they do their work well and truly. They provide new and growing communities with all kinds of equipment which enables the borrower to produce goods enough, and more than enough, to meet the debt charge; and they provide the old-established communities with sound securities for the investors, and a profitable market for the manufacturers and merchants and shipowners, and so indirectly for the shipbuilders. When the work of the loan issuers was not done well, then the borrowing countries got the equipment, or goods of some kind sent by the lender, and the lending country got the consequent increase in export trade, but the investors lost their money, or part of it, and the annual payment in the form of goods sent by the borrower was not, or not fully, forthcoming.

Foreign lending in the form of loans has thus a very important influence on the development of world trade and its careful handling by the loan houses is a highly responsible task. The private firms which handle it form a kind of plutocratic aristocracy in the business world, with high prestige in the eyes of the investing public, which attaches more importance, perhaps, to the name of the issuing house than to the terms and conditions of the loan. In this the public's instinct is shrewd; it knows that it has little but guesswork to go on in judging about the probable solvency of a borrower, and is content to leave this decision to firms with long experience and tradition behind them, and a name and reputation, with a value beyond many kings' ransoms, to maintain.

When we come to company promoters, it is a different matter. For the big issuing houses do not condescend to the small fry of company promotion, and there are no recognized institutions, known to the general public, that handle this business. Companies come into being, nobody quite knows how, and enterprises are offered concerning which investors have nothing to guide them except estimates of probable profits if the venture is new and a statement of profits earned in the past, if it is an old one. The all-important question of future management and earning power is shrouded in mists of obscurity, illuminated only by the names of the directors and of the brokers to the issue, concerning which the general public cannot be expected to have knowledge enough to discriminate. It is small wonder that the path of company creation has been strewn with many failures, though the domination of the joint stock company in all spheres of business life is a sufficient proof that its development has been, on the whole, profitable both to the investing public and to the manufacturing and commercial community.

Companies and company promoters are all the more important because a new school of investment doctrine has lately arisen which tells us that the old-fashioned theory of safety in investment to be achieved by a preference for what are called gilt-edged securities is a mistake, and that real safety is to be got by diversified holdings of common shares in companies, or corporations as they are called in America.

A well-secured first charge with a fixed and certain rate of interest was what the old-fashioned public, and its old-fashioned advisers on investments, believed to be the kind of security that one could go to sleep on. If this was what people wanted they could obviously find it best among the debts of Governments and public bodies described in previous pages, or among the debts of important companies supplying a commodity or service that the public was certain always to need (if such commodities and services exist).

A government or municipal debt is charged on the taxpaying and ratepaying capacity of the area governed, and if the area is wide enough and rich enough, must be better secured than any promise to pay issued by an enterprise that works one line of business and is subject to the ups and downs of trade.

But public debts, owing to this higher rating of their security, give a comparatively low yield to the buyer – there was a time, in 1896-97, when British Consols could only be bought at a price which made the return to the holder less than $2\frac{1}{2}$ per cent. on the money that he put into them. And so investors in search of a better return went to look for what they thought the safest securities issued by public companies.

Public companies had securities to suit all tastes. They come into being because somebody thinks, for instance, that it will be good business to start a soap factory, to work a process that will produce a particularly alluring soap and as he has not enough money of his own to set it going, he sets the mysterious machinery of company promotion to work and invites the public to put money into it. He gets a board of directors together, some of whom knew something about soap and some of whom are known to be people who would not lend their names to an enterprise unless they believed that it was, as far as they could determine, honestly conceived and likely to be successful. And the public is asked to subscribe for debenture stock, or bonds if the concern is American, preferred or preference and common or ordinary stocks or shares.

The debenture stock or bonds are a debt owed by the company similar to the Government debts. They are a first charge on its net revenue – that is, on the income that it gets by the sale of soap after the payment of all expenses, wages, salaries, directors' fees, auditors' fees, taxes, rates, rent, materials, upkeep of buildings, plant and machinery. When all these charges have been met the bond or debenture holders take the first slice out of the profits to the extent of the fixed rate of interest due to them, and probably a sinking fund charge held on their behalf by trustees. They are creditors of the company and if their charge is not met they can put it in the hands of a receiver who will manage it or sell it on their account and if it is sold they have first charge on whatever price the business and its assets may fetch.

Holders of the preferred and common stocks or shares are in a different position. They are not creditors but owners – partners in the concern to the extent of the money that they have put in. After the debtholders have been paid their interest and sinking fund, the preferred holders take the second slice usually at a fixed rate, rather higher than that paid to the debtholders because they rank second and so the security is not quite so good; and after their claim has been met the common shareholders are entitled to any remnant that there may be as dividend, though the directors, if they are sensible and prudent as most of them are, will certainly keep back some of the net revenue, or profits, and put it to reserve or carry it forward.

This fact, of regular allocations to reserves out of profits, is the foundation of the new investment theory that common shares are safer than fixed interest securities; because, if the sums regularly put to reserves are prudently used either in developing the business or in the purchase of securities, the revenue of the company, and consequently the margin available as dividend on the common shares, will tend to rise steadily. The common shareholder will thus have a rising income and his shares will have a rising value, while the holders of fixed-interest securities – debts, bonds and preferred stocks – get their fixed rate and no more. At present, owing to general depression and diminished earnings of industry of all kinds, the theory is under a cloud. But if it is in the main true, as, with certain qualifications, it seems to be, it will win its way back to favour with the recovery of trade; and its birth and growth have made the whole machinery of company promotion and of stock-exchange dealing and stockbroking and speculating even more important than they were before it appeared.

They have been growing in importance ever since the adoption of the limited liability principle made investments in joint stock companies possible to people of small means. Before that time, 1858 in England, if a company went bankrupt, shareholders were liable for its debts to the extent of all their possessions. Limited liability meant that anyone who bought a share that had been fully paid up was liable for no further payment in respect of it. Since then, joint stock companies have gone forward steadily to domination in enterprise, but their common stocks and shares have hitherto been looked on as more or less speculative investments, as they certainly are, and the fixed-rate securities were thought to be the safe medium of investment for those who could not afford to take risks. If common shares are now to be raised to the dignity of the best investments, if only one holds a sufficient variety of them, the business of company promotion and company direction acquires a new responsibility. Already they have an importance which is quite incalculable, because on them depends the provision of the sinews of energy for all enterprise that is new and risky and doubtful. Loans to governments and public bodies have done a great work in assisting development, but they have necessarily been spent chiefly on such things as railways, docks, lighting and

'public utilities' – services for which a steady demand
may be counted on with fair confidence. They are
proved enterprises and can be run successfully on
lines of routine, though there is something to be said
for the view that even they are more likely to prove
themselves adaptable and expansive and receptive of
new ideas if in the hands of managers who have the
spur of private enterprise behind them. But for new
notions, new inventions and new enterprises – and it
is on these novelties that the progress and growth of
the world's pool of wealth depends – companies, formed
with the capital and managed by the brains of those
who are prepared to take a risk, are, under present
conditions, the only bodies that do the work of starting
and testing.

Hence the necessity for sound company promotion,
good directors and managers, intelligent and well-
informed stockbrokers to advise the public, and a free
market in securities. This market is provided by the
dealers in securities and made freer and steadier by
the professional speculators who can take long views
and back them, buying when no one has a good word
to say for markets, and 'selling a bear' – that is, selling
stocks in the hope of buying them back cheaper – when
prices are soaring.

For better company promotion we want more companies formed for this purpose with influential and
well-informed people in charge and good financial
backing; so that if a promising venture is put before
them they can nurse it through its infant ailments
and only put it before the public when it is, to a
reasonable extent, proved. As it is, too many eggs

are put into the public's basket before they have been really laid, and properly managed incubators are very much wanted. Such a service is of the highest value both to the trade of the world, which can only grow if new ideas are encouraged, fostered and financed, and to the investing public, which ought to be given a fairer chance when it ventures into speculative enterprise.

Speculative investment means investment in securities carrying a considerable risk and used to be looked on as rather naughty by the strait-laced stockbrokers of an earlier age; but it is not only legitimate but a duty for those who can afford to take the risk. If we all stuck to 'safety first' loans and bonds there would be no money for untried enterprise, and progress would be paralysed. All the more reason why the risk should be diminished, as far as it can be, by the honest and careful handling of companies in their early stages.

And in their later ones also. Management, which means the qualities of the men in charge, makes all the difference to success or failure. If ill-directed, the work of the most skilful body of wage-earners and of the best machinery that can be bought, will produce loss instead of profit. On the whole the management of companies has evidently been honest and prudent, as is shown by their growth and dominance. But there have been too many scandals and mistakes, and when these happen there is apt to be a cry for stricter company laws.

This is not the place for a discussion of this prickly problem, but I lately heard a very practical suggestion from Mr. Henry Morgan, the President of the Society of Incorporated Accountants and Auditors, for enabling shareholders to exercise better control of their property. In his view the present system by which directors send out proxy forms in their own favour for shareholders to sign, gives the Board almost overwhelming power and deprives shareholders of any opportunity of using their voting power except by attending the meetings of the Company, which only a small proportion of them can do. Accordingly he proposes that the present complicated and unfair proxy system should be abolished and that, in every case where a poll is demanded, the Board should be required to send to each shareholder notice that the poll is to be taken, together with a voting-paper setting out the resolutions submitted, so that the shareholders would be provided with a simple method of voting for or against the various resolutions. This system would, he believes, cure many abuses of their power by directors.

There is no need to insist on the value, when it is well done, of the work done by stockbrokers, bondsellers and others who help the public to find investments and by the dealers who make a free market in securities. We have seen that the filling and swelling of that pool out of which we are all (more or less) provided with what we want, depends now chiefly on company enterprise; and company enterprise would not be possible unless there were a free market in the stocks and shares that companies issue, for investors would not subscribe to them or buy them, unless they knew that, if they wanted their money back, they could sell in a market which would give them perhaps more, perhaps less, than they had paid, but always something, except in the comparatively rare cases that have led to complete disaster.

As to the pure speculator, who buys only to sell again and sells only to buy cheaper some day, he is usually looked on, if he loses, as an ass who has got his deserts, and if he wins, as a parasite who preys on the public, brings the City into disrepute, and ought, if only it were possible, to be hounded out of existence.

But it is necessary to discriminate. We have seen that a free market in securities is essential to company progress, which means, as things are, all of our progress in getting things that we want; and a free market in securities is greatly facilitated by the existence of the right kind of speculator.

If stocks and shares could only be bought and sold, if there were a real seller or buyer to perform the other side of the bargain, stock exchange business would be much slower and more difficult, and consequently more expensive. The professional dealers could do something to fill the gap, but their power to take and provide stock is not unlimited, and business is made much easier and cheaper by sales and purchases which finally cancel themselves out by book entries.

The reward of the speculator is precarious and probably, on the whole, small. When the general public speculates its reward is generally a minus quantity, except in such abnormal time and place as America in the boom years of 1921-29. Then, with an immense expansion of banking credit and huge and almost unbroken rise in stock-exchange prices, the public made a regular income by buying stocks and selling them at a higher level, until the inevitable crash came. But this speculators' Paradise has only happened once. Usually, what the public makes out of the stock markets it makes at its own expense, for A's profit is B's loss, roughly and in the aggregate, and both A and B have to pay the commissions and other charges of the game. Moreover, the general public is almost certain to pay toll also to the professional speculator, who is on the spot, and 'in the know' – though being in the know is often a costly advantage – and gives his whole time to a pursuit which is much too technical and risky to be indulged in by amateurs.

And it has been already noted that speculators are often useful in steadying the market in securities, though these are only those cool and detached operators who are strong enough to resist the herd instinct and have courage enough to sell, at times when all the many-headed that can scrape together the necessary cover are rushing in to buy. Such operators in the first place help to stem the upward rush of prices by providing fictitious sales. Later on there comes a time when the public has suddenly discovered that prices cannot rise indefinitely, and is tumbling over itself to sell, and then the beneficence of those who had previously 'sold a bear,' and are now ready to buy back, is plainly apparent. They provide a cushion for prices to fall on, just as they had previously steadied the upward rush. And so they help to flatten out the curves of security prices – and it may incidentally be noted that speculators in commodities work a similar and perhaps even more important benefit. By providing a 'forward market' in, for example, cotton, they

enable the spinners and weavers to 'hedge' against a
fall in the price before the process of manufacture is
finished. For the price of cotton goods is influenced
to some extent by the price of raw cotton. If raw
cotton, bought in April, is ready for sale as piece goods
in June, and in the meantime there has been a heavy
fall in the cotton market, piece goods will fetch less,
owing to the prospect of supplies, later on, of goods
made out of cheaper cotton. Against this risk the
weaver can protect himself, thanks to the existence
of the speculator, by 'selling a bear' of cotton in April
against his purchase. If cotton goes up he loses on
his 'bear' sale and gains on his cloth. If it goes down
his gain on his 'bear' sale goes against his loss on the
price of his cloth.

CHAPTER VII

THE ORGANIZERS

Pioneers and Plodders – The Importance of the Pioneer – His (sometimes) Huge Reward – His Qualities – Is his Power Dangerous? – Its Limits – Our Hard-working Servant, if we use him Right.

'THERE are always two kinds of people in the world – those who pioneer and those who plod. The plodders always attack the pioneers. They say that the pioneers have gobbled up all the opportunity, when, as a plain matter of fact, the plodders would have nowhere to plod had not the pioneers first cleared the way.'[1]

So says Mr. Henry Ford, and he is certainly right in his two kinds of people, though I think he exaggerates, if he does not invent, the persistency of the plodder in attacking the pioneers. I speak as a member of the army of plodders, by which I mean people who just peg away at the job which they find themselves doing, and never make any adventurous move to expand or develop it, and never move out of it unless somebody asks them to come into another. If all the world were like us, there would never be any progress or adventuring, and the business machine would just jog along as it is – or rather would slowly fall to pieces, for it needs new ideas and driving power even to keep it going.

---

[1] *To-day and To-morrow*, by Henry Ford, p. 2.

But this we quite recognize, when we take the trouble to think the matter over; and far from attacking the pioneers, we admire their energy and their power of finding, borrowing or stealing ideas and making them into facts, and we wish them more power to their elbows.

These pioneers are those who are included under the heading of this chapter as the organizers. Their reward varies from immense wealth and world-wide reputation, or at least notoriety, down to ruin and poverty; and whatever they can get out of the rest of the community, they are evidently cheap, because they are the people with whom we could least of all dispense, if material progress is our object. They are the driving power which makes the whole machine move. If the bankers were truly described as the linchpin of the wheel, the organizers are the electric spark that makes the explosion that sets the wheel spinning and keeps it spinning.

Formerly they often worked with their own money or with money borrowed by themselves for their own account. Under modern conditions, they are usually chairmen or managers of big companies, working for them and rewarded by commissions on the turn-over or the profits, and by many opportunities, given them by their position, of fishing in the troubled waters of industry and finance.

They are a curious race, and their faculty of seeing what is worth doing and getting it done, is often associated with quite elementary powers of mind, as judged by ordinary standards of intelligence. As the world is at present arranged, the object at which they

aim is, naturally, success in earning money; because
success in doing things and getting things done seems
to be the spur that incites their tireless energy; and,
under our present arrangements, the hall-mark of this
kind of success is the possession of a big balance at the
bank. But money, except as a symbol of success,
often – perhaps one might say generally – interests
them very little. Their personal needs are often
extremely simple long after they have acquired great
wealth; and the anxieties of their work and their
absorption in the sedentary tasks of business in cities
are apt to impair their digestions and strain their
nerves. These drawbacks leave these unfortunate
conquerors unable to enjoy those solid and real
pleasures of life – health and good food and good
companionship – which their efforts put more easily
within the reach of the plodders who work for them.
According to the popular fancy they win the whole
world and enslave all the rest of us through the power
of their money. In fact they spend lives of harassed
effort hunting for fresh fields to conquer, and often
losing in the course of the hunt most of the things
that are really worth hunting for: and we plodders
win in the last lap, because the pioneers can only
succeed in their search for monetary success by getting
things done which we want to be done. We are the
general consumers who finally decide, by our purchases, whether any venture shall bring profit to the
pioneer.

Earnest reformers tell us that we should have a
better world if the object of industry were not profit
but service. But as it is, profit can only be earned by

providing us consumers with a service that we want and will buy. We often make big mistakes about the things that we want; but if the decision is taken out of our hands, who is to be judge about the service to be produced by industry? Are we prepared to hand over our choice to a possibly capricious committee, perhaps composed of cranks who want to make us something quite different from what we want to be ourselves?

At first sight it appears that the dependence of the world on the organizers for productive progress, and the consequently great rewards that they earn, are a serious danger. For it has already been noted that they are often people of quite ordinary intelligence apart from the instinctive flair that they possess for 'propositions,' as they would call them, that are likely to prove profitable. Immense energy and driving power and self-confidence, based largely on a half-superstitious belief in their own luck, are the qualities which, combined with the profit-earning instinct, bring them through to success.

Such qualities do not help the successful organizer to make a judicious use of the great wealth that he may acquire; and fastidious observers have some justification for wondering what is going to be the future of our civilization, if it be true, as Mr. Wells has foretold in *William Clissold*, that Big Business is going to take charge of it. 'With this immense money power, at one end, in the hands of commonplace and half-educated adventurers, and with a gullible and half-educated public at the other, that can be hustled by advertising cheap-jacks into buying any rubbish that the organizer chooses to sell it, what,' ask the shades of Matthew Arnold and other apostles of culture and refinement, 'is the outlook for humanity?'

This question is serious enough, but not quite as serious as it looks at first sight. In the first place, as better, and better educated, brains go into business, the outlook and sympathies of the average organizer are likely to improve and widen. In the second, the power that big money puts into hands that do not know how to use it is really very limited. When a man has satisfied his own personal needs for sustenance and clothes and shelter he is bound, in fact, to hand the rest of his income over to others to spend it for him. This is obvious in so far as he gives it away; and the benefactions of rich men, especially in America and to a less extent in England before high taxation made it difficult, are on an enormous scale. If he invests it, it is again obvious that all those whom he sets to work on the enterprises that his money finances, whether they are managers or wage-earners or makers of machinery or suppliers of raw materials, are spending the organizer's income for him in return for rendering him a service or selling him something that is needed for his enterprise.

He, it is true, initiates the enterprise and decides what is to be made or provided. But he knows that he can only make a profit out of it if you and I, the general consumers, approve and buy the product. We, if we use our power aright and refuse to be bullied by the bawling cheap-jack, are the ultimate arbiters of business success.

But the rich organizers – and all the other very rich people – can also spend money on many things which have some ulterior object in furthering a cause or influencing public opinion; and the use of great wealth for such purposes as these is resented by those who do not possess it. An obvious example is the habit lately developed by successful newspaper organizers of rather violently pushing their political views down the throats of the public that reads their journals. It may, however, be doubted whether this power is really very effective. Public opinion is, in these times, at least on this side of the Atlantic, so critical and suspicious of Big Business when it ventures into politics, that this kind of propaganda probably irritates more people than it convinces.

The position of the public press to-day, with its dependence on advertising revenue for profits, is not the sort of arrangement that anyone would devise who was thinking out a sound scheme for providing the public with news and information and guidance in forming judgments. Nevertheless, the system has certain advantages. Thanks to the huge revenue that is poured by the advertisers into the coffers of the papers that attract them by a big circulation, the press is now able to sell its wares, with an organized celerity that has no parallel, in the remotest hamlets, telling the inhabitants something about what is happening in the world and giving them pictures of the leading actors on the public stage. A country rector in a small parish tells me that whereas forty years ago three papers came into his village every morning, all delivered to the houses of well-to-do people, every cottage now has its daily. Some people may think that this is a pity and that the readers of the modern sensational press get more harm than good from it; but on balance the advantage is surely very great in the amusement and wider outlook that the immense growth of newspaper reading has given and created. And recent political events have shown that the political influence of the press is not nearly as great as many of its critics fear. People read the papers to be entertained by seeing and hearing what other folk are doing and to know what is happening in the world of sport (often with a view to amusing themselves by betting) and, above all, to be thrilled by tales of crime or wickedness. 'News is sin and sin is news,' said that profound philosopher, Mr. Dooley, and this is so, not because the average man and woman are sinful, but, on the contrary, because sin is something exceptional and out of the common, and interesting for that reason. But the number of newspaper readers who are guided in their political views by those expressed in the leading articles is apparently quite small, to judge from recent election results.

But if we have no need to fear the effects of the big pull on the pool of wealth secured by the organizers, in dominating our minds and ambitions, how much does it otherwise benefit them, and what is much more important, how much harm does it do us?

Let us look at the position of a great industrialist or financier with an income of £100,000 or £200,000 if you like, and see what he can do with it.

Touching those things that really count towards comfort and happiness, he is no better off than most of us, and probably much worse. He cannot wear more than one lot of clothes or sit in more than one chair. As to food and drink, he can buy the most expensive, which is by no means always the best, but he is lucky if he can enjoy much of it. On the contrary, the wear and tear of his life have probably confined him to a strictly moderate diet, aerated waters and other such unpleasantnesses.

As to friendship, cynics and satirists of all the ages have depicted for us the hollowness and hypocrisy of the friends of the wealthy and their tendency to vanish from the picture if any doubt arises about the wealth. All which is largely nonsense, because people are not really like that, as anyone knows who has been 'down on his luck.' Still, in this matter of friendship, which, in the widest sense of the word is by far the most important thing in life, the organizer is not helped by his big money reward and is probably hampered by his many preoccupations and anxieties.

So these unfortunate benefactors of the human race do not do themselves much good, except by earning the satisfaction that comes from big things done. Do they, by the huge rewards that they collect, do us much harm?

This question will seem absurd to many who are sincerely convinced that the inequality of incomes is one of the most serious causes of evil in the world and that it would be much better for all if the wealth of the rich could be taken from them and divided among the poor. If this process were really going to benefit the poor, most of us, I think, would be in favour of it, because the existence of a number of people who do not get a real chance out of life is a continual discomfort which we should like, merely from the point of view of our own selfish satisfaction, to be spared. But I think that if we look at what happens to the incomes of the Big Rich we shall see that, even as things are, they are and inevitably must be, distributed to the less wealthy and so find their way down into the pockets of the neediest of those who work, and of those who cannot find work to do.

Obviously, the typical millionaire has many houses, estates, motor cars, yachts and other apparatus and a host of secretaries and servants to do his bidding. Unless he is extraordinarily well served, most of these assets and retainers are probably more or less a nuisance; because, especially if he has a businesslike mind, he feels that he ought to be making some personal use of them all at once, which is physically impossible. But does their existence in his possession do the rest of us any harm?

On the contrary, when we come to look into it, they are the channels through which these big rewards collected by the organizers and others flow down among the rest of us. We, by buying the stuff that the organizer makes and handles, give him a reward beyond the dreams of avarice; and the only thing that the poor fellow can do with it is to hand it back to us, in return for services that he does not really need, for us to spend on services that we do need, or at least are more likely to need. Because the smaller the amount of anybody's income, the more likely it is that a pound or a shilling or any other monetary fraction of it will be effective and useful, when spent.

This principle of what economists call Marginal Utility is very real when applied to money incomes.

It tells us, for example, that each mouthful of bread that a hungry man eats gives him less satisfaction, until, as he becomes less and less hungry, he enjoys the bread less and less until at last he wants no more; and that though, owing to the unfortunately limited capacity of the human stomach, this principle works most evidently in the case of food, it is in a less degree applicable to most other things that we consume or enjoy – 'When everything is cloth of gold,' as Gilbert sang, 'up goes the price of shoddy.' It is certainly true of money. The less we have of it, the more useful what we have is to us; and when once we have satisfied the real needs of civilized men and women, the more we have the less use it is, until, if we are troubled with a sense of duty about money matters, we arrive at last at the harassed lot of the conscientious millionaire, who spends a life of anxiety and toil in trying to find good and noble uses for his surplus funds.

'But,' it will be objected, 'all these goods and services that the great wealth of the successful organizer enables him to buy have been taken out of the common pool, and so there is less in it for the rest of us. It may be true that he passes his income on – so do we all, whenever we buy things – but in doing so he takes a bite out of the common cake, and his big bite makes a big hole.'

There is some truth in these objections. The rich organizer's demand for luxury goods certainly tends to put capital and effort into the making of them which might otherwise go into making things that we of the common herd need, and so might make them more plentiful and cheap for us; if scarcity were the problem of the moment more might have to be said about the need of more rational spending by the successful organizer and by all the rest of the very rich. But, as we all know, the problem of the moment is quite other – it is that of enabling the world to consume all that it might make and grow, instead of paralysing itself with its own success in producing things for which, owing to reasons which will have to be examined later, it cannot find a market.

All this question of money-spending, however, is more relevant to the question of the reward of the hereditary wealth owners and the Idle Rich. At present we are concerned not with them but with the Sweated Rich, the toiling few who, 'grunt and sweat under a weary life,' working much harder than the rest of us, so that they may, by their initiative and driving force, keep the wheel of the world's business running, and so that the common pool may always be kept full and even fuller. We have seen how little they get out of the game, apart from the fun of playing it, which is really all that most of them want; and how immensely important their work is to the world which they are sometimes believed to enslave, but which in fact enslaves them, because the whims of the ordinary men and women, expressed through their buying power, are the final arbiters of profit in these days of mass production.

It is important to note in support of the contention that the big reward of the organizer is generally gained by benefiting the community, that those countries in which the inequalities of wealth are greatest are also those in which the general standard of life is highest. America is an obvious example.

In England, progressive taxation, screwed up to a terrific and perhaps dangerous pitch, takes a huge toll of the organizer's income while he lives and of his estate when he is dead. His wealth is thus one of the sources out of which provision is made for national security and for social betterment. By and large, in view of the immensely important work that he does, the net material reward that he actually keeps for himself looks, at least in Britain, pitifully small.

As to the danger to civilization involved by the money power wielded by the organizer and his myrmidons, it ought to be clear from what has already been said that this danger lies not in the organizer but in civilization, that delicate plant that certainly needs all the care and attention that it can get. The organizer works to supply our material needs. If his work is successful and we do not discourage him by criticism and penalize him by taxation that he thinks excessive, he will show us the way to meeting these needs with ever-growing ease. The result will be, if we make a reasonable use of this ease, that we shall enjoy an ever-growing amount of time and energy for what may be called, by way of shorthand, the higher needs. But if we allow the organizer to hustle us into buying all kinds of absurdities that we do not want, just because our next-door neighbours have got them – in other words, if we allow Respectability rather than Satisfaction to be the test of our ambitions – we shall make the organizer into a tyrant instead of letting him be what he ought to be, the hard-working servant of our pleasure.

In the course of time, as the whole productive machine is evolved and improved, it may be that we shall dispense with the organizer as we know him, at least in some lines of business. We may see the wage-earners providing their own capital and their own organizers and carrying on industry on their own account. They could have made a good beginning in this direction in 1930 merely by saving the bonus that they pocketed owing to the fall in the cost of living. Sir Josiah Stamp, in a broadcast address delivered on 23rd January 1931, observed that 'there was no particular reduction in money wages in 1930 and the purchasing power of these wages rose considerably. On a total wage bill of, say, £1,800,000,000 the increase in the spending power of the masses of the people, despite unemployment, was of the order of £100,000,000.'[1] So that this handsome sum could have been available in one year, without any sacrifice of the wage-earners' standard of living, for setting up their own industries with their own organizers in charge.

Hitherto, such experiments in 'self-employment' as practised by the Co-operative Movement, have not been a conspicuous success. Mrs. Sidney Webb in a pamphlet on the *Discovery of the Consumer*, after giving a record of 'disastrous results,' culminating in the experience of the builders', furniture makers' and other guilds initiated by the National Guilds League, 1919-20, and supported by a few of the trade unions,

---

[1] *The Times*, 24th January 1931.

accounts for them by saying that 'the ideal of the control of industry by the workers concerned had the supreme demerit *that it would not work.*' But need this always be so?

In the meantime, owing to the discredit of political and bureaucratic control that has made State Socialism of the old-fashioned kind an obsolete anachronism[1] our Socialist friends are developing a system of public boards, to be managed by men of business experience, to provide services such as electricity supply and London's transport, for which there is an assured and regular demand. This system, if successful, may extend its scope and widen its net. But it seems likely that there will always be corners of the business field in which we can make use of the energies of the private organizer looking for profit in out-of-the-way places and finding new ways of amusing us and administering to our comfort.

[1] See Mr. Morrison's speech in the House of Commons on the London Traffic Bill, *The Times,* 24th March 1931.

CHAPTER VIII

THE SALESMEN

The Suspected Middleman – An Old Story – The Cost of Selling –
An Argument for Socialism – If it could Work – Our Bad Spend-
ing – The Service of the Middleman – Tending to be Short-
Circuited – The Function of the Advertiser – 'Sales Resistance' –
Responsibility of Women.

By salesmen I mean all those who work directly or
indirectly to put the goods and services that industry
grows, makes and otherwise produces, into the hands
of the consuming public. They thus include the
advertisers, the merchants, middlemen and dealers of
all kinds through whose hands, or through whose
books, the goods pass, and finally the shopkeepers and
retailers and the great multiple stores at which the
public finally buys.

These are the folk about whose reward most of us,
I think, are most inclined to be critical and suspicious.
We want to know why there should be such a big
difference between the price that the farmer gets for
his cattle and that which we pay the butcher for the
beef, or between the price of coal at the pit mouth and
the price that it costs us by the time we have got it
into our cellars. Surely, we think, somebody must be
making too much out of us.

If somebody is making too much out of us, it is a

very old story, if that be any consolation. All down the ages the merchant and the dealer have licked the cream off the milk. Mr. Dibblee, in his very interesting book on *The Laws of Supply and Demand*, tells us that one of the 'prodigious difficulties' to be faced in economics is 'the predominance in wealth and capital of the mercantile as compared with the manufacturing cities of the world. This was no less true in the days of Tyre and of Carthage, or during the commercial predominance of Florence, Genoa and Venice. Each of these mercantile queens had probably for purposes of military protection to make, as well as to market, some of her own wares, but it was the marketing that brought the profits. In our own day' (his book was first published in 1912) 'the great cities of Glasgow and Philadelphia, both of which are great ports as well as manufacturing centres, are nearer than most to the ancient model; neither are yet quite in the first rank, and they stand noticeably behind the great commercial capitals, while the purely manufacturing centres are forgotten in some row still further back. . . . A hundred years ago Liverpool was the selling and buying centre, while Manchester manufactured. There was a certain rivalry between them, with a balance of wealth in favour of Liverpool. Now Manchester, with Salford and her continuous suburbs, has a population of well over a million and stands the second city of the Empire; this place has been gained by her becoming the mercantile centre for cotton goods, as Liverpool remains for cotton, while Manchester cotton manufacturers have left her for more special and less wealthy centres. Coarse yarns are spun at Oldham, finer counts at Bolton, the weaving centre is at Blackburn, while bleaching and calico-printing are carried on throughout the district wherever the water facilities are sufficient. But the two mercantile cities are incomparably more wealthy than any of their rivals and almost equal to all of them together.'

And lastly, there is London. 'The greatest and wealthiest city in the world,' as Mr. Dibblee was then able to call it, 'grows ever fatter and richer without herself using more than a fragment of modern industrial power. Only the equally commercial cities of New York and Chicago are likely to surpass her in the near future or in the more distant future Buenos Aires or Montreal.'[1]

Such 'lumps of raw fact,' as Mr. Dibblee truly says, are staggering when thrown at one suddenly. It is not production but marketing that is costly. He wrote before the war had added so enormously to the cost of national and local government and of the transport of goods, all of which goes into the price of what we buy if those who handle the goods can get it out of us; but even then he believed that it was roughly true to say that it cost more to sell most articles than to make them 'even in the case of the most highly organized and most eminently specialized industry in the world.' He concluded that, 'since apparently the greater part of the rewards of industry go to those members of our commercial organization who are engaged in the adjusting duties of selling, buying, and selling again, we have also to infer that there is some

[1] *The Laws of Supply and Demand*, by G. B. Dibblee (Constable), pp. 50 *et seq.*

corresponding difficulty in these tasks which enables those engaged in them to gain these great rewards. It cannot be all chicanery and thievery.'

In his interesting analysis, which those who want to go deeper into these matters will do well to study for themselves, Mr. Dibblee finds that it is very difficult even to begin to compare the cost of making with the cost of selling, because we cannot be sure about the net cost of making, for there is no manufacturer in the world who does not devote some of his capital, part of his salaries and wages and most of his own private energies to building up his 'connexion.' In other words, the first manufacturer, before the article has left his hands, has 'already spent on it indirectly in one way or another anything from one-fifth to one-tenth of the net manufacturing cost of the product in obtaining for it its first market. In America, the proportion might very likely be greater, because the public there seems to enjoy high prices, and the manufacturers and middlemen have more margin in which to let themselves have their fling in advertising, semi-advertising and generally building up their connexions. All of which costs money and has to be added to the price.'

Also many articles pass through the hands of several manufacturers and each of these has his selling costs; and most of them pass through the hands of carriers by land and sea, all of whom have had to spend money by advertisement and otherwise on selling the transport service that they produce, and their selling costs also go into the price. And when at last 'the bantling typical commodity emerges into the hands of the first middleman, it finds the loading up of selling cost comparatively only at its beginning stage. The middle-men will have understood their duty badly, if they are not able to run up . . . anything from 20 to 30 per cent. on the first wholesale net price. It is our final friend, the retailer, who succeeds in putting on the biggest increment, because he has had the hardest task in selling to the consumer and he also, I am told on high authority, is the last person to consent to any cutting down of his share of the plunder when times are bad.'

All this 'plunder' looks, to put it mildly, a little excessive and unnecessary, and the public will need a good deal of convincing before it believes that these intermediate charges are reasonable. The subject wants thorough investigation. In 1930 the British Government made an effort to pass a Consumers' Council Bill with powers to examine traders' books and, if necessary, fix prices. It was a well-meant measure and the proposal to fix prices (which no Government can do) was only dangled before the middleman as a threat. It was thrown overboard in a stormy session, but has been fished up again in 1931; and something like it is wanted, especially in the interests of the shopkeepers, if they are unjustly suspected of making too much out of us.

The great costliness of the process of getting a finished article from the finisher to those who buy it is a strong argument on the side of those who contend that life would be made cheaper and easier if all our wants were met by a wise and beneficent Government, which would tell us what things to want and make them for us. If everything were standardized and we all wore the same kind of clothes, ate the same kind of food, lived in the same kind of houses and indulged in the same kind of amusements, the task of making and distributing necessaries and comforts for us would, obviously, be simplified and cheapened to an extent that is almost incalculable. The Government, knowing the number of its consumers and the articles which it was going to provide for them, could set its army of makers and distributors to work with a quiet confidence that would be in striking contrast with the harassed uncertainty that accompanies the efforts of the producers and distributors who work under our present system, making all kinds of different articles on the chance that they will be able to sell them, and then putting into the task of selling them efforts which double their cost before we get them. If all the waste and friction of advertising and competition could be done away with, what an easy and simple life mankind might lead!

And so it might, but could it be done? And if it were done, could we submit to the loss of personal choice that this rationing system would involve?

In the first place, we have seen that this contention assumes the existence of a wise and beneficent Government, and already[1] in discussing the question of nationalizing the banks we have seen reasons supplied by earnest Socialists for not being able to count on enough wisdom from politicians to entrust them with the task of controlling currency and credit. Would they then be wise enough to tackle the much more complicated business of providing us with all our

[1] Pp. 92, 93.

material needs? And when wisdom is lacking, beneficence is more likely to be well meaning than efficient.
Moreover, this rationing system is usually associated
with complete equality in sharing the goods produced,
as advocated by Mr. Bernard Shaw. As to this plank
in the Socialist platform as designed by some Socialists,
we are able, as so often happens, to cite the damning
evidence of other Socialists. Mr. G. D. H. Cole, in a
book in which he very frankly recants much of the
doctrine that he preached in his earlier works, deals as
follows with the notion of the completely equal distribution of the national means of life. It has, he says,
'a tremendous fascination for the social Utopian,
because it seems to dispose, at one blow, of so many of
the sources of our troubles – of the sordid struggle for
gain, of the ungentlemanliness of being richer than one's
neighbour, and of the equal ungentlemanliness of
being poorer. It puts economists once and for all into a
back seat in the affairs of life. This complete equality,
however, plainly postulates a very different set of
economic conditions from those we know now. It
fascinates a narrow group of enthusiasts; but it is
repudiated no more energetically by the successful
business man than by the ordinary worker in industry.
The latter will, as a rule, have none of it. It strikes him
as mad and wrong that the man who is less skilled than
he, or works less hard at the same job, should get the
same money. He believes that the world's goods are
badly distributed, and he is quite prepared to agree to
a minimum distribution according to need as a basis
for the protection of childhood and for other special
purposes; but he still wants to reward each according

to his works – according, that is, to his own revised estimate of what each man is worth. He will explain, as volubly as the business man, that he would never work hard without a financial incentive: in short, he believes in a wage system shorn of class exploitation, and not in a society based on Communistic principles.'[1]

We can, then, claim high Socialist authority for the belief that Governments are not likely to be wise, and that the ordinary worker in industry will not work without a financial incentive any more than a business man. This belief goes far to show that a system of governmental production and distribution of goods, getting rid of all the waste and friction of competition, is not likely to work well.

But if it did, how should we like to have no choice in the matter of the material goods that we enjoy? What would be the feelings of a lusty meat-eater if the Government were captured by vegetarians? And what about clothes and their present appeal to human vanity, which does so much to brighten the world of to-day? It is true that a certain uniformity is imposed by fashion and habit; but the opportunity for choice and variety is still great enough to give an enormous amount of amusement and pleasure and colour to life.

If it be objected that the sacrifice of choice in these material things will make our lives so easy that it will be worth suffering in order that we may develop our higher faculties, can we feel any confidence that a Government would give us any more freedom with regard to art and study and culture?

[1] *The Next Ten Years in British Social and Economic Policy*, by G. D. H. Cole (Macmillan), pp. 199-200.

Mr. Bertrand Russell, a very advanced thinker, whose views on politicians in general have already been quoted,[1] is quite sure that it would not. 'The fundamental conception of Socialism,' he says, 'in regard to our present question, is that all who can should be compelled to work, either by the threat of starvation or by the operation of the criminal law. And of course the only kind of work recognized will be such as commends itself to the authorities. Writing books against Socialism, or against anything embodied in the Government of the day, would certainly not be regarded as work. No more would the painting of pictures in a different style from that of the Royal Academy, nor producing plays unpleasing to the Censor. Any new line of thought would be banned, unless by influence or corruption the thinker could crawl into the good graces of the pundits.'[2]

A state of things under which any new line of thought was likely to be banned, does not promise much to those who are anxious about culture and the higher faculties. And to the great mass, who are more concerned with living a comfortable and pleasant and jolly life, the drilling and regimentation and rationing that would be involved if competition were eliminated would be dearly paid for by greater ease, to be spent in rationed amusements. The exercise of choice, to the extent of one's resources, in what one takes out of the common pool, is surely one of the most precious rights that free men and women can have.

All this is much less irrelevant than it looks. For

[1] P. 93.
[2] *Roads to Freedom*, by Bertrand Russell (Allen and Unwin), p. 117.

when we have seen what competition does for us, we have gone far to explain (if not to justify their number and costliness) the existence of this army of advertisers, middlemen and salesmen, who work to make our choice easier for us, though each member of the army tries to force our choice into the product that he is pushing. In this matter of spending we need all the help that we can get. Mr. Dibblee, in the book from which I have quoted above, is almost venomously severe with us on this point. He speaks of an assumption that, whatever his deficiencies otherwise may be, a man at least knows what he wants, and knows also when and how to buy an object to satisfy him. 'This assumption,' he continues, 'is so far from being true that for at least half his expenditure an ordinary individual does not know what he wants, and out of the other half for at least a half he does not get what he wants. It is only by becoming the creature of habit and the victim of mimicry or stimulation that he accomplishes very badly a task which is really more difficult than that of earning his income.'[1]

These are hard sayings, and perhaps the writer puts rather too much force into them. He is certainly quite right, however, when he says that spending one's money is a more difficult task than earning it; and as this subject is of huge importance and contains the key to happiness, as far as material things can help us to it, let us hear a little more of his description of our stupidity about it.

As to the 'middle and upper classes,' he thinks that 'half the furniture of any house is mere mimicry of

[1] *The Laws of Supply and Demand*, p. 22.

other establishments whose use is in display without beauty or comfort. Half the clothing of either children or adults is dictated by fashion and discarded before consumption. Half the wages of most of those who pay for domestic service are for the performance of ceremony useless, boring and time-wasteful. Few of us are perhaps willing to admit this specifically in our own cases because all kinds of useless waste and ceremony have for ourselves associations to which, out of habit or traditional sentiment, we attribute supposed importance. But it is easier to see the truth of such a generalization in the habits of others, particularly of the very rich, whose estates and stables, yachts, gardens and pictures are bought for them, kept going for them and regulated for them down to the last boot-button by a whole army of officials and experts with only an occasional reference to any personal enjoyment, which their owner may expect from them.'

With regard to the 'great masses of the poor,' Mr. Dibblee notes that at least four of the vital necessities of their existence – education, sanitation, insurance and provision for old age – have to be procured for them by the State or the municipality, 'and another, their food, is injudiciously chosen and, in this country, wastefully and unattractively prepared.'[1]

These strictures upon all classes, considered as spenders, were written before the war, and since it shook our lives to their foundations, some of them have become truer and some less true. Nevertheless, this mirror is held up to us by a highly intelligent

[1] Mr. Dibblee, *op. cit.*, pp. 23-24.

observer – Mr. Dibblee was a scholar of Balliol and a Fellow of All Souls and had, before he wrote this book, spent many years in active business as manager of a great newspaper.

There is no need to lay stress on the importance of being wise in our spending. The justification of the present business arrangements of the world, which may be roughly described as the capitalist system, is found in the freedom that it gives to all of us – if we choose to use it – to put what we can into the common pool of wealth and to take out of it what we choose, to the extent of the money income that we get in exchange for what we put in.

This freedom, like all other kinds of freedom, is a priceless gift if we use it well and a disastrous mockery if we use it ill. With regard to the work that we put into the pool, freedom is limited in the case of most of us by the nature of our abilities and the range of our energies, and also by the fact that we are probably shoved into some sort of a job by the advice of our elders, or because the job happened to be offered, long before we are old enough to make any sort of choice on our own judgment, and to make a change later takes a good deal of determination. Nevertheless, the fact remains that those who have a strong enough desire to do a certain kind of work and will try hard enough to do it, generally will find a way.

Freedom in spending is unlimited. To the extent of our earning power, we are lords of creation and can help ourselves from a pool which the business intelligence of all the world and of all the ages are working or have worked to fill for us.

The people whose reward we are considering in this chapter work to tell us what to buy and to bring it from the producer to our doors or over the shop counter into our hands. Their work is of enormous value, if we keep them in their right place as useful servants and do not allow them to be hectoring tyrants.

As to the middlemen and dealers, they have done a job in former ages that was immensely important when the means of communication and transport were slow and fitful. In the days of pack-horses and sailing ships, the man who made it his business to know where things could be got and where they were wanted and would take the risk of bringing them from one to the other and could provide the money for financing the purchase and wait for many months before he saw it back, did work for trade and international intercourse that fully earned any rewards that he got – when he got them, and was not cheated out of them by ship-wreck, pirates, highway robbers or a change in the whims of buyers before the goods came to market:

> 'Have all his ventures failed? What, not one hit?
> From Tripoli, from Mexico, and England,
> From Lisbon, Barbary and India?'

The lot of the Merchant of Venice in those times was a daily round of surprises, lucky and disastrous, and of long-drawn suspenses that must have needed amazing toughness of mind to bear them.

In these days, the merchant is being short-circuited. Submarine cables and wireless messages and the development of the commercial news-service enable every one who will take the trouble to know all that is happening in the markets of the world at every minute of the day; the speed of steamships, railways, motor lorries and aeroplanes moves goods about with a rush that has immensely shortened the space between the buying and delivery; Governments have policed the highways and cleared the seas of pirates, though they have set up, or kept up, customs barriers that obstruct and take toll of trade; and bankers have perfected a system of international payment, by bills of exchange and telegraphic transfers, that enables the seller, in China or Peru, to get money from New York or London in as many hours as it once took him months.

All these things are making the merchant and dealer less necessary and industry is gradually shoving him out of the way as a costly survival of barbarism. Manufacturers to an increasing extent are doing their own buying of materials and their own selling of finished articles to the final retailer. This process is especially active in the United States, and it is interesting to note that the squeezing out of the independent middleman, by pressure from both ends, has there tended to increase the cost of distribution, which makes the manufactured article so unconscionably dear to the final buyer. This striking fact may give pause to some people here who are inclined to ascribe to the extortion of middlemen all the sufferings of the consumer. It is stated in a Department of Overseas Report, published in May 1931, and compiled by two officials of the British Embassy at Washington, on *Economic Conditions in the United States of America, March 1931*.

'Intensive selling,' it tells us, 'means direct marketing,

or the nearest approach to direct marketing that the product and the circumstances will permit. It means, in short, that the functions formerly performed by middlemen – jobbers or wholesale merchants – in many trades have been transferred to the sales departments of manufacturing establishments. These intensive direct sales efforts, however, proved extremely costly. They ate up a good proportion, in some cases nearly all, of the economies in manufacturing costs by large-scale production methods. Costs of distribution increased all round and with them the difficulty of maintaining the flow of goods to home consumers necessary to keep the mass machinery in full operation.'

In England the great combines usually control the supply of the materials that they need and sell direct to shopkeepers, often on terms that give the latter no choice about the price at which they sell to the public – a matter about which we want more light.[1] Was this arrangement made by the manufacturers or by the shopkeepers? And in whose interest? There is also here a manufacturer of cheap clothing who buys cloth in quantities that give him a great advantage over the ordinary tailor, makes it into clothes, ready-made or to measure, and sells them direct to the public through shops in different parts of England. Another successful venturer has founded first a private business and then a joint-stock company which has been a pioneer in cheap retailing and goes direct to manufacturers and educates them in the production of the articles that its public needs.

If the middleman is thus retiring to the twilight of

[1] See below, p. 408.

the unnecessary, the advertiser and the boosting salesman seem to be more and more aggressively evident
in spite of trade combinations and amalgamations
which might have been expected to reduce their
number and their vociferations. We all know that
there is a tobacco combine and a soap combine, but
the newspapers are covered with appeals for our
patronage of this and that brand of cigarettes and the
young lady who so pleasantly displays 'that schoolgirl
complexion' is all over the hoardings.

All these things – cheap ready-made clothes, cheap
domestic articles turned out in standardized millions,
and loud-voiced cheap-jacks shouting at us from every
side – are an offence to the fastidious. The superior
persons who sneer at what they call 'bungaloid growths'
– the millions of little houses dwelt in by little people,
if we measure stature by the cash yard-stick – see in
these movements a lowering of the national taste
and culture. Well, it depends on what we want. Those
of us who believe in what the Utilitarian Radicals of
a hundred years ago put forward as the object of
political and business effort, the Greatest Happiness of
the Greatest Number, want to see as many people as
possible leading jolly and comfortable lives and we
welcome all the methods by which modern industry
makes things cheap and plentiful. And were the
national taste and culture so much better in the days
when the superior person had more say in the matter?
It is difficult to walk far in London without seeing some
disgusting blot left as a legacy from that time.

Advertisers claim that, far from adding to the cost,
they concentrate business in the hands of the big and

efficient producers and give the public the benefit of mass production. The rewards that they get and the cost of their activities are paid, they contend, not by the public which buys at their bidding, but by the small and dead-alive producing firms and companies, which are driven out of business, because, in the first place, they do not know how to advertise, and, in the second, do not sell an article that is good enough to deserve to be advertised. For it is one of the convictions of the enthusiastic advertiser that to advertise a bad article is to throw money down a sink, and that consequently he, the advertising expert, is not only a heaven-born seller but a heaven-sent purifier of production; and that whenever he is given his way the public is better served. As to which the public is still sceptical. It sees the point and recognizes that, by and large, the most loudly advertised goods are likely to have merit, but it also knows that the rule is not universally true, and that it does not follow that advertising clamour is necessarily based on fact and that all that glitters in advertisements is gold to the consumer. At the same time, it knows, if it thinks the matter out, that advertising is of enormous use in telling us about the contents of the pool of wealth. We cannot dip into it with judgment unless we allow those loud-voiced advisers to tell us what is to be had; and if we relied on our own limited knowledge of what the organizers and makers are doing for us, and only bought things that we saw displayed in shop windows, or heard about from our friends, our range of purchase, and therefore also of activity and enjoyment, would be seriously narrowed. Opportunely, as I write, on a

damp and dismal autumn day, there comes to hand a
catalogue setting out the virtues and prices of plants,
trees, shrubs, hardy perennials, roses, bulbs that will
make spring and summer lovely. I am spurred to
drop my fountain pen – a producers' miracle that
advertising has made cheap for all of us – and seize
a long-tined fork and get the soil ready to increase the
beauty of the world, to which the gardening advertisers
so cunningly contribute.

Moreover, we may remind the fastidious critics that
there is room for everything in the business world.
Side by side with what they think to be the mass-
produced abominations of ready-made clothes to be
worn in cheap little houses, the exponents of the distinctive and costly article can, and do, still flourish.
All that has happened is that the ready-made stuff
has been improved out of all recognition, thanks to
the advertiser and the mass-producer. But there will,
however much the multiple shops may multiply,
always be room for the specializing retailer who under-
stands quality and distinction. Most of us like, if we
can afford it, to have some of the things that we use
or live with first-rate in quality and finish, though we
may accept standardized articles, and welcome their
cheapness, in the bathroom or in whatever domestic
departments seem to us to be less important. When
we are looking for quality a first-rate shopkeeper
who knows his work is a most valuable friend.

But all this matter of wise spending requires constant
attention. It has been said that the price of liberty is
ceaseless vigilance, and certainly our freedom of choice
in buying will lead us into mistakes if we allow the

salesmen to dominate us by their insistence. What the Americans, who have examined this problem with some of the seriousness that it merits, call 'sales resistance' is a quality that we have to develop and exercise. There, the much greater development of buying on the instalment system – by which the buyer pays for the article in sums spread over weeks and months and sometimes years – gives the glib salesman an enormous chance of selling things to his customers that they do not want. Want of cash is no longer a protection. One can take the goods and pay some day. And so we hear of 'the poor devil who has to borrow money from his boss each week because he has overbought on contract goods,' and how 'every town seems to have at least one unfortunate whose sales-resistance is so low that his contracts total more than his earning power for the next year.'[1]

In this matter, the women of all classes have enormous influence, and especially those who do the all-important work of laying out the family income of the wage-earning classes. Is it true that the cost of production is high in England, not because the British wage-earner's standard of life is really higher, but because his wife lays out his money to such poor purpose, as compared with her Continental rival, that he has to be paid a large money wage in order to get anything like equality of standard? Some people who ought to know think so. For instance, M. André Siegfried, a disinterested foreign observer, says in his

---

[1] From an article by Arthur Pound, in the *Atlantic Monthly*, February 1926, quoted in the *Economics of Instalment Selling* by E. R. A. Seligman (Harper and Bros.), p. 269.

book on *England's Crisis* that 'the English workman spends freely, chiefly because he is not clever at organizing his life. His wife is also somewhat lacking in *savoir-faire*. She does not take a keen delight in shopping economically nor does she pride herself on her cooking. . . . She is honest and loyal, but slipshod, and her household often lives on tinned goods and prepared foods. As a housekeeper she has no sense of, nor delight in, economy as we have in France, and therefore she requires higher wages to maintain a very ordinary standard. . . . The English standard of living means, to a certain extent, the right to live shiftlessly without exertion and at the same time to be well paid for doing so.'

Women, in fact, as our domestic Chancellors of the Exchequer, are the corner-stone of the business temple. Every one who has had much chance of looking at the domestic arrangements of the less wealthy members of the community will tell you that what makes most difference to the comfort and pleasantness of the home is not the income of the breadwinner, or the joint incomes of the breadwinners if several of the family are earning, but the way in which the wife or sister, or whoever does the job, manages the income and lays it out.

We depend on women for most of the important material comforts – good food to eat, good beds to sleep in, good chairs to sit in, clean, pleasant and tidy (but not too tidy) rooms to live in. This spending job which, as Mr. Dibblee has truly told us, is more difficult than earning an income, we hand over to them, as far as it is concerned with domestic enjoyment. We give them no pay, directly as such, for doing this work which makes so much difference to our happiness. But long before they got the vote they had the massed spending power which rules, or could rule if it chose, the world of business. We do not want them to stint and scrape and squabble over sous, as the French women are said to delight in doing; but we do want them to take reasonable care in dealing with their domestic budgets.

CHAPTER IX

THE CAPITALIST

Services of the Saver – Alleged Injustice of Capitalism – What it has done for us – Growth and Improved Distribution of Wealth – The 'Functionless' Shareholder – Inherited Capital – The Idle Rich – Their Utility as Amusement – And as Patrons of New and Costly Inventions.

So far we have considered the right to draw on the common pool of wealth that is earned by various kinds of workers. Now we have to face the difficult question of rewards given to people who are not working to-day, but are living on work that has been done, by themselves or by somebody else, in the past.

If the work has been done by themselves, there is no difficulty about justifying the reward. For in this case we are dealing with men and women who took, during their working time, less out of the pool than they might have had, and handed over part of their earnings to other people, so that it might be spent on furthering the world's business, or sometimes, in the case of Government loans, on defending their country against attack or helping it to attack other countries. In other words, we are considering the reward of those who have saved instead of spending, and so helped to provide the world with capital; and we are face to face with the capitalist, that person who gets so much abuse and yet does a job for society without which it could not make progress in increasing its wealth, or even maintain its present rate of output of the good things that we want and enjoy.

The world's capital consists of the tools and equipment of industry in the widest sense of all these words. We saw in Chapter I how many industries and how much equipment and construction devoted to their development are necessary in order to provide a cup of tea in a teashop; and this parable can be applied all round, if we think of anything that we use from a railway to a tube of tooth-paste and consider the number of people who have had to work in the past and present to fill the great pool of goods and services, the existence of which we take as a matter of course, as if it had been created for us by a beneficent fairy godmother.

In fact it has been created for us by the toil of millions of wage-earners directed in their work by adventurous organizers, using the capital provided by those who did the dull and tiresome work of saving, instead of spending all that they earned on immediate enjoyment.

When the tools of industry were simple and easy to make, every man may have been, more or less, his own capitalist. Perhaps Adam when he found that he had to eat bread with the sweat of his face, fashioned for himself some sort of a hoe to deal with the thorns and thistles that were part of his punishment. If so, he was providing himself with capital, by devoting part of his time and work to constructing a tool that would make his later work more easy.

153

Another capitalistic effort that he almost certainly made to win his bread was saving part of his own crop, instead of eating it, in order to sow for next year's harvest. Herein he is the exact counterpart of the modern capitalist, keeping part of the reward of his work and sinking it in industry in order to get a better return later, and taking the risk of losing it altogether owing to frosts, drought or other vagaries of Nature.

Nowadays when industry, on a scale great enough to meet the ever-growing demands of an enormous population, has to have equipment costing millions of pounds, workers and organizers are powerless without the help of capital. As was shown in an earlier chapter, we have Mr. Ramsay MacDonald's authority for the statement that 'a man can go into the forest and tear boughs off trees with his hands for his fires, but he cannot fell trees without an axe of some kind, which is capital.'

But though capital is thus admitted to be necessary it does not follow that the present system, by which it is provided by the savings of private individuals like you or me, is the only possible one. When the Socialist critics point to the private capitalist as a blot on the system, they are not so foolish as to suppose that capital is unnecessary. They think that its accumulation in the hands of individuals gives them too great a power which they are likely to abuse, and that the business of providing capital for industry ought to be handled by the Government or by some body representing the community. If this were done, the effort of saving would still have to be made, because the controlling body would have to set a certain number of people to work, not in making things for immediate enjoyment, but on making machinery and other kinds of equipment so as to increase the community's output later on. While they were at work on this job, those engaged on it would have to be fed and provided for out of the common store, and the same self-denial for future improvement would thus be exercised as is now provided by the individual saver.

As to what might happen under Socialism, however, is not our concern at present. This digression was only necessary because defenders of our present system sometimes think that when they have shown that we cannot live and grow without capital they have proved that the capitalist, as we know him, is essential to progress. This is not so. With his help the world has made marvellous conquests in the field of wealth-earning, but it is quite possible that he may some day be superseded.

For the time being he holds the field and has been, in spite of failures and blunders, so successful in widening and deepening the pool of wealth, that it will be well to be quite sure that we have got a better servant before we dispense with him. We saw in Chapter VI how the world's business is now chiefly done, in the most highly developed countries, by joint-stock companies, the capital of which is subscribed by the investors whose claim to a reward we are considering.

In the eyes of some of its critics this claim is based on injustice and robbery. In one of his early works – *Self-Government in Industry* – Mr. G. D. H. Cole said that 'To do good work for a capitalist employer is merely, if we view the situation rationally, to help a thief to steal more successfully.' This is a bad example of the way in which clever people throw bad words about. With his two Firsts and his Fellowship at Oxford, Mr. Cole might have known that a thief is a person who takes something that he knows to belong to somebody else; and the average capitalist certainly does not do this. When he takes interest on money that he puts into industry, he fully believes that he is taking what is fairly his own, earned by a service rendered. He may be wrong about this, though it is difficult to see why; but if so, he is acting on a mistaken conviction that does not justify his being branded as a thief.

In his recent *Next Ten Years in British Social and Economic Policy*, however, Mr. Cole is much milder and seems even to think that the capitalist should be encouraged and provided with a National Investment Board, to guide and control the placing of his funds. 'The State,' he says on page 77, 'has both to prevent the misuse, from the national standpoint, of the limited economic resources in the possession of its citizens, and, by positive means, to foster their use in the right way.'

Mr. Bertrand Russell thinks that 'the existing capitalist system is doomed. Its injustice is so glaring that only ignorance and tradition could lead the wage-earners to tolerate it.' He thinks that through the influence of America, it may 'linger for another fifty years.' But these observations were made in a book called *The Practice and Theory of Bolshevism*, which was first published in 1920, and in which Mr. Russell also said that 'If we continue to antagonize the Bolsheviks

I do not see what force exists that can prevent them from acquiring the whole of Asia within ten years.'

These ten years have passed and there has not been much improvement in the relations between the Bolsheviks and the rest of the world, though whether we 'antagonize' them or they us, is open to argument; but they have not yet acquired a square inch of Asia that they did not possess ten years ago.

As an economic tipster, then, Mr. Russell cannot be relied upon for accuracy in dates. Which is no reason why he may not be right in his indictment of what he believes to be the glaring injustice of the existing capitalist system. The brilliant clearness of his thought and style make his works a joy to his readers, but I venture to suggest that in his judgment of his fellow-men and of the institutions under which we live he mars his teaching by a certain sourness. His sweeping indictment of the whole race of politicians has already been quoted as a picturesque over-statement of certain truths that must not be ignored by those who think that we shall improve our enjoyment of life by national-izing industry. From a review[1] of a new book of his, *The Conquest of Happiness*, that I have not yet had time to read, I gather that he thinks that no system for the avoidance of war 'has a chance while men are so unhappy that mutual extermination seems to them less dreadful than continued endurance of the light of day,' which seems to show that he has been singularly unfortunate in his choice of friends and acquaintances; and an even more startling indication of his state of mind is his observation on page 23 of *The Practice and*

[1] In the *Morning Post* of 7th October 1930.

Theory of Bolshevism that 'hatred of enemies is easier and more intense than love of friends.'

To the average sensible man and woman hatred is as difficult, because one has no 'enemies' to hate, as friendship is fortunately easy under modern gregarious conditions; and before we have lived very long most of us recognize that such hatreds as we cherish are worse than a waste of effort, because one's power to hurt the other fellow is probably very limited if one has any at all, while the mere feeling of the hatred is an uncomfortable poison which hurts one's own mind and probably impairs one's digestion. If we find certain people unpleasant, it is much more comfortable, instead of hating them, to recognize that they are like that because they cannot help it, having been brought up under unfavourable conditions; also that it is quite possible that they are not unpleasant at all and that we are wrong in thinking them so.

There is nothing irrelevant, in spite of appearances, about the above digression. The world's business – the growth of the pool of wealth and the ease and satisfaction with which we dip into it – are seriously checked and hindered by the prevalence of bad temper and misunderstanding. And when great thinkers lay down the doctrine that hatred is easy, whereas in fact it is abnormal and stupid, they are helping to stem the flow of material wealth as well as libelling human nature.

To the ordinary mind, believing that mankind is groping its way to a great increase in material comfort, which may, if rightly used, be of the highest service in achieving more important conquests, the capitalist system appears to be an arrangement which has enabled an enormous forward stride to be taken along the path of progress, in spite of the huge obstacles which various stupidities, chiefly due to bad temper and misunderstanding, have put in the way. It has many imperfections, sometimes seeming to scatter its prizes with as much logic as a lucky-bag, and involving great waste, as already noted. But, working with the help of science, it has enabled an immensely greater population to lead much more comfortable lives.

In the century before what is usually considered to be the capitalist era began – 1651-1751 – the population of Great Britain rose from 6,378,000 to 7,392,000 – an increase of 1,014,000; in the next century, while capitalism was getting on to its legs, the figure rose to 21,185,000 – an increase of 13,793,000, and in the following sixty years – 1851-1911 – it rose by 19,350,000 to 40,535,000.[1] Nobody contends that capitalism was the sole cause of this huge addition to the population of this island, still less that a teeming multitude is the only test of prosperity. It may very well be true that if we had not bred so fast, the allowance of comfort per head might have been greater. And if Mr. Bertrand Russell's view that everybody is unhappy is correct, we may here find the real reason for which he accuses capitalism of glaring injustice – that it brought so many people into this miserable world. But most of us get a good deal of fun out of life and prefer to stay alive as long as we can; and according to Sir Josiah Stamp's estimate the real wealth per head

[1] See an article by Dr. Shadwell in the *Encyclopædia of Industrialism*, p. 304.

of the population of Great Britain was roughly multiplied by four during the century before the war, and this increase was evenly distributed through all classes of the population.

If this be injustice, some of us would like to see a little more of it. Since the war, the distribution of wealth has been in favour of the poorer classes. Dr. Arthur Bowley, Professor of Statistics in the University of London, published in September 1930 a book called *Some Economic Consequences of the Great War*, into which he has packed, with amazing skill and conciseness, an enormous mass of information. On page 165 we find: 'In summary we may say that great progress has been made towards the extinction of remediable poverty, considerable inroads have been made on excessive wealth and generally income is less unequally distributed than it was ten years ago.'

As to injustice, we can cite Mr. Ramsay MacDonald in contradiction of Mr. Bertrand Russell: 'Capital,' says the first Socialist Prime Minister of England, 'has its value, a simple fact which means that under the freest economic conditions interest will be paid. It may be interest of five per cent., it may be of a tenth per cent., but the utility of capital in production will always have an appreciable value which the labourer who uses it will pay without suffering exploitation or injustice.'[1]

Moreover, the labourer who uses the capital – the tools and equipment supplied by the investor – only pays for the use of it if the goods produced are sold at a profit sufficient, after paying his own wages, to find

[1] *The Socialist Movement*, by J. Ramsay MacDonald, p. 2.

a reward for the investor in the shape of interest or dividend. The wage-earners' wages are a first charge on the gross profits of industry, and are paid week by week, often long before the work that is being done can have brought in any return. After wages come taxes, rent, salaries and other administrative expenses, then interest on debt to bankers and bond-holders, then the claims of upkeep and depreciation – the sums put into keeping plant and equipment in proper condition and providing against the day when they will be obsolete – then the dividend to preference holders, if any, then, if the Directors know their business, something handsome is put to reserve funds or added to the amount carried forward, to provide for expansion of the business and against adverse turns in the wheel of fortune. And finally, after the wage-earner and all these subsequent claimants have had their share of the receipts of the business, the ordinary shareholder or common stockholder takes what is left, if anything.

And then the finger of scorn is pointed at him as an 'absentee' who is 'functionless.' Certainly he is an absentee, and he would be an amazing fool and an intolerable nuisance if he were anything else – if he adopted the habit of dropping in at the works and making well-meant suggestions about carrying on the business, is it likely that his presenteeism would be helpful?

As to his being 'functionless,' he may well only wish that he were so in these days of 1930 and 1931, when every day as he scans his paper he sees the prices of his investments dropping and reports of companies appearing with reduced profits and lower dividends, or no dividends at all, for him and his like. His function is the very real one of providing the labourer and the organizer with tools and equipment and with the means of paying for materials and transport and all the machinery of making and selling the stuff or service that the business turns out, and taking the risk of getting no return on his money, if the business is ill-managed, or if, as is happening to-day, some creeping paralysis that nobody can quite explain has slowed the spin of the trade wheel so that many of the best-managed businesses are limping instead of running.

This risk-taking function of the shareholder was never more apparent than at the present time. And by an amusing trick of Fate, that most sardonic humorist, just as he is ruefully licking the wounds that risk-taking has inflicted on him, the British investor is accused by a Canadian critic of having shirked his risk-taking job, and played for 'safety first.' Such is the charge brought against him by Dr. Stephen Leacock, whose book on *Economic Prosperity in the British Empire* has already been cited on page 105. It was published in the summer of 1930, and in it he tells us, in effect, that the investing class in this country has been distinguished by a somewhat timorous caution. He begins by referring to the penetration of American capital into Canada, which took, in growing proportion, the form of establishing branch distribution houses inside the Dominion, as compared with the flow of British capital which 'consists overwhelmingly in the purchase of Government securities, municipal loans, and the stock of railway and public utility companies.' This, he says, is the 'form of investment which prefers safety to adventure and where the aim is not so much to make money as to keep it without losing it.'

And then he goes on to tell us about the British investor in general, such as he was before the redistribution of all social values effected by the Great War. Till then, says Dr. Leacock, 'England possessed, more than any other country in the world, an investing class consisting of people of limited means. The money of these people came to them by descent, and they knew more of Latin Iambics (*sic*) than of business.[1]

'With them was a landed gentry whose only flight of business enterprise was the pursuit of agriculture by proxy. These people, in their other aspects, were the pride and bulwark of England. They wrote its poetry, they preached its sermons, and they fought and won its battles. But of business they knew nothing. Beside them, the leaders and magnates of the business world used to be a mere minority, viewed with a mixture of contempt, awe and envy. This investing class of financially ignorant people, anxious only to keep their money and not hoping to increase it, set the peculiar tone to British investment which still shows itself in the location of British capital in Canada,' as already described.

In the present state of the stock markets, a great many investors – in England and everywhere else, and especially in the spacious lands across the Atlantic – are wishing that they had followed the cautious lines that Dr. Leacock describes so contemptuously. Investment

[1] We wrote Iambics in Greek, but 'it's of no consequence.'

which endeavours, not so much to make money as to keep it without losing it, seems to have been rather justified by results at a time when prices of the most well-established common shares have been shrinking under the Wall Street slump and the world-wide trade depression, while those of 'safety first' securities have been comparatively steady, especially since cheap money came to their rescue.

But is it really true that the old-fashioned English investor was as ignorant and timid as Dr. Leacock thinks he was? As to his attitude towards investments in Canada, he might have a good deal to say for himself on the subject of the many millions that he lost in the Preference and Common Stocks of the Grand Trunk Railway Company. Dr. Leacock seems to think that the stock of railway companies is the kind of security for those who want to keep their money without losing it. The Grand Trunk stockholders could give him a few telling truths on that point. English investors were, I fancy, no more ignorant about business than those of any other country, and on the whole they were as well advised as most others, and it was in England that the great principle of co-operative investment through Investment Trust Companies was first worked out and applied, and by means of it British capital (apart from the little job of equipping British industry) has been spread all over the world and into all kinds of enterprises and all classes of securities with an amazing record of success, thanks to diversification of risk and a careful financial policy.

And is it not rather absurd to accuse the British investor of thinking only of keeping his money safe, seeing that English money has made the rubber industry more to the advantage, just at present, of the motor manufacturer and user than of the shareholder? Again, English capital has always been ready – perhaps too ready – to go underground if anybody told it there was a gold reef down below, and it opened up the goldfields of Australia and of South Africa and poured millions into Rhodesia to the tune of Cecil Rhodes's Imperial pipings.

Railways Dr. Leacock now seems to regard as safe and steady investments, and so they have been on the whole, in most countries, in spite of the Grand Trunk example, though they do not look so solid at present; but they had not been proved as such when English capital first built them at home and then all over the world, and the English investor, now accused of always having played for safety, must only too often have wished that he had been a little more cautious.

Any capitalist who has made and saved the money which he has handed over to industry or to public bodies to be turned into equipment or spent on public purposes, has thus been shown to earn any reward that he gets. With the best secured 'safety first' investments some element of risk is inevitable; and with common stocks and shares he comes last in a long line of claimants to the profits of industry, which without his money could not, as things are now arranged in the world of business, earn any profits at all.

When we come to capitalists by inheritance – those who receive income from property that has been left to them – the claim to reward is much less easy to establish. They are living on work done or service

165

rendered by someone in the past, perhaps in a very remote past, when people, such as Charles the Second's mistresses, acquired enormous properties by rendering services which were, according to modern judgments, very much over-valued.

Such examples are the stock-in-trade of some critics of the capitalist system. But the evils attached to them are due, not to capitalism in the ordinary sense of the word, which is less than two hundred years old, but to the more ancient institutions of private property and of inheritance. These examples are rare and are unlikely to happen in these days, when there is more chance that a stupid public will give fortunes to those who sell it rubbish, than that a Merry Monarch will give away slices of his kingdom to ladies who amuse his fancy.

But apart from examples of this kind, there can be no doubt that the right of those who acquire wealth, even in the most legitimate and socially desirable way, to hand it on to any heir that they choose to name, is a cause of inequalities which many regard as unfair. The complaint is as old as the days of Wat Tyler:

'When Adam delved and Eve span
Who was then the gentleman?'

Why should 'happy undeserving A' be born with a golden spoon in his mouth, while 'wretched meritorious B' has to earn by toil that he possibly detests, every stiver that he spends?

In the first place, let us note that it by no means follows that those who are born rich live happily.

Some of them seem rather to be apt to look on their position not as a stroke of luck to themselves but as part of the scheme of the universe, and to feel aggrieved because they were not born richer. The futility of riches as a means to happiness is, in fact, a commonplace of moralists, and we saw in Chapter II that work is pleasant to a great number of those who have to do it. Happiness is secured, or made easier to secure, not by wealth, but by feeling well off in the widest sense of the phrase. This feeling comes more easily if we have a certain amount of material comfort, but this amount is quite moderate in most cases and depends largely on what we have been used to. If we are all going to embitter our lives because somebody round the corner has better luck than we have, there will be no end to bitterness, because inequalities of some kind, in wit and beauty and stature and health, can never be abolished.

Which is no reason for not trying to abolish the inequalities of wealth if they do more harm than good. But do they? Let us look at these 'idle rich' folk good-temperedly, remembering that even if they are a public nuisance, as some think, it is not their fault; for they did not make themselves so, but were born to idle wealth just as the rest of us were born to toil.

How much harm does their existence do us? As we saw when we looked at the big rewards given to successful organizers, the only thing that the very rich can do with their money is to hand it on to the rest of us to spend, either by spending it themselves or by investing it. Whichever they do, they set some of us to work and their big incomes are a stream in the flow of wealth. It is true that when they spend themselves they take from the pool of wealth certain goods and services, but these are only to a very small extent the kind of things that the rest of us want. Their spending on luxuries and frivolities may often be 'anti-social'; but on the other hand it often, as will be shown when we come to see what good they do, provides us with a good deal of amusement which is an immensely important contribution to the supply of immaterial goods. If the world were faced with scarcity, we might want to check this luxury spending and divert the energy that goes to meeting its whims, into making things that are needed for the health and comfort of humble folk. But we shall find as we go on that what is puzzling the world at present is the problem of using all the goods that it could easily produce if it took off its coat to the job. If luxury spending were stopped to-morrow, it might not make necessaries cheaper for those who need them, though it probably would tend to do so. But necessaries are dear to-day, not because they are scarce, but partly because it costs so much to put them where they are wanted, and partly because restrictions on output, imposed by employers' agreements and trade union regulations, add to the cost of working up the cheap materials with which the world is flooded.

But here again we have the support of Mr. Bertrand Russell, who says, on page 158 of *The Practice and Theory of Bolshevism*: 'I do not think that mere inequality of wealth in itself is a very grave evil. If everybody had enough, the fact that some have more than enough would be unimportant. With a very moderate improvement in methods of production, it would be easy to ensure that anybody should have enough, even under capitalism, if wars and preparations for wars were abolished. The problem of poverty is by no means insoluble within the existing system, except when account is taken of psychological factors and the uneven distribution of power.'

As to power, in these days of democracy and mass production, it is dispensed by the popular voter and the general consumer; and the future of mankind depends on the discretion, or want of it, that these ladies and gentlemen may show in dispensing it. But at least we have the support of this distinguished Communist in thinking that inequality of wealth does not hurt the community much. Inequality of wealth is not quite the same thing as the right of inheritance and the consequent existence of an 'idle rich' class, but it is very much the same. For if we all started from scratch and no one could inherit the right to help himself, without effort, from the pool of wealth, there would be much less, if any, ground for any sense of unfairness among those who are left behind in the race. Whether, as things are, such sense of unfairness really exists in many minds I am inclined to doubt. One can only judge from one's own narrow range of experience. But having been one of, and having chiefly lived among those who have had to make their own way in life, I have never felt, and have rarely heard expressed, any envy of those who were provided for by the proceeds of work done by somebody long ago.

If, then, these idle rich do not do the rest of us much, if any, harm, let us see whether we can chalk up anything to their credit, in these critical and sceptical days, when, as Falstaff says, 'The poor abuses of the time want countenance.'

One justification for them, though one that is rapidly weakening, is that the desire to 'found a family' and leave their heirs beyond the reach of fortune's malice is an important spur to the energy of the organizers. We saw, in the chapter devoted to the reward of these queer folk to whom we owe so much, how little of the really good things of life they are able to enjoy themselves; but it is alleged that they are often kept more closely on their treadmill, and induced to rotate it with a more vigorous kick, by the knowledge that they will be able to leave their money to heirs, the seed of their own loins or any others that they may choose.

If this be so, we have gone far, from a business point of view, to justify the existence of the idle rich. For we have seen how immensely important to the material comfort of us all is the ceaseless activity of the pioneers, as Mr. Ford calls them – those who provide energy and driving power to get things done, and strike out new lines.

But this incentive is probably weakening as more sensible views are spread concerning the benefit conferred on young people by immense fortunes left to them. Nevertheless, the desire to heap up wealth and leave it as one chooses to leave it is still one of the spurs that keep the pioneers busy, and the terrific scale of death duties, rising to half of the big fortunes, now imposed in England, is perhaps one of the reasons for a certain lack of eagerness and vigour of which many of her business men are nowadays accused. 'Why should we risk our time and money in fresh enterprise,' they ask, 'if the State takes income tax and surtax on profits, if any, shares none of the losses, and then takes anything up to a half of what we leave when we go?'

If then the existence of an idle rich class can be claimed as an indirect incentive to activity on the part of the organizers, the surplus income that it invests is also a benefit to all of us who want to see the pool of wealth grow. They are the people who can invest with least effort; and unless somebody invests, the equipment of the world with the plant that turns out and distributes the things that we all want cannot be maintained and increased. One reason why certain kinds of industries – those which provide the plant for production and transport – have been depressed in recent years is because people nowadays save less than they used to. It has been estimated by the Colwyn Committee, which investigated problems of national debt and taxation, and issued its report[1] in 1927, that the amount annually saved in England is less by £150,000,000 to £200,000,000, after making allowance for the reduced value of money, since the war. This is partly owing to the greatly increased taxation, partly to the better distribution of the nation's income noted on page 160 on the authority of Dr. Bowley, partly to the general inclination to get the best out of life while we are alive and take less thought for those who come after us, and partly to the general uncertainty and political unrest, due to international and domestic bad temper and discontent, which saps the confidence that encourages

[1] Stationery Office, Cmd. 2800.

investors to save. These tendencies are more or less visible in most, if not all of the countries that used to provide capital for the rest of the world, and it will be shown later that one of the causes of the present world depression is the drying up of the international capital market. So that those who save and invest as the very rich can and do, unless the tax-gatherer shears their fleece too closely, supply a felt want. And here we do find a real objection to the luxury spending of the idle rich. For if they spent less on frivolities they could save more, and so further trade and development.

Another very real benefit conferred on the rest of us by the so-called 'idle rich' is the immense amount of effort – some of it of a kind that involves ceremonial and pomp and fuss to an extent that must be quite maddening – that they make from mere sense of duty and on the principle that *richesse oblige*. They attend banquets and listen to speeches, they entertain distinguished visitors from the Dominions and abroad, not comfortably and pleasantly as you and I entertain domestic and foreign friends, but to the accompaniment of flashlight photographs, bands, reporters and society paragraphists. They further all kinds of work for the public good and – Heaven help them! – spend years of their lives in sitting on committees. 'They enjoy it all,' you say? If so, I for one feel all the more gratitude to them.

And those of them who shirk these duties and are merely frivolous and sometimes slightly, or even exceedingly, scandalous, are worth a great deal to the rest of us in the entertainment and amusement that their vagaries provide as described and pictured in the newspapers and in popular novels and in semi-imaginative memoirs. Life would be a much duller affair for millions if they could not watch day by day the bright and gaudy farce that is played for them by the more notorious performers on the stage of what is called society. High-browed critics may tell us that this enjoyment got by the multitude from the spectacle of the frivolous and naughty only makes frivolity and naughtiness worse. No doubt they are right from their point of view, and when the apostles of 'uplift' have taught the multitude to enjoy a better kind of amusement and the idle rich cease to be what we newspaper men call 'good copy,' the world will perhaps be a better place. But at present the world is in a horrible mess and life, in spite of great improvements, is dismally dowdy for far too many of us. I want everybody to get as much fun as they can as long as they do not harm anybody else; and it may be suggested to those who want to sweep away the idle rich, that they provide a brilliant and useful puppet show, which thrills and dazzles and amuses those whom they regard as their social inferiors.

And then, sport. Take the example of fox-hunting, the 'pursuit of the uneatable by the unspeakable,' as Oscar Wilde called it, a form of amusement that is, at first sight, the least easy to defend from a business point of view. Just because a number of people want to ride across country in pursuit of a 'varmint' which delights in killing poultry for the mere joy of slaughter, a costly organization is maintained for the preservation of the fox, which otherwise would long ago have gone the way of the wolf, and for the breeding and training of hounds and horses so that the devotees of the 'sport of kings' may indulge in it. To promote this anachronism, say the critics, thousands of chickens are destroyed every year and a large amount of energy and money, which might have gone into the production of real goods, is wasted year by year.

But the object of production is enjoyment, and fox-hunting provides enjoyment not only to those who indulge in it and to all the country folk who profit by it and love it, but also to millions who have never seen a pink coat and do not know one end of a horse from the other. How many laughs and thrills should we lose and have lost if there were no more hunting pictures in *Punch*, and in all the newspapers, and if we had never read Surtees, and Whyte Melville's novels and *Some Experiences of an Irish R.M.* and many other such books? Production is not an end in itself, as some people seem to think. It is said that Mr. Ford does not allow any but teetotallers in his works, because he thinks that even the smallest consumption of alcohol lowers the energy of the workman and reduces his skill in handling machines. Even if this be true (which is very doubtful), what is the use of being the most efficient producer alive if it means that one cannot have a glass of beer with one's supper if one likes it? Too much asceticism is as bad as over-indulgence, and we want to spread and increase brightness and pleasure, not cut them out in order to produce more dull things.

Huntsmen, grooms and kennelmen might be set to ploughing and so there might be more wheat in a world which at present finds itself overstocked with cereals.

More probably, as things are, there would be more unemployed.

A more practical benefit that the idle rich confer on us is the stimulus that their money and leisure give to the production of inventions which at first are expensive toys, but are developed later into useful servants of the whole community. The example of the motor car at once suggests itself. For years only the very rich could afford to own one, and it was at first so untrustworthy as a means of conveyance that no one whose time was important could depend on it. And now, as we all know, the idle rich folk's toy has become the servant of all and has sent most of the population scurrying about the country in cars and buses and brought down the price of railway tickets and given everybody a wonderful power of movement and vision. This power, of course, has been abused, like all the other powers enjoyed by man; but the benefit, on balance, given to us by the automobile, thanks to its early patronage by the idle rich, is surely immense. It has taught thousands of us how to handle machinery, and this is a lesson in accuracy and carefulness. For a machine makes no excuses and does not forgive slack work. The horse, good, patient beast, when it had its mouth pulled about and was flicked with a whip by a rough and stupid driver, generally made allowances for human weakness and took him home in safety. A car shows no such tolerance.

When all this is said in favour of the existence of inherited wealth, the sentiment against it is, I think, strong and growing in England, especially with regard to the most enormous fortunes. The terrific scale of death duties is shattering them to pieces – possibly, as we shall see, too fast – and all down the scale the fine paid to the State by those who receive inherited wealth is big enough to check accumulation. Side by side with the work of the tax-gatherer's 'two-handed engine at the door' through which all who possess have to make their exit, is the growing belief that it is better to fit those whom we leave behind to fend for themselves and to justify by their own work their pull on the pool of wealth, than to give them the chance of leading idle lives on the fruits of work that others have done before them.

CHAPTER X

THE UNEMPLOYED AND
THEIR MAINTENANCE

Those who cannot work – Those who cannot get Work –
Owing to Inventions and Mechanization – Or Trade Crises –
Responsibility of the Community – 'Work or Maintenance' –
From Severity to Sentimentality – Abuses of the Dole.

In the last chapter we considered the power which is
given, by the system of inheritance, to those who
accumulate wealth to hand it on to their heirs, so
allowing them to live on the proceeds of work done in
the past, without any necessity for earning a living for
themselves. We have now to look at the problem of
those who have no store of past work – their own or
other people's – behind them and are unable to earn
a living by working for it. This is the problem of
unemployment.

One class of the unemployed consists of those who
are called 'unemployables' – those unfortunate people
who, owing to some weakness of mind or body, cannot
stay the course of life at the pace at which it is
now run, and sometimes cannot even line up for the
start.

The second are those who are strong and skilful, in
varying degrees, at some particular job, but find that
owing to a change of fashion or the invention of a

M 177

substitute, the article that they have worked to produce is no longer, or much less, wanted, or that the introduction or improvement of machinery has made it possible to produce the article with the help of a much smaller amount of manual labour.

As an example of those displaced by inventions we may take the hansom-cab driver, with his marvellous skill in steering the 'gondola of London' at a pace that then seemed reckless, through London's then practically unregulated traffic. He has vanished and no kindly novelist has given us a portrait of him, as Dickens immortalized the stage-coach driver in Tony Weller. As an example of those whom machinery has made less necessary, we may note, among many, the farm-worker, that most versatile and skilful craftsman. He used to wield flail, scythe and sickle, and some of us can still remember what haymaking looked like, when a dozen good mowers were swinging their scythes in an even line under the June sunshine. It was a picture of human strength and skill and beauty. Now a machine does the work and it, too, and many others like it, are pictures of human ingenuity and skill that have worked for the benefit of those who get cheaper food, but have saved the effort of many human mowers and reapers and threshers and made their strength and skill useless to them for earning a living by exercising them in that particular way. This sort of unemployment, due to the development of machinery, is so common a feature of our modern conditions that it has been given a special name – 'technological' unemployment.

For all these classes of workless folk, a decently

minded modern community feels itself responsible, and
the extent to which it approaches this problem in a
humane and generous spirit and deals with it either
out of charitable or public funds, is a good test of the
degree of a nation's civilization. This is one of the
tests that shows very clearly and hopefully how much
more decently and kindly men nowadays behave to
one another, and refutes the silly assertion that one
hears so often, that human nature cannot be changed.
If that were true there would be no hope, but in fact
human nature is changing always and it is everybody's
business to help to make it change in the right
direction.

In the good old days those who had no 'visible means
of subsistence' were apt to be regarded as incorrigible
rogues, and to be clapped in the stocks or branded.
Nevertheless it was something that in a Tudor England,
as recorded by Mr. G. M. Trevelyan, 'the provision
for the poor, formerly left to the monasteries and guilds
and to private charity, was provided for as a duty
incumbent on society at large and enforced by the
State.'[1] A few pages later he tells us that 'the sudden
suppression of the monasteries before the Poor Law
had been fully developed to take their place as an
agency of relief, naturally increased distress, as much
perhaps by turning adrift the large companies of
monastic servants as by stopping the monastic alms.
. . . The "beggars" became the objects both of fear
and of pity. Their entry into a village (usually called
a "town" by our Tudor ancestors) has been immortalized in nursery rhyme:

[1] *History of England*, p. 269.

'"Hark! hark! the dogs do bark; the beggars are
   coming to town."

'And then we know how

   '"Some gave them white bread, and some gave them
      brown,
   And some gave them a good horsewhip and sent
      them out of the town."

Both bread and whip, at first the expression of individual
charity and self-protection, were organized as compulsory social duties by the series of Tudor Poor Laws
culminating in the Poor Law and parish Poor Rate of
Elizabeth. Gradually the distinction between the
able-bodied who would not work, the aged and feeble
who could not work, and the unfortunate who could
not find work, became clear to Tudor society and took
its place in the Poor Law.'[1]

By the end of the reign foreigners marked with
surprise in England an absence of beggars to which
they were unaccustomed in other lands, and the diary
of a Duke of Stettin's Journey, dated 1602, is quoted
to the effect that 'it is a pleasure to go about for one
is not molested or accosted by beggars. . . . For in
England they do not suffer any beggars except they
be few in number and outside the gates. Every parish
cares for its poor.'[2]

Nevertheless, though England's lead in the matter
of caring for her poor is a thing of which we may well
be proud, for many centuries the spirit in which the

[1] *Op. cit.*, pp. 284-5.   [2] *Op. cit.*, p. 358, note.

work was done seems to have been based largely on the 'bread and whip' principle, which again was based on the idea that those who have no work to do, or have not enough strength of mind or body to work, ought to be fed as sparingly and treated as severely as possible, in order to spur them to try to find or to do work. Society recognized that it had to provide for them, but its attitude to the job implied that both the 'work-shy' and the workless were sinners and failures who ought to be driven, by the unattractive conditions under which they were given relief, to repairing their fault and turning over a new leaf.

This attitude produced a reaction and a challenge. It was argued that those who are too weak in mind and body to work are so, not from any fault of their own, but owing to the conditions under which they were conceived, born and brought up, and that their weakness is due to the failure of society to organize itself in such a way that every one born within its boundaries shall be – apart from inevitable accidents – a proper man or woman reasonably equipped in mind and body. And if we consider what you or I should probably have been, if we had been bred by slum-dwellers and brought up in slum surroundings, we shall admit that this contention is sound and unanswerable.

Still stronger is the case for humane and generous treatment of the able-bodied workers who cannot find work. From the examples given of the hansom-cab driver and the farm-worker, displaced, one by the invention of the motor car, and the other by farming machinery, it is clear that under modern industrial conditions workers are subjected to risks, owing to

economic forces which are completely beyond their
control, and that it is entirely unjust to lay the whole
burden of facing these risks upon shoulders that are
quite unable to bear them. The claims to 'work or
maintenance' voiced by the Socialists was a cry for
mere justice. William Higgs, a farm-labourer born of
a line of such, and a skilled haymaker, horse-master,
reaper and binder, finds that he is not wanted because
a machine can do his work much better and quicker.
Should he, therefore, be forced into a workhouse?
Society has benefited by the mechanical invention
which has cheapened its food and so increased its
wealth. It can well afford, and ought to be glad to
afford, to treat William Higgs, not as a sinner but as
one who, owing to a change that has benefited it, has
suffered completely undeserved ill-luck, from the consequences of which he has every right to be protected.

And the case is still stronger when, as at the present
moment, the whole business arrangements of this
planet have been subjected to a jolt, or rather a series
of jolts, which has resulted in the curious paradox, so
ridiculous if it were not so tragical, of destitution and
depression due to too much plenty. The Great Ones
of the Earth, who rule us politically, financially and
commercially, have made such a mess of the job that
mankind is smothered under a mass of goods that it
cannot consume, and there is not only 'technological'
unemployment, but unemployment due to the too
great generosity of Fortune's Cornucopia. When the
business world has thus been ridiculously turned
upside down, the workers who are thrown out of work,
owing to the blunders of those who have handled our

destinies, are the last who ought to be asked to suffer, because they are the least responsible for the mess, and have the least store of resources to fall back on.

And yet I was lately talking to a quite intelligent, decent and kindly member of the lower middle class, a sort of secretary-clerk, and he said: 'I wonder what would happen if the dole were abolished? Of course it ought never to have been started.'

This bitter feeling, very strong in certain classes in England, about the unemployment relief commonly called the 'dole' has most unfortunately been aroused by the stupid way in which public money has been wasted, owing to the violent reaction against the severity of the old methods of relieving those who were out of work. Governments, like all weak bodies and institutions, generally swing from extremes of severity to extremes of sentimentality. From the principle that any able-bodied man who cannot find work can expect no help from the community unless he goes into a workhouse, England went over to a system under which anyone who could not find a job at his or her particular trade was entitled to maintenance on terms which did not encourage him or her to look for another.

Moreover, the Act was so drafted and the system was so administered that extraordinary examples were given of the loopholes through which those who were ingenious enough to take advantage of them were able to increase their incomes at the public expense. One was that of a labourer employed by a printing firm for two nights a week, one of which was Saturday, and thereby earned rather more than £4. He was entitled to draw, and did so, unemployment benefit for the rest of the week, although his pay for his two nights' work was more than was earned by many mechanics.[1]

There were also examples in which in certain industries it was a regular arrangement between the employers and workers that the latter should be idle during so many days in the week, and draw unemployment benefit.

Unemployment became a normal profession for many whose wants were modest, and in fact the modesty had not to be too excessive. An example was given[2] of a dole-drawer who told the official who regularly paid him that he would not be coming for it next week as he was going to Liverpool to see the Grand National, and was told by the paying official that he would be enabled to draw his weekly honorarium at Liverpool.

Or, if we want official evidence, there is that of Sir Alfred Watson, the Government Actuary, given before the Royal Commission on Unemployment Insurance. Among many examples that he gave was that of 'the coal trimmer who works regularly and for very long hours on two or three days in each week, during which he earns from £5 to £7 a day,' and yet receives unemployment benefit.[3]

All these absurdities, due to exaggerated sentimentalism and the respect of politicians of all parties for the votes of the unemployed and of the possibly some day about to be unemployed, produced a state of things which led to a gross waste of public money and serious

[1] Article in *Morning Post*, 20th August 1930.
[2] In a letter to *The Times*, 5th August 1930.
[3] *The Times*, 30th January 1931.

demoralization of those who were thus stupidly encouraged to lead lives of idleness. Incidentally, they also proved that the old severity of Poor Law administration, though often terribly unfair and inhuman, did at least protect the community from being exploited by those who prefer to take ingenious advantage of its slackness and sentimentality. As to their attitude, concerning the wickedness of which it is easy for those who have never done a day's work to wax eloquent, let us remember before we distribute damnatory epithets the temptation that was put before them. They saw benefits being handed out by the community which they believed, as most people do, to have a bottomless purse, and they did not see why they should not take their share. We may deplore the decline of the old spirit of self-reliance which made people prefer to support themselves rather than 'come on the parish,' though whether that spirit was ever more general than it is to-day is open to question. In old days the self-reliant spirit was encouraged by very rough methods. To-day it is discouraged by well-meaning sentimentality. If it has declined, let us put the blame in the right letter-box, addressed to those who have invited this decline by making the task of living on the community too easy and attractive.

But having seen the two extremes at work, we can now consider what is the fair and sound principle on which the relief of the unemployed should be carried out. If we agree that those who are thrown out of work by industrial changes ought to be protected against destitution by the community which has benefited by them, we shall also agree that in fairness to the community the unemployed should be expected to take any kind of work that is offered, or else should be obliged to accept a scale of subsistence which is substantially less than that earned by those who are at work. To ask a man or woman to do any work that is offered them is not imposing on them any hardship that is not shared by all classes, except those who are independent. We all live on the pool of wealth to which all the rest of the community contribute, and we have to contribute, if we are lucky, work that we want to do, but if that is not what the community wants from us, we must make the best of it and do the work that somebody wants and will pay for. In the course of a rather rolling-stone life, I have earned my living in five different kinds of business and professions, only one of which (for which I was in many ways unfitted) gave me work that I really wanted to do. But there was no hardship about it. One gets used to any sort of work and one gets some fun out of most of them.

Only if this principle is insisted upon can the really sound and satisfactory cure of unemployment – by absorption of the unemployed in new or expanding industries – be expected to work. If because a country goes 'dry,' all those who have worked in breweries expect to be maintained for the rest of their lives by the community, in spite of the increased demand for labour that would be forthcoming from the manufacturers of temperance drinks, there could be none of that adaptability and power of readjustment on which the progress and expansion of industry depend.

Given this condition – willingness to take any work

that is offered – the mobility and elasticity of manual labour, combined with the constantly varying demands of consumers and the ready adaptability of machinery, should lead to a great variety of new forms of productive activity. And the mechanization of industry makes the transfer of workers from one job to another easier and less irksome than it was when manual skill and craftsmanship were more important and long training was required. Now that machinery does more and more of the work, a good mechanic, knowing the tricks and manners of one sort of mechanical assistant, can master the whims of another more easily than an old-fashioned cobbler, for example, could have learnt to become a bricklayer.

Should we go further and say that it is fair to demand from the unemployed that they should be ready to accept work wherever it is offered, at home or in the Dominions? In his scheme for the re-integration of the British Empire, Dr. Leacock, the Canadian economist, whose severe judgment of the British investor has been quoted on page 163, suggests a great system of redistribution of the Empire's population by emigration and settlement, organized on business lines, and subsidized by the State. He tells us that even the accumulated wealth and productive power of England cannot continue indefinitely to support our unemployed. 'The unemployed,' he says, 'have got to go. And the outside Empire, properly organized, needs them. The burden would turn into an asset. The word "man-power," forgotten since the war, would get back its meaning. Any and all of these people would emigrate to the outer Empire if they were given free transit and a job on arrival. If they wouldn't, it would be a fair proposal to suggest to them that they die of starvation.'[1]

Such threats of starvation are fortunately out of date; and it remains to be seen whether the outer Empire is prepared to be peopled as Dr. Leacock suggests. Until that point is clearer and until it is also clear that Dr. Leacock is right in thinking that it is not likely that the unemployed can be turned into productive workers in England, it seems hardly fair to expect them to forfeit a claim to maintenance because they do not want to leave their country.

[1] *Economic Prosperity in the British Empire*, p. 197.

CHAPTER XI

OTHER STATE BENEFITS

Old Age Pensions – Social Services – Mr. Tawney's Blessing –
Some Critics' Cursing – The Balance of Advantage – How Much
can we Afford?

BESIDES providing for those who cannot get work to do,
a modern State spends large sums on public health and
education and on the maintenance in old age of those
who have not been able to make provision against the
time when they are no longer able to work. 'Since
1900,' said Mr. Tawney in his book on *Equality*, 'some
sixteen European nations, four of the British Dominions
and several States of the American Union, have
established systems of old-age pensions, defrayed from
public funds, or by means of insurance, or by a combination of both. Though state-aided insurance against
sickness, invalidity and unemployment is somewhat
less general, it advances year by year.'

It has already been noted in Chapter III that the
cost of these social services, as they are called, has risen
by more than £300,000,000 since 1911, and that this
expenditure, in so far as it is not paid for by their own
contributions, is a further addition to the increased
share of the pool of wealth that has been secured by
the wage-earners.

To some critics of our present tendencies, this process

appears to be an almost unredeemed evil. They admit that there is a certain amount of sentimental philanthropy, and desire to relieve poverty, behind it; but they attribute it largely to the desire of politicians to get votes by giving away public money, and they believe that the result of this expenditure is the demoralization of those who receive the benefits, the loading of the back of enterprise with a burden that it cannot stand, and the imminent bankruptcy of the national finances.

Mr. Tawney, on the other hand, finds nothing but satisfaction in the widening of what he calls the 'range of requirements which are met by some form of collective action'; and his book is an admirably reasoned, if occasionally overstated, argument in its favour. Listen to his description of the days before this distribution of what he calls 'social income' had begun:

'Undismayed by progressive taxation, the property-owner could spend on himself, or invest as he pleased, almost the whole of the fortune which the tide of economic expansion washed to his feet. Unfettered by legal restrictions, the wage-earner was free to do everything which cholera, typhus, and enteric, a working day of anything from twelve to eighteen hours and an absence of facilities for education so complete that as late as 1870 only two-fifths of the children between six and ten were in attendance at school, would permit of his doing. In such conditions the most fundamental of inequalities was simple and unmistakable. It was not that one class was rich and another poor. It was that one class lived and another died. A "gentleman" in London, the Commissioners of 1844 were told, lived on the average twice as long as a "labourer"; while the corresponding figures for Leeds were forty-four and nineteen years, and for Liverpool thirty-five and fifteen.'

But we must not forget that there was another side to this picture. The Colwyn Committee gives us a glimpse of it. 'In the Victorian era,' says page 241 of its report, 'it is generally true that saving was left as a monopoly in the hands of the wealthier classes, who were allowed to remain in almost complete control of their riches. In our view it is impossible to justify the old distribution of taxation, even though it reduced interference with saving to a minimum. It is true that under it industry advanced enormously and the standard of living improved for the whole community more than in any comparable period.'

This last sentence seems to support the case of the critics of the social service expenditure and of the taxation which provides it. While they were practically non-existent, industry advanced enormously and the whole community's standard improved more than ever before or since. If that state of things had continued, might not the wage-earners have been able to secure for themselves out of the greater growth of production and wages that might have ensued, the lengthened span of life and all else that the social expenditure had given them? And might it not have been better for them to have done it for themselves, cultivating the spirit of independence, on which we used to pride ourselves? Such a contention Mr. Tawney would flout with scorn. To him this combination of communal provision and progressive taxation (which means taxation that falls chiefly on the well-to-do) has great and special advantages. 'Unlike a rise in wages secured by a trade union, it taps, not merely the resources of a particular industry but wealth of all kinds, whatever its source, including that arising, not only from production, but from finance, speculation, commerce and the unearned increment of urban ground rents.' He thinks also that it can be continued and extended in periods of depression, though those who pay the taxes could argue with much force that attempts to do so at such a time would certainly increase the depression and prolong it, and so do the wage-earners more harm than good. 'By concentrating surplus resources,' Mr. Tawney continues, 'directing them to the objects of primary importance and applying them, as in the case of the services of health, housing and education, under expert advice and in accordance with a specialized technique, it makes possible the attainment of results which no body of individuals, even though they spent ten times the sums involved, could achieve for themselves by their isolated action.'

He is also able to cite the growth of the accumulated savings of small investors and to show that, according to expert opinion, 'there is no evidence that the advent of state schemes has led to a slackening of individual effort to provide against the changes and chances of life.'

There is evidently some weight in this contention that surplus resources, concentrated in the hands of a responsible body and scientifically applied to important objects, can do much better work for us than when left, as the old-fashioned theory told us, 'to fructify in the pockets of the people.' To be entirely true, Mr. Tawney's contention assumes a degree of wisdom on the part of the responsible body and care in the use of public funds such as are apt to be conspicuous by their absence. We have seen in Chapter V, in dealing with proposals for nationalizing the banks, the weaknesses of politicians and of governmental action exposed by very earnest Socialists; and we have seen in our last chapter the absurdities in which we have wallowed, thanks to a well-meant but ill-considered scheme of unemployment relief, designed by politicians and executed by bureaucrats.

Nevertheless, these questions have to be decided by the balance of advantage, and those who believe most strongly that Governments make a mess of everything and should do as little as possible, have to admit that public action, with all its faults, is inevitable in certain fields. None of them would want to hand over the provision of a police force to private enterprise, and few would contend that education should have been left to the choice of parents to be exercised, if at all, among teachers who provided it in schools organized on competitive lines with a view to profit.

If education had been left voluntary, and no taxation had been raised to provide it, it is possible that some of the wage-earners, out of the higher wages that untaxed industry might have provided, might have given their children as good an education as they get now, perhaps even a better one. But whether the children got any education at all would have depended on the whims and incomes of their parents, and this is not a position in which any civilized nation could leave those who have to grow up to exercise the rights of citizenship.

And as with education, so with health. We could not leave sanitation to the chances of private enterprise, the whims of landlords, and the capacity of tenants to afford it. Within limits, then, expenditure on social services is clearly not only inevitable but desirable. As to the limits, we have to be guided, first, by how much we want to see done, and secondly, by how much the country can afford to spend. A comfortable and pleasant old age is a benefit that all ought to enjoy and most especially those who have worked at the dullest and least interesting jobs. We may feel that it would be better that all who earn a living should earn one good enough to enable them to acquire, by their own exertions, sufficient to give them a comfortable and pleasant evening to their lives, and that they should also all possess the thrift and foresight necessary to provide it. As it is, these things are not so, and so old age pensions are provided by the States mentioned at the beginning of this chapter. Few of us would now be inclined, in the interests of independence and thrift, to condemn to penury or the workhouse those who have had the bad luck to be born without the qualities that would have enabled them to avoid it. When we remember how strong is the element of luck in all our business lives and how largely material success depends on the circumstances in which we start and work and the qualities with which we happen to be born, we must admit the justice of any public action that tends to outwit the freaks of Fortune in distributing her favours, as long as such action does not check enterprise to a dangerous degree.

There remains the question, how much a country can afford and what is the extent of the 'surplus resources' that can be placed at the disposal of the social services. If we all worked heartily together and if machinery were allowed to work as hard as it might for us, this question would bother us much less. As it is, it insists very urgently on being faced. If so much is spent on the social services that industry is taxed to a degree that takes the heart out of the organizers, and the springs of capital are dried up, then this kind of expenditure is carried to a point that hurts those whom it is designed to benefit. Whether that point has been reached will have to be considered when we come, in Chapter XX., to the question of taxation.

CHAPTER XII

THE WORLD AS WORKSHOP

International Trade – Barriers, Natural and National, against it – Trade Balances – Of the United States – Of Great Britain – Strength of America's Position – England's 'Invisible' Exports – Interdependence of the Nations – The Effort towards Self-Sufficiency.

IN 1928, according to a League of Nations publication, a world population of 1,962,000,000 did a total trade, in imports and exports across the frontiers, of $66,708,000,000, or £13,341,600,000, and just half of this trade – $33,832,000,000 – was done by the continent of Europe, excluding Russia, with a population of 372,000,000 – less than one-fifth of the whole.[1] If the rest of the world could work up to Europe's standard in international trade, what a business we should all be doing!

Such was the result of the aggregate effort of this curious ant-heap working under private enterprise for purposes of profits, which can only be earned by growing, making or doing things that people want and can pay for. An immense, unregulated (but not, as we shall see, unrestricted) flow of goods, guided by foresight, chance and hazard, and guesses about what we

[1] Memorandum on Production and Trade, League of Nations, Geneva, 1930.

are likely to want, pours day and night into the pool of wealth. To many of us it gives plenty. To all of us it gives plenty compared with the share that our forebears enjoyed. But there ought to be much more of it.

But trade between the nations is, inevitably, complicated by many difficulties that do not impede the exchange of goods and services between the citizens of any one of them. First of all there are what may be called the natural barriers, such as the geographical difficulties of distance, oceans, mountain ranges and so on, which make it a costly task for the workers in China, for example, to exchange their goods with those in Peru; differences of language which make it difficult for workers to tell one another what they want to buy and sell; differences of money which complicate the task of payment; and differences of taste, which cause a good deal of wasted effort because those who make goods which, in their opinion, ought to find a ready market in the places to which they are sent, discover that they are not in accordance with the local view as to what is attractive.

All these barriers are part of the nature of things as they are, and their effect in checking the free flow of trade between worker and worker has already been enormously reduced and will be reduced still more, perhaps in some cases abolished.

Last century's work, in covering the earth with railways and good roads and the oceans with fast steamships, has immensely cheapened the cost of sending goods from one end of the world to the other; and this process should go on much further by the spreading of the network of railways and roads, the improvement of motor transport and the development of carriage by aeroplane. The language difficulty has been greatly reduced by the spread of education and may be largely eliminated some day by the adoption of English as a universal trade language among the chief nations; the laziness of Englishmen about learning foreign languages has already done much to further this end; and it is now being quickened by America's immense power as world creditor, trader and money-lender. Differences of money count for much less in these days, owing to the general use of the gold standard[1] by the leading commercial nations, a system which may easily be extended and simplified. Already the exchange of the money of one nation into that of another is carried out with marvellous celerity and cheapness by the international market in what is called foreign exchange.[2]

As to differences in taste, let us hope that they will increase and become more varied as the general power to make things grows. As consumers, we want our whims and preferences to be studied and catered for; on the other hand, because it is easier and cheaper to make millions of one article than thousands of a hundred articles, the producers and their cunning army of salesmen naturally try to train us all to want the same thing. It will be a disastrous day for civilization if they succeed and 'standardize' our wants about things in which individual taste ought to count.

In this matter of buying and selling there is a queer

[1] Explained below in Chapter XVIII.
[2] As to which see Chapter XIII.

difference between individuals and nations. You and I want to sell our work as well as we can to anyone who will buy it and also, if we follow our natural instinct, to buy any goods that we want as cheaply as we can and of the best quality that we can get for our money. Nations also want to sell their work to other nations, but, for reasons that will be set forth later, they feel uncomfortable about buying the work of other nations. A large volume of exports, which are goods and services sold abroad, is regarded with satisfaction and pride; but a large volume of imports, which are goods and services bought abroad, is thought to be a weakness; and this feeling is cherished by those within the nation who make goods of a kind that are imported, and demand that such imports should be restrained by duties imposed at the frontier.

In fact, as we shall see, a nation cannot export unless it imports something. And so the reluctance to import is continually thwarted by the desire to export, with the result that, in spite of the import duties, trade between the nations does manage to grow in normal times.

Owing to this common prejudice against foreign goods, besides the natural barriers that impede the free flow of trade, artificial barriers, known as customs duties or protective tariffs are set up at the frontiers by the great majority of nations. Import duties are imposed on goods which are being brought in for sale from any other country. In a few countries export duties are levied on goods that are going out; as in Brazil, where import duties are collected by the Federal Government – the Government of Brazil as a whole –

and export duties by the various States into which Brazil is divided, San Paulo, Para and the others. But import duties levied on goods coming in across the frontier are the more popular and general. If not too high, they have a double convenience that accounts for their popularity. They provide the Government with revenue and at the same time keep out some foreign goods and so make it easier for the home growers and makers of similar goods to increase their output and earn profits; but if they are raised beyond a certain point they cease to produce revenue, because they effectively prohibit foreign goods from coming in, and secure the whole of the home market for the home producer.

There can be no doubt that these import duties and other forms of Protection are an obstacle to the free flow of goods and that the pool of wealth would be deeper and fuller if they could all be abolished. Whether they are a good or bad thing for the nations that impose them has long been a subject of controversy. Before we can discuss it, we must consider the position of a nation as a producing and trading unit.

A nation is a conception that is not as easy to grasp as it looks; it has been defined by Mr. H. G. Wells as a body of people who suffer from a common Foreign Office. For our present purpose we can get near enough to the root of the matter if we say that it is a body of people living within definite boundaries, using (more or less) a common language, ruled over and taxed by the same Government, and using the same kind of money.

As in the case of an individual, the earnings of a nation, due to the sale of its exports of all kinds of goods and services, must periodically balance with its expenditure on all forms of goods and services imported, though the balance may be arrived at by borrowing or lending, or by increasing or drawing on its store of cash. You as an individual earn or receive an income, we will suppose of £500 a year, either for work that you are doing or for work that somebody has done in the past. You spend £420, put £30 into premiums on your life policy and the odd £50 is added to your bank balance or invested in National Saving Certificates or any other investment that you may fancy. As an individual, you have delivered £500 worth of service to other members of the community, received £420 worth of goods and services and lent £80 worth to your life company and the Government or your bank, knowing that you or your heirs will get it back some day, with additions from the life company and the Government and perhaps from the bank, if the money has been placed on deposit for a definite period and not on current account to be drawn at any time. Your yearly account is thus balanced.

Then you have a bad year with sickness at home or you find it necessary, and pleasant, to help a friend who is in a corner, or perhaps some special opportunity for enjoyment makes you give yourself and your family an extra treat which means that you outrun the constable; and at the end of the year you find that you have disbursed, including your life premium, £550.

You have paid out £520 and invested £30 in insurance, but you have only earned £500. But you must have found the £50 of which you are 'shy,' either by drawing on your bank balance, if it will stand it, or by borrowing from your bank, if it will allow you an overdraft, or by cashing Saving Certificates, or by running up bills with the tradesmen who supply you – which means to say that you have borrowed the money. Somehow, by realizing investments or by drawing on your store of cash at the bank, or by a little of each of these devices, you have, after a fashion, balanced your account.

In the matter of international trade, a nation works on just the same lines. As far as the rest of the world is concerned, its exports of all kinds – goods and services – are its income; its imports of all kinds are what it spends, what it invests abroad, if anything, are its savings, what it has to pay to foreign lenders on account of interest and debt redemption are its liabilities on account of debt, and its imports and exports of gold are its receipts and payments of cash. And these items on both sides of the account must balance year by year, unless the nation can balance them by borrowing; if it cannot, it or some of its citizens will have to repudiate their debts or arrange a postponement of them by means of what is called a moratorium, or period of delay.

The business is complicated by the fact that the nation does not, as such, buy or sell abroad at all. Its Government may do so to a small extent, and in these days most Governments owe money to foreign lenders, and some have money due to them on account of loans or war indemnity charges, and so they come into the picture through having to make or receive interest and reparations payments. But by far the greater part of what may be called the foreign balance sheet of the nations consists of payments due on one side or other of the account owing to the sales and purchases or lending and borrowing by private individuals and private companies, firms and institutions. There is thus an immense number of cross-currents and entries on both sides and the aggregates published represent nothing but a roughly approximate picture of the huge transactions of foreign trade.

All the leading nations, however, sell goods abroad and buy goods abroad, and the totals in quantities and values of these merchandise transactions are officially declared. The declaring officials doubtless make every possible effort to get the figures correct, but even in this matter of tangible merchandise there is room for a good deal of error. In the case of goods that are liable to duty there is a strong temptation, especially when the duties are stiff, to under-statement of quantities and values by the firms that handle them, and in countries where most people think that there is no harm in cheating the Government – and is there any country in which some people do not think so? – and where the customs officials are ill-paid and slack, there may be a good deal of falsification of this kind.

Still, for what they are worth, and they are certainly worth a good deal, there are the figures of what are called the 'visible' items of merchandise sold and bought; and we also have figures, which may be taken as probably correct, of the imports and exports of precious metals, gold and silver.

But besides these items, as to which there is a reasonable amount of certainty, there are many others concerning which there is no definite record, and they can only be calculated by means of such investigation as is possible, assisted by a certain amount of scientifically conducted guesswork.

For instance, England balances her international account by means of the service rendered to other countries by the ships of her mercantile fleet, and by her bankers, insurance companies and merchants, and by the interest due to her from investments made abroad in the past by her citizens, partly offset by the investments which her citizens are making at the moment. America balances hers by enormous expenditure on the part of her citizens on foreign travel and by the large sums sent across the sea by immigrants to their relatives in the old countries and by charitable and missionary contributions. None of these 'invisible' items can be exactly measured, but the patient work of official and other statisticians, constantly investigating and inquiring, gives us a picture of the trade balance of the leading countries, which shows roughly how they make both ends meet in their business relations with the rest of the world.

Let us take the figures of America's and England's balance of payments in 1929 and see how they look. Here are America's as compiled by the United States Department of Commerce, and published by it in its Trade Information Bulletin No. 698, and sorted and condensed by me so as to help those readers who are terrified and confused by rows of figures:

AMERICA'S BALANCE OF PAYMENTS, 1929

'Visible' Trade	*in £ millions.*
Exports sold	1098
Imports bought	951
Balance in America's favour	147

'Invisible' Trade	*in £ millions.*
Spent abroad by tourists	132
Sent home by immigrants	44
Sent abroad by charities	10
Spent abroad by Government . . .	18
Paid to foreign shipping and railways . .	4
Total paid abroad	208
Interest received on private investments abroad .	112
War Debt payments received (interest and capital) .	41
Other items received	5
Total received from abroad	158
Balance against America in £'s, 208 — 158 = . .	50

SUMMARIZED, America's position is therefore thus:	*in £ millions.*
Favourable balance on Visible Trade . .	147
Unfavourable balance on Invisible Trade . .	50
Net favourable balance	97

Many of these figures give the net balance of the
items. For instance, the amount spent abroad by
American tourists has had deducted from it the sum of
£36,000,000 which foreign tourists are believed to have
spent in America. Interest received from abroad is
shown less the interest (estimated at £82,000,000) due
from Americans to foreign investors; shipping and other
freights are less the £18,000,000 earned from ocean-
borne passengers by American shipping. And once

more it must be remembered that all these figures are necessarily estimated and give merely a rough picture.

Rough as it is, however, and after making allowances for possible errors, it is a picture of an amazingly strong position. Looking at it again, we see that America sold abroad £147,000,000 worth more goods than she bought abroad. She also had £112,000,000 due, on balance, on account of interest on investments abroad (which means an invisible export of coupons – claims for interest and dividends) £41,000,000 on account of war debts from the European belligerents, and £5,000,000 for oddments such as motion - picture royalties, cable charges, etc., making a total due to her on visible and invisible trade of over £300,000,000.

Against this huge sum due, the payments that she had to make were the trifle of £18,000,000 spent by her Government and the £4,000,000 net due for freights and transport charges. The other items of expenditure were voluntary and charitable and could be cut off altogether without inflicting material discomfort on her citizens – foreign travel, help sent to relatives overseas, subscriptions to charities and missions abroad account for £186,000,000 and she is left finally with a balance of £97,000,000 with which she adds £74,00,000 net to her investments abroad and £24,000,000 to her already enormous stock of gold and so ends the year with a discrepancy of £2,000,000. In other words, if at any time she were hard-pressed and found it necessary to reduce the sums that she has to pay abroad, all that she would have to do would be to cut down the luxury of foreign travel, the altruistic pleasure of foreign charity and the thrifty practice of foreign

investment. If she reduced by one-half her foreign payments on these accounts, desirable but not, in time of
crisis, necessary, she would increase her pull on the
wealth of the rest of the world by nearly £100,000,000.
To say nothing of what she could do if she chose to
part with some of the enormous holding of gold that
she has acquired during and since the war, raising her
total stock (at the end of 1930) to £920,000,000 and
the gold resources of her Federal Reserve Banks to
£588,000,000.[1] It is a position of immense strength
that is shown by America, as trader, creditor and
holder of a huge – wastefully huge, it looks – reserve
of cash in gold.

England's position is also very strong, but her
strength is not so well distributed as America's and
consists chiefly in the big income due to her on account
of foreign investments made in the past, to which she
is not now adding as rapidly as she used to, and in fact
at the moment (1931) may not be adding at all.

But let us look at the figures for 1929, as being the
last year that may be considered normal, though we
have to reckon with the fact that that 'normal' period
may have passed away for ever. In that year, as trader
in 'visible' goods, England showed an unfavourable
balance of £382,000,000, this being the amount by
which the cost of her imports exceeded that of her
exports.

(The use of the words favourable and unfavourable
in this connexion is sometimes questioned, as implying
that a country with a favourable trade balance is
necessarily strong and rich, and *vice versa*. This is

[1] *Federal Reserve Bulletin*, 31st January, pp. 9 and 43.

certainly not so. An unfavourable trade balance on visible goods may be due to various causes – in England's case it arises, as we shall see, because she has a big income from invisible trade and a big income from foreign investments, that is to say, because she is strong and rich. In that of a young developing country it may arise because capital is being poured in from outside in the form of goods to equip it and promote its power to create wealth. A so-called favourable balance may arise because a country has large payments to make abroad to meet interest charges on borrowed capital, and so has to send goods to be sold abroad and provide these sums. In this case it may be a sign of weakness or at least of dependence.

A 'favourable' balance of trade is thus a misleading phrase if it is taken to mean more than just what it does mean, namely, that as a buyer and seller of visible goods a country receives more than it pays.)

Coming back to England's international business activities, we can set them out as follows, remembering the caution necessary in taking the estimates on which they are based. These estimates, however, are framed with the utmost care by the highly trained experts of the Board of Trade:

ENGLAND'S BALANCE OF PAYMENTS, 1929

'Visible' Trade	*in £ millions.*
Imports bought	1221
Exports sold	839
Balance against England	382

'Invisible' Trade	*in £ millions.*
Net income from –	
Shipping	130
Oversea investments	285
Banking and commissions	65
Receipts by Government	22
Other sources	15
Balance in England's favour	517
LESS Adverse Balance on 'visible' trade . .	382
Net Balance in England's favour . . .	135

So here we see that when all the items visible and invisible are put together, England had a substantial favourable balance on the year, in fact some £40,000,000 bigger than America's.

(To complete the picture, we may add that England drew on her cash balance by exporting £16,000,000 worth of gold, and so was believed to have £151,000,000 available for investment abroad, on the total transactions of the year.)

But England's advantage is apparent rather than real. In the first place, it will be remembered how large a part (£186,000,000 out of £208,000,000) of America's invisible imports consisted of luxury and eleemosynary spending which could easily be cut down if necessary. England's balance sheet shows no such items big enough to be considered.

Again, her income of £130,000,000 from shipping – the gross receipts of her mercantile fleet – looks and is magnificent; but it is won in the teeth of competition with heavily subsidized foreign vessels and in spite of all kinds of restrictions with which foreign countries try to keep their carrying trade under their own flag.

That British shipowners succeed so well is a splendid achievement, but carrying goods for other peoples and for British Dominions who try, and are ready to spend money on trying, to carry their own, is a not too solid source of income.

An even more questionable item in the British balance sheet is the big income from overseas investments – £285,000,000 – especially when it is compared with the much smaller amount – £135,000,000 if we leave out the gold exports – that was invested abroad during the year. To the extent of £150,000,000, according to these figures, England was living, not on her capital as we are sometimes told by domestic croakers and foreign critics, but on the income earned by past effort, much of it made at a time before she had shown the rest of the world how to industrialize itself and lent it money and sent it men to do it with, and so her industries made profits more quickly and easily than they do to-day.

She is thus in the position of a wealthy manufacturer who has been in business a long time and has saved a great deal of money. He is still doing a profitable trade, but he chooses to spend not only all that he makes by trade but more than half of the income that he gets from his investments.

'And why not?' may very naturally be asked. Why should either a man or a people that has a big store of invested wealth accumulated out of past effort be expected to reinvest every year every penny received by way of income on the investment? If they are to continue this policy until the crack of doom, always accumulating and never enjoying, making money for others to take, how shall it have profited the man or the nation?

In this contention there is a good deal of truth and common sense. Storing wealth at compound interest for the benefit of posterity is a process that can be carried too far. Our forebears, and those of us who are old enough to remember it, lived hard fifty years ago, with the result that when the Great War came we had reserves of financial strength the extent of which astonished us. But it is a mistake to suppose that even they always invested abroad the whole of their current income from overseas investments. The *Economist* of 22nd November 1930, page 952, tells us that in only three years between 1880 and 1914 did we invest abroad more than our foreign interest. 'Since the war, with reduced savings and a larger need for capital at home, our foreign investments have recently amounted to about half our foreign interest, whereas during the thirty or forty years before the war, we normally reinvested abroad 62 per cent. of our foreign interest.' The man who did not see why he should do anything for posterity because posterity had never done anything for him, had a certain amount of reason behind him.

But only a certain amount, and the principle cannot be carried too far. A man or a nation that relies too much on income derived from investments gives hostages to fortune by making his or its livelihood depend on the power and willingness of debtors to pay interest. One that is paying for all that he buys or all that it imports, by means of tangible goods sold or real services rendered at the moment, is clearly in a stronger position.

In 1930 the net balance in England's favour was reduced to £44,000,000, out of which she took £5,000,000 in gold, so that the estimated balance left for investment was only £39,000,000. There were estimated declines of £25,000,000 in her income from shipping and £50,000,000 in that from overseas investments, as originally estimated, £10,000,000 in that from banking and commissions, and £1,000,000 in Government receipts; while the adverse balance on visible trade had increased by £5,000,000.

When we look into the details of the visible imports and exports of America or England, the comparative weakness of the latter becomes more evident still – and a glance at a world map showing the relative sizes of the two countries throws a good deal of light on the point.

America, with her 3,000,000 square miles of rich and fertile area and a climate ranging from sub-Arctic to sub-tropical, produces nearly everything that heart of man can desire for a population of 123,000,000 of souls. Apart from tea, coffee, and rubber, she can, or could if she liked, grow or dig out in her own borders, everything that is necessary to civilized life and have a big surplus for export.

The United Kingdom of Great Britain and Northern Ireland, with about 45,000,000 packed into an area of 95,000 square miles grows less than half (44 per cent. in 1929[1]) of the food that its inhabitants need, and also has to import all the cotton and many other raw materials that its factories need to make into the goods

[1] See 'The Case for Agriculture,' put by the National Council of Industry.

that they sell abroad. Mr. Hugh Butler, in the United States Department of Commerce's Handbook on *The United Kingdom*, tells us that 'to a degree almost unparalleled elsewhere, Britain is dependent upon the exchange of products of the mine and the factory for foreign foodstuffs and raw materials.'

Since food and raw materials – the primary products, as they are called – are the basis of life and industry, a country that grows them itself is clearly in a sounder position than one which has to get them in from abroad in exchange for goods and services that it sends out.

England's livelihood, and the actual existence of a certain number of her inhabitants, depends on the smooth-working of international trade, the willingness and ability of other countries to accept her goods and services in exchange for food and raw materials, and, consequently, her power to produce goods and services at a price that her foreign customers can and will pay.

At the same time, her readiness to buy the food and raw materials that other countries produce has made her the chief world market, as the biggest importer, and this fact gives her a position of great strength. For other countries cannot flourish unless they sell to her; and if they sell to her, they, or some country to whom they pass on the claims so created, must take something from her in exchange.

If the world were civilized enough to go on quietly with its business of making and enjoying good things, a country in England's position could rely, with a fair amount of confidence, on the smooth working of trade between the nations. But when the machinery of international trade is jolted by a world-wide war and its consequences, then those countries – among which England is pre-eminent – that depend most for prosperity on its smooth working are hardest hit.

Nevertheless, so clearly is all the world dependent, in matters of trade prosperity, on the activity in selling and buying of each of its parts, that no country that has any real share in world trade can ignore misfortunes and depressions that may occur anywhere, preventing the smooth flow of goods and services into and out of the common pool of wealth.

Those countries, such as Canada, Australia, New Zealand, Argentina, Brazil and India, which chiefly sell food and raw materials abroad, depend on the general prosperity of trade almost as much as England, Germany and the other sellers of goods manufactured by industry; and their dependence is in one respect even greater because they are generally debtor countries and so are obliged to sell their goods abroad in order to meet the service of their debts, unless they can meet them by fresh borrowing, which is difficult if the machine of world prosperity is seriously out of gear.

If the industrial countries are not prospering and their factories are working short time, their demand for wool, cotton, hides, timber, metals and other materials will evidently be less. And at the same time those who own and work in the factories will have smaller profits and less wages to spend and their demand for food, clothes and other comforts will be to some extent affected. Thus every part of the great machine acts and reacts on the others.

When those countries which chiefly sell primary

products – food and materials – beyond their borders aim at greater self-sufficiency by fostering manufacturing industries at home, they are sometimes apt to forget that by so doing they are reducing the power of their foreign customers to take their products. When, for example, Brazil sets up a textile industry and consequently buys less cotton goods from Germany and England, she has no right to be surprised if she finds it less easy to sell abroad the coffee that is her chief staple export. She may argue, with perfect truth, that there will be no need for her to sell so much coffee as before, because she is making her own cotton goods, or some of them, instead of buying them from abroad; but this will be no consolation to the coffee planter who has sunk capital and energy on a big estate and finds his foreign market shrivelling, especially if, as is probable, he also finds that the cotton goods that he buys from the local factory are much dearer than, and not as good as, those that he used to get from overseas.

The net result of the process seems to be that the Brazilian public pays more for inferior cotton goods and the Brazilian coffee planter has a less ready market abroad for his bags of coffee; against which we have to set the profits made by the Brazilian manufacturer of cotton goods and the wages earned by those who work for him, and the fact that Brazil has to this extent made herself self-sufficient and independent of world trade and its fluctuations and shocks.

Does this effort at self-sufficiency pay the nations that make it? And, if not, does it carry with it advantages that balance any material loss that may be involved? In other words, do we want Free Trade or Protection?

Before we can face this question, we must look more closely at the method by which payments for all these goods and services are carried out, and see what is meant by 'foreign exchange.'

CHAPTER XIII

GOODS, SERVICES AND MONEY

Foreign Purchases and Sales – How paid for – The Market in
Exchange – Shipments of Gold – 'Gold Point' – Australia's Experience – A Self-curing Disease.

IT was stated in the last chapter that all nations want to
sell goods abroad, that in order to do so they have to
take something from abroad in exchange for them, and
that consequently, in spite of the reluctance of most
nations to buy goods from abroad, and the duties that
they impose to obstruct their entry, the trade of the
world does succeed in growing. To make this clear we
have to get a rough idea of the way in which the
exchange of goods and services between the nations is
paid for.

In this respect, again, a nation and an individual are
in much the same position. You and I sell our work
and receive money in payment for it. But the money is
no use to us until we have turned it into some article
or service, such as a hat or a bus-ride, that is provided
by somebody else, or invested it in some loan or
security from which we expect to receive interest in
future and which we hope to be able to turn back again
into money if a day of need comes. We may stack up a
hoard of money, but this is a most wasteful proceeding,
and if everybody adopted it there would soon be a

217

scarcity of money with the awkward consequences that follow from it, as we shall see later on.

Nations, as such, do not receive money from one another, except in so far as certain Governments owe one another debts, on account of reparations and war-time loans. Trading, as we all know, is carried on almost entirely by individuals within the nations, and so the payments that take place between one country and another are, so far, chiefly the result of an immense number of transactions between individuals or firms or companies. But it is usual in considering international trade to neglect this detail and to talk of a nation's imports, exports and payments; and as long as we do not altogether forget the detail, this way of thinking about the matter is simpler and easier.

Owing to the different kinds of money that nations use, there is a complication in international payments that does not arise in payments between members of the same country. If you, a Londoner, sell goods to a customer in Birmingham he pays you in British money which you can spend wherever you like in Great Britain. But if you sell to a customer in Chicago, he may pay either in dollars or in pounds, according to the arrangements that exist between you. If he pays you with a cheque in dollars on his own local bank, those dollars are of no use to you here until you have turned them into sterling money, which your bank will very easily do for you, because there is a market in London and in all the great trade centres in what is called 'foreign exchange,' which means the turning of foreign into local money, and *vice versa*, or of one kind of foreign money into another.

But your dollars can only be sold here because somebody here wants them, wherewith to make payment to someone in America, for something – goods or services or securities or property – that he has bought there. And in the same way if your American customer pays you in pounds for what you have sold him, he, or his bank, can only buy those pounds if someone in America has pounds to sell, which are due to him for something sold to somebody in England. In normal times these claims of one nation on another, for goods and services mutually sold, or for securities purchased or loans and advances made (which are maybe regarded as sales of promises to pay) either roughly balance or can be balanced by means of claims on other countries – as for example when British merchants who have bought raw cotton from America and sold cotton goods to Argentina can pay the American sellers of the raw cotton with dollars bought in Argentina from an Argentine cattle-breeder who has sold beef to America.

But there come times when, on this general balance of payments, England, for example, wants more dollars than are offering in the exchange market, and then the price of dollars in London, which usually fluctuates within narrow limits, will go up and, in the language of the market, the New York exchange will move against London. The quotation for this exchange is given in dollars, so when the price of dollars in London goes up, this will mean that the pound will fetch less in dollars, and so the rate will go down. When the exchange is at par a pound is worth $4·86·66, but if dollars are scarce and in demand, the rate will move down towards $4.85½. This movement will tend to induce anyone who can sell goods or anything else, or can borrow, in America to do so, so as to get the advantage of turning the dollars so raised into pounds at a favourable rate; but if this stimulus is exhausted without producing a recovery in the exchange and the balance is still against London, the rate will go down to what is called gold point, which is the rate at which it pays to send gold to New York, and turn it into dollars at the fixed statutory rate of $4.86⅔ to each pound's worth of gold.

Gold point depends on the cost of shipping and insuring the gold, and the amount of interest that is lost on it in transit. Lately (in the early part of 1931) these charges have come to about a cent and a quarter, and so the point at which it has been more profitable to provide dollars by shipping gold to New York to buy them with, has been in the neighbourhood of $4.85⅜.

As long as there is plenty of gold to be shipped, and it can be shipped fast enough to meet the demand, the exchange between any two countries that use gold as the basis of their currency cannot fluctuate in either direction beyond the limits of the gold points. But when there is great pressure, and also difficulty about shipping and insuring gold, these limits no longer apply; and in the early part of August 1914, when British bankers and financiers were calling in money from all over the world and the whole machinery of finance was out of gear, rates ranging up to seven dollars to a pound were paid in New York to anyone who had pounds to sell.

International accounts are thus balanced by an exchange of claims (embodied in what are called bills of exchange) established by sales of goods, services, securities and promises to pay; or, if these do not suffice to strike the balance, by shipments of gold, as long as there is gold to be shipped. If the gold stock is exhausted, or cannot be drawn on further, then the exchange, no longer governed by the gold points, expresses the depreciation of the country's currency and at the same time checks it by making the country a bad one to sell to and a good one to buy from.

This has lately happened to Australia, owing to a combination of misfortunes, chief among which were a disastrous fall in the price of wheat and wool, her principal exports, and the shutting up, in 1929 and 1930, of the international capital market, in which Australia had been, to an extent that had provoked some criticism, a chronic borrower. But if she borrowed too recklessly, some of the criticism should be posted to the address of the London money market, which did the lending. 'The national income of Australia,' says the *Economist* of 14th February 1931, 'whose total production is estimated at about £450,000,000 a year, has suddenly been cut down by £100,000,000 a year, or even more. The export of wool in the financial year to June 1930 brought in only £36·5 millions, against £61·6 millions in the previous year; and the export of wheat £10,000,000, against £20·3 millions. And since June 1930, wool and wheat prices have continued to fall. Apart from the loss of export income, long-term overseas borrowing, which had been proceeding at the rate of £30,000,000 a year, has been entirely eliminated since 1929. It is small wonder that . . . in spite of drastic import restrictions and prohibitive tariffs and the formation of an exchange pool in London, the Commonwealth Government has been unable, without banking help in London, to secure sufficient sterling exchange to meet the £36,000,000 interest due each year on the external debt of the Governments and public authorities.'

Australia thus found herself in the position of an individual who is faced by a fall in the value of the articles that he produces and so is less easily able to pay his way, and at the same time is cut off by his banker in the matter of the borrowing facilities that he has been enjoying. What an individual has to do in these circumstances is to cut down purchases and draw on his store of cash. This Australia did, by prohibiting some imports, putting higher duties on others, and by shipping, in 1930, some £24,000,000 of gold.[1] These measures did not suffice and so she was obliged to do what an individual would have to do under a similar combination of misfortune, and to tell some of her creditors that they would have to wait, because she had not sufficient claims to English pounds, created by sales or by borrowing, to meet the needs of all who needed them to meet their obligations in England. The Government, perhaps naturally thinking that the credit of the Dominion and of its States came first in importance, arranged that it should have the first right to any English pounds that were to be had and left private companies and persons who wanted them to get what they could under a

[1] *Economist*, 14th March 1931, p. 559.

rationing system. Australians who wanted to travel abroad and asked their banks for a stock of British and foreign money to spend on the journey, were told that they could only have a fraction of what they required. Companies that had earned profits in Australia could not pay dividends to their English shareholders because they could not send the money earned to England; and British holders of house property and other investments in Australia were obliged, for the time being, to go without the whole or part of their interest or rents, and were told that, if they came to Australis, they could have the money due to them and spend it there.

In spite of these measures and restrictions the Australian pound fell in exchange-value until, as the chairman of the Bank of Australasia told the shareholders' meeting, it was worth in March 1931 about 15s. 4d.[1] in English money; and it was interesting to see how such a depreciation in the exchange value of a country's money tends to correct itself by its own effects. For British merchants who had money owing in Australia and could not bring it home because they were not allowed to buy English pounds with it, solved the problem by using it to buy wool in Australia, bringing the wool to England and there turning it into English pounds; and everyone in Australia who could sell anything abroad made a handsome profit on the exchange of English pounds so realized for Australian money, while any Australian who wanted to buy foreign goods, found that they were made so much dearer that his demand was checked.

This tendency is always at work to correct exchange

[1] *The Times*, 27th March 1931.

fluctuations. If we like, for example, to imagine such a depreciation in the pound as compared with the dollar, that the pound, instead of being worth 4·86 odd dollars was only worth $2·43; then a Northampton bootmaker in England who had been selling boots in America at $5 a pair and getting rather more than a pound for each pair sold, would be able to sell at only three dollars a pair and still get more than a pound for each pair; and so he, and all other exporters from England, would be assisted by the depreciation of the pound in selling abroad. On the other hand, American exporters of automobiles to England would be hampered and checked by the low value, when turned into dollars, of the pounds for which their cars would be sold. In other words, as a country's money depreciates in exchange value, it becomes a bad country to sell to and a good one to buy in. As long as it has goods to sell, buyers from other countries will be taking goods from it, owing to this exchange advantage, while its purchases abroad will be severely checked by the dearness of everything imported when measured in its currency. And so the disease tends to cure itself by its own remedy if the remedy is given free play.

This rough sketch of the working of the exchange machine shows us why it is that a country that sells abroad must take something in return for them – either goods or services or securities or promises to pay or gold; because if it does not do so, the exchange values of other countries' money will be depreciated to such a point that it will no longer pay to sell goods to them. If it takes nothing but securities and promises to pay, it is piling up claims on other countries which will have to be settled some day, if at all, by imports of goods or services; if these claims are not settled it will mean that the goods will have been given away at the expense of those who bought the securities or made the advances. If it takes gold in large enough quantities it will cause tight money in other countries, dry up the flow of international capital, and upset the apple-cart of international trade. Free international lending is essential to the free flow of world trade, but it is by the exchange of goods and services between the nations that the soundest trade is done. And it is interesting to see how the natural desire of individuals to get what they want tends to defeat the efforts of Governments to confine their purchases to home-made goods. America puts a stiff tariff on goods that come in, but the wealth of her citizens and their preference for high-priced goods enables British and European goods to come in over the barrier to some extent; and at the same time Americans, as we have seen in considering the United States' balance of payments, go abroad in shoals and spend their money, that they are not allowed to spend at home on foreign goods, abroad on hotel accommodation, railway fares and other things bought in foreign countries.

We also see, from this glance at the exchange market, that we may accept with caution the terrors with which we are threatened owing to the industrial development of Russia with its alleged slave, convict and conscript labour, and of China with its millions of cunning workers who are, we are told, ready to work for a pittance such as no European – to say nothing of an American or British – workman would look at. Their goods, we are told, are going to swamp our markets. But what will they take in exchange? And if they take nothing in exchange how will they take payment? Their competition in neutral markets may be severe and serious, and this is a matter to be pondered deeply by those who think that a nation like England, which must sell abroad if it is to live, can nevertheless maintain any standard of life that it likes to choose, without reference to the humbler demands of its competitors. But if our own markets are to be swamped, it can only be in return for something produced by some form of business activity in England.

CHAPTER XIV

PROS AND CONS OF FREE TRADE

Reaction towards Protection in England – How Import Duties
Work – Protection or Revenue – Or a Bit of Both – The Consumer – Must Protection raise Prices? – Mr. Amery on the Moral
Aspect – The Products of Cheap Labour – Import Duties a Popular Form of Taxation – Bargaining Power – Confidence Secured
to Industry – *Laisser-faire* and Free Trade – Protection and Unemployment – The War Risk.

In the course of 1930 there was a marked reaction in
England, the classic home of Free Trade doctrine, in
favour of a Protective policy; a Liberal Summer School
at Oxford, in August, was startled by a bombshell
thrown by a Liberal M.P., who expressed doubts as
to the wisdom of Free Trade, and though the Labour
Government gave no countenance to this change of
opinion, a large number of its supporters have uttered
sentiments that showed a strong inclination towards
Protection in one form or another – if not by import
duties then by some kind of organized buying through
import boards, which would favour home products,
and the products of the British Empire. The Conservative party has always been inclined to a policy of
Protection, though containing many stout champions
of Free Trade. And we have thus arrived at a happy
state of affairs in which this difficult problem is no
longer a matter of party politics – for all the great

parties contain those who hold, in varying degrees, different views on it. It is thus, at long last, possible to discuss it as a matter of public expediency, and without political bias.

Do we want to buy the best goods that we can get as cheaply as possible, wherever and however they may have been made? Or do we, or ought we to, want to buy those made at home just because they are made by our own fellow-citizens? If we have this preference for goods made at home, are we prepared to give the Government the power to induce us to buy them by putting an import duty on foreign goods?

Since one cannot be sure that quite everybody knows exactly what import duties mean, all those who do will excuse me if I explain that they are taxes levied on goods that come into the country, such as the tax, amounting to one-third of the value of the goods, now levied on automobiles, watches, clocks and musical instruments coming into Great Britain. These duties were put on during the war by Mr. McKenna, then Chancellor of the Exchequer, in order to save shipping space – needed for the import of munitions and necessaries – and to check the importation of articles that were then thought to be luxuries for a people that was fighting for its life.

The practical effect of them is that if a motor car valued at £200 comes to Britain's shore, somebody has to pay £66, 13s. 4d. before it is allowed to enter and be sold; and that if a Swiss watchmaker sends a watch valued at £1 to an English dealer, the dealer must pay 6s. 8d. to the customs official before he can get possession of the watch and sell it to a shopkeeper who puts it in his window for sale.

Owing to this high duty on foreign goods of this kind, the British maker gets an evident advantage. If he can sell a similar automobile at £250, or a similar watch at 25s., he can beat the American or Swiss invader. If, on the other hand, the foreign manufacturer wins his way in by good workmanship or cheapness, the Government gets revenue. If, for example, an American car comes at a price of £150 which is a little better – or better advertised – than a British car priced at £200, it can pay the one-third duty of £50 and still come in and be sold. In that case the British manufacturer has been beaten in spite of the advantage given him by the duty, but the Chancellor of the Exchequer has received £50 and to that extent has to squeeze less out of you and me by other forms of taxation.

When duties are not high enough to be prohibitive and to keep out foreign goods, what happens is that a certain amount of both these advantages are secured – the home manufacturer sells more at a better profit than he would without the shelter of the duty; and the Government gets a certain amount of revenue from the protected articles that force their way in in spite of the duty. But it is not correct to argue, as some Protectionist enthusiasts are inclined to do, that both these advantages can be secured to the full – that we can at once secure the whole of the home market for the home manufacturer and also a nice revenue for the Treasury. We can have a little bit of both, or the whole of either, but not the whole of both.

But what happens to the man or woman who buys

the goods – the general consumer? It appears at first sight that import duties are definitely contrary to his or her interest. If foreign goods are kept out, it seems that consumers pay a higher price or get a worse article. If there is a 10 per cent. duty on boots, the British maker can sell a 20s. pair of boots at 21s. 6d. and still beat the foreigner, whose 20s. pair would be taxed to the extent of 2s., and so would cost the buyer 22s. If the foreign buyer makes a sacrifice of profit and sells a 20s. pair of boots for 18s., then the Government gets the duty and the British manufacturer is undersold; but the British consumer, instead of benefiting by the sacrifice made by his foreign supplier, sees it handed over to the Chancellor of the Exchequer.

This, however, is one of the points on which, I think, Free Traders are too dogmatic and positive. A recently published statement of their case, *Free Trade or Protection?* by Arnold Godoletz, says very definitely that the 'effect of Protection is to raise the price of the protected article inside the country – or to prevent its falling where it otherwise would. Thus the manufacture of this article is stimulated. It is sometimes contended that Protection does not raise prices, but if this were the case how then could it encourage?' He adds that what is probably meant by this assertion is that an industry may be so assisted in its early youth by protective measures that it ultimately is able to manufacture as cheaply as or even cheaper than before; that this does not often happen; and that such exceptions do not affect the 'main rule that the immediate and principal result of duties is – higher prices.'[1]

[1] *Op. cit.*, pp. 46, 47.

But here, I think, he does his opponents less than justice. The 'infant industries' argument is a very old one and a stronger one than Mr. Godoletz admits – so strong that it was recognized as valid by the great Victorian economist, John Stuart Mill. But modern industrial tendency to production on a great scale has put a new argument into the hands of Protectionists, to which I have not yet seen a convincing answer. This is, that if the home maker is given the home market free from foreign competition he can organize his business on a large scale, buy materials more cheaply, keep his machinery running full time, get a larger turn-over with the same amount of work done by his selling agency and managers, and with the payment of the same amount for rent and rates and interest. These 'overhead' charges, as they are called, go on running whether the factory is working half-time or full-time or overtime, whether it is turning out, for example, 50,000 or 150,000 pairs of boots per week. And so the greater the output of boots or whatever the article may be that is manufactured, the smaller will be the proportion of 'overhead' charges that enters into the cost of each. And hence the manufacturers who want Protection have a reasonable argument when they say, 'Give us the home market secure, keep out the foreign stuff, and our cost of production will be so reduced that we can give the public as cheap an article as ever, set more hands to work, and relieve the Exchequer of some of the cost of maintaining the unemployed.'

A reply commonly given by Free Traders to this argument is that if this is so, all that manufacturers have to do is to expand their business, get the advantage of reduced overhead charges and so beat the foreign importer without the help of a tariff. But it is hardly reasonable to expect industry to take this bold line in view of the many handicaps from which, as we have seen,[1] it suffers in Great Britain.

If there are plenty of manufacturers at home competing with one another in the home market, it is quite possible that an import duty need not raise the price of goods affected by it; but in these days when manufacturers have a habit of amalgamating into one or two big concerns and making agreements with one another to regulate the price at which their goods are sold, the consumer is justified in suspecting that, if the home market is secured for them, he is likely to be delivered into their hands to be shorn close.

This question is of very great importance to a country like England, which must sell goods abroad. If Protection raises the price of food and materials, it will hit our export industries, already suffering from many handicaps in competition with other countries. Some Protectionists, as we have seen, argue that this would not happen. Others suggest ingenious devices for compensating the export industries by a bonus on exports, to be paid for out of the revenue derived from the tariff.

My own bias has always been in favour of Free Trade, but for reasons which have not much to do with the business aspect of the matter. They are that:

(1) Protection tends, in my belief, to make a

[1] *Ante*, pp. 55, 56.

country's politics a nasty business. When all the industries are 'out for a slice of tariff pie,' as they say in America, politics are likely to stink unpleasantly.

(2) Whatever a Government does, it is likely, owing to the obvious weaknesses attached to any political machine, to make mistakes – and trade is a very delicate machine and the result of Governmental mistakes may be surprising and disastrous; therefore the less it meddles with trade the better, apart from its necessary job of seeing that neither employers nor employed abuse their powers, and that industry is carried on under wholesome and decent conditions.

(3) I dislike being 'bossed' and interfered with more than is necessary. Freedom of thought and speech and action seems to me to be a priceless possession. It has to be interfered with if it becomes a nuisance to one's neighbours. But I do not like the idea, when I spend the money that I earn, of being fined by customs officials because I may choose to spend it on goods made in some other country.

(4) It stirred my patriotic pride to see this little country, with its slow-minded and easy-going inhabitants (assisted by some quick-witted Jews and hardworking Scots and ex-Germans), almost the only one in the world that had the pluck to throw its market wide open, and to say to all the rest: 'Send your goods along and we will buy them if they are good enough'; and prospering with the world prosperity that it helped to create.

But all these things are a question of degree and of opinion and of the balance of advantage. It does not follow that politics must be made nastier by being mixed up with trade questions; it may be possible to produce a Government that can handle trade matters sensibly; one has to be bossed about many things and if it is for the common good that one's desires in purchasing should be thwarted and fined by a tariff one has to put up with it; and if Britain's courage in opening her markets did us harm on balance it was a mistake.

From the economic history of the half-century before the war, it would seem that the question of Free Trade or Protection is not nearly as important as some who argue on both sides of it maintain. Immense progress was made in that period by Germany and America, for example, under Protection and by Great Britain under Free Trade. It is true, as urged by Protectionists, that Germany and America were advancing more rapidly than Britain. On the other hand they were starting, more or less, from scratch, and their relative progress was thus naturally more rapid than that of the old trader who had a higher standard to improve on. Moreover, Free Traders are justified in arguing that Germany had knocked down a great network of internal barriers by the formation of the Zollverein, which made trade free between the various German States, so that her progress may have been due, in part, to more freedom rather than to more Protection; and that the United States, with its immense area free from all customs barriers, may also be claimed as an example of prosperity under Free Trade.

In favour of Protection it may be argued that it has

always been the policy of the great majority of civilized nations, but this argument seems to be very weak when we consider the number of blunders and crimes that have been committed down the ages by the great majority of nations that have considered themselves civilized – the silly wars that they have fought about things that are now seen not to have been worth the bones of a transport mule, the tortures and horrors that they have inflicted on one another in the name of religion, and their treatment of the working classes at home and of subject races abroad. Any appeal to the general wisdom of the nations, as a confirmation of the soundness of fiscal or any other policy, breaks down when we consider the exhibition that European civilization has provided in the last twenty years.

One of the most brilliant Protectionist champions of to-day, Mr. L. S. Amery, has found a new argument for his case by contending that Free Trade is immoral. This is an amusing retort to the rather unctuous attitude of some Free Traders, who regard their doctrine as a sort of inspired gospel which is only questioned by those who are depraved in mind. Cobdenism, he says in his pamphlet, *Empire and Prosperity* (p. 16), 'was, and is, essentially an immoral policy. Its fundamental thesis is that the immediate interest of the individual must, somehow or other, coincide with the general welfare. For the individual to consider, in his purchases, whether he is helping his own fellow-citizens or foreigners, paying for good work done under fair conditions, or for sweated or even slave labour, is in the eyes of Free Trade sentimental folly. For the State by legislation to enforce or encourage such consideration is the sin against the economic Holy Ghost. If the test both of private and of public morality is the limitation of individual selfishness by consideration of the general interest, then, by that test, Free Trade stands condemned as an immoral doctrine. Its motto has always been: "Each man for himself and the Devil take the hindmost." '

But no Free Trader would accept Mr. Amery's description of his beliefs as correct. He would say that the essence of them is the view that if we all do the best we can for ourselves and our families, unhampered by official red tape and vote-catching politicians, the general welfare is more likely to be secured than if trade is dragooned by a horde of bureaucrats backed by wirepullers and vested interests. But this question of a moral duty with regard to the goods that we buy is interesting. Ought we to make sure that we know all about the conditions under which all the goods that we buy are produced? And if we tried to do so would not the life of every consumer become a series of harassing inquiries that would hold up the world's trade in a way that would be bad for everybody? And if we know that we are offered goods made by people who are poorly paid, according to our standard, do we really help them by refusing to buy for that reason? The Balfour Committee on Trade and Industry thought otherwise. 'To exclude,' it said in its final report, 'the importation of goods which we need because the workers who make them, judged by our standards, are poor can only diminish still further their already restricted power of taking British products in exchange. Some of the most important foreign markets for British goods are those which, under such a system as is proposed, we should be bound to penalize, and the result would be, not only a heavy blow to British trade, but a lowering rather than a raising of the standard of life of the more primitive races, who would no longer be able to sell their products or to take ours in exchange.'[1]

We are coming nearer to the business aspect of the problem when we look at the advantage of Protection, or of import duties, as a source of revenue to Governments. They are popular with Governments that like to collect taxes without the taxpayers knowing what is happening, and with peoples that prefer to pay taxes without knowing it. This, perhaps, is one reason why they are everywhere so popular, because Governments and peoples all have this preference for deluding and being deluded. Adam Smith may tell us that every tax is, to the person who pays it, a badge of liberty, and that 'the time of payment, the manner of payment, the quantity to be paid, ought all to be clear and plain to the contributor and to every other person.'[2] He may be right in thinking that every sensible taxpayer in a civilized country ought to demand this knowledge. But in fact most people prefer to pay their taxes when they think that they are purchasing articles, and to forget that the price of the article includes a certain amount of tax. The income tax, with all its forms and inquiries, is an unmitigated nuisance. The duty involved by the price of a bottle of beer is lost among its winking bubbles.

---

[1] Final Report Committee on Industry and Trade, Stationery Office, Cmd. 3282, p. 271.
[2] *Wealth of Nations*, Book V, Chapter II, Part 2.

This pleasant delusion can be secured whether the tax takes the form of an import duty on articles that come in across the border, or of an 'excise' duty, as it is called, imposed on articles such as beer and whisky that are made at home. But import duties are the most popular form because there is a notion that they are – as they are sometimes – paid by the foreign seller; and also because they give a certain advantage to the home producer. This fact makes some patriotic taxpayers ready to accept them, even if they may involve some addition to the price of the goods, and it also secures to the Government that imposes such duties the support of all the makers of the articles that get the protection involved.

It is also contended that a country must have a protective system in order to give it bargaining power in making trade treaties with others. This argument, I believe, has had a great deal of weight with many of the Free Traders in England who have lately been converted to a belief that her fiscal policy must be changed under the conditions that exist to-day, with new and higher tariffs rising against her in so many places. Other countries, it is urged, when they come to discuss trade arrangements with us can menace us with a high explosive shell in the shape of a tariff increase against our goods. We have no weapon but platitudes – true but ineffective – about the desirability of international co - operation and goodwill. The Free Trade reply to this contention says that trade arguments conducted by tariffs have nearly always led to higher tariffs all round, and that free-trade England gets the benefit of any tariff concessions secured through them by other countries, owing to the action of the 'most-favoured-nation clause,' in her commercial treaties, which secures for her any advantage or concession given to any· of her rivals – if Germany induces Spain to lower the duty on German textiles, British textiles, owing to the working of the most-favoured-nation clauses, have to be similarly relieved. This may be so, but many well-informed and reasonable folk who look on Free Trade as the only sensible and civilized system to be aimed at, think also that at the present moment the best way of aiming at it is for England to adopt a policy of Protection. Her market, they contend, is so important to all the leading nations that the threat of its whole or partial loss would do more than anything else to induce them to modify their own policies, and bring their tariffs down.

A still more practical argument in favour of Protection is the confidence that it gives to producers and to those who invest in the producing industries. Nowadays in a Free Trade country those who make and grow things that are consumed at home feel that they stand exposed to every blast of competition from every part of the world, as other countries improve their power to produce. They are, it is true, on the spot, but carriage by sea is now so cheap, as compared with carriage by rail or road, that foreigners have an actual advantage in sending goods to any market that is on the seaboard.

British manufacturers and producers are especially liable to this feeling of defencelessness, because they have many special difficulties to face – high wages, as compared with those paid by their Continental rivals, high taxation, official regulation, trade union restrictions. They are told to rationalize and reorganize their industries, which grew up anyhow, as most things do in England, at a time when foreign competition was unknown or much less severe; but they must have hearts of superhuman stoutness to start on this business with the confidence that is essential, in the conditions of unrestricted foreign competition that now prevail. 'Our country,' they say, 'is now the dumping ground of the world.' By this they mean, though dumping is a difficult word to define exactly, that producers in other countries, with their home market reserved (more or less) to them, can run their plants knowing that they will get a good price for their goods at home and can shoot the surplus into the British dumping ground for what it will fetch, and so their big turn-over keeps their overhead charges low.

This may be very pleasant for the British buyer of the goods shot here, but if the process takes all the heart out of the home producers, and leaves them limp and dispirited, is it going to pay us in the long run?

But, says the Free Trader, these foreign goods have to be paid for by some kind of an export. This, as we saw in the last chapter, is true, but the Protectionist can reply that the export may be in the form of shipping or banking or insurance services or claims for interest on money lent abroad. The Free Trader can fairly contend that shipping, banking and insurance are highly profitable industries and their product is at least as good as that of foundries and factories; and that unless we are to make a present to people overseas of all the capital that we have invested abroad, we must take goods in payment of interest on it. But the Protectionist, I think, has popular prejudice behind him when he looks on the factories and foundries as more important, especially at a time when unemployment among manual workers is a national problem; and contends that owing to the many special difficulties that beset their owners, a slice of tariff pie is only fair compensation.

In view of the immense importance, in business matters, of the temper and spirit in which people do their work, this argument is of great weight. When a man feels that all the dice are loaded against him and that he does not get a fair chance, and is cowed and dispirited by this feeling, he works with a dogged despair and with none of that happy determination that is so necessary to success.

Nevertheless, many cautions are necessary before the psychological argument in favour of Protection – as a tonic for the mind of British producers – can be accepted as conclusive. In the first place, there is the grave danger that the process of reconstructing British industry may be retarded rather than promoted by the granting or even by the prospect of Protection. In fact it may be contended that it has for some time been retarded by the mere possibility of Protection. It is significant that the industries in which most progress has been attempted towards reconstruction – cotton and shipbuilding – are those to which little or no benefit can be expected from a tariff. Reconstruction or rationalization, as it is called now, has been well defined as the application of common sense to industry; it generally implies consolidation of an industry into larger units, so as to secure economies in buying and selling and overhead charges, and the elimination of out-of-date or otherwise inferior plants; it is thus an uncomfortable process for those parts and parties of and in an industry that are obsolete and inefficient, because it cuts them out; and every attempt at reconstruction is likely to be hampered by the opposition of folk who know that it will involve their elimination, as part of the purging process. If Protection encourages them to stiffen their backs and argue that they will be quite useful behind a tariff wall – in other words, if the tariff is used to shelter inefficiency, and to keep alive diseased and useless growths that ought long ago to have been dealt with surgically – it will do industry more harm than good.

It may be possible only to grant Protection to industries that have made themselves worthy to be helped by helping themselves first as far as possible, but it is very difficult. Who will decide? That Protection necessarily fosters and promotes inefficiency, as is often asserted by Free Traders, is one of those overstatements that are only too common on both sides in this discussion. But it undoubtedly does so sometimes, and this is one of the dangers that have to be considered.

And as to the confidence and stability that are alleged to be given to the industries of a country when once they are safe behind a tariff wall, these are only secured when industry can be sure that the wall will not be removed next time there is a change of government. The recent state of affairs in England with the McKenna duties and 'safeguarding' duties first being taken off and then clapped on again, and then a long time of doubt as to what the Chancellor of the Exchequer will do, was a harassing addition to the doubts and uncertainties that are inseparable from all kinds of enterprise. The question for industry is, is it better to be at the mercy of competition from all the world and to organize itself so as to meet it successfully, or to organize itself on the assumption that it is going to have Protection which may be taken from it by a swing of the political weathercock?

Another argument that is often heard from those in favour of import duties is, that Free Trade is part of the old Manchester School system of *laisser-faire* – 'leaving us to do our business' – which is now out of fashion. The idea underlying that system was the belief that Government should interfere as little as possible with trade, and that everybody should be left free to make his own bargain, buying and selling as he pleased; and that in this way, with each man doing his best for himself and his dependents, the general wealth and welfare was most likely to be secured and increased. This doctrine, as has been acknowledged, could not be carried out to its logical conclusion, partly because of the relative weakness in bargaining power in the hands of the manual workers, with no store of accumulated wealth behind them, and so compelled to take work on any conditions that were offered; and partly owing to the ignorance and short-sightedness of employers who made uses of their power that may have been profitable to them at the moment, but left a legacy behind them that has ever since been a bar across the path of industrial progress in England.[1]

Complete *laisser-faire* could only work in an ideal community, with industry officered by wise, far-seeing and humane employers, whose horizon was not bounded by their next balance sheet. A certain amount of control of industrial conditions was necessary, as things were. And we have got it – much too much of it, in the opinion of many who are responsible for the conduct of industry. Hours of work, factory conditions and wages are regulated in many industries by law, and further restrictions and regulations are imposed by the trade unions which have also acquired immense political power. This being so, say our Protectionist friends, it is evidently absurd and illogical, when you regulate everything else, to leave uncontrolled the import of goods made abroad under conditions that would not be tolerated for five minutes in this country.

This argument is a very shrewd thrust between the ribs of those who look on *laisser-faire* as a wicked doctrine, and are in favour of the maintenance and extension of the regulation and control of industry. But it is easily parried by those who think that regulation has been carried much too far, that industry has been hampered rather than helped by much of the grandmotherly legislation that has wrapped it in swaddling clothes, and that *laisser-faire* is a doctrine that would do us all good if we saw a little more of it. Those who hold such old-fashioned views as these are entitled to cherish free imports as one of the few relics of freedom left to us and to argue that they waft a

[1] *Ante*, see pp. 48-50.

healthy breeze of competition upon our industries, which, without them, would lead sickly lives in a hot-house atmosphere of pampered regulation, that would not be good for the increase of the nation's wealth.

It is also commonly asserted that Protection would cure unemployment. A pamphlet called *The Case for Agriculture* and issued by the National Council of Industry and Commerce, says that 'the *theoretical* gain from Free Trade is offset by this enormous *actual* loss,' which it calculates at £126,000,000 odd per annum, of providing for the unemployed. That Protection, applied as a fresh tonic to industry, might have some effect in increasing employment, may be admitted. But to assume that it is a certain and permanent cure for unemployment, as is implied by the eminent gentlemen who compose the National Council, is surely unwarranted, in view of the fact that protected Germany had five millions[1] of unemployed, and protected America had about eight millions, in February 1931.[2]

One unfortunate result of this fiscal discussion is that the Protectionist champions so often think it necessary to tell us that the country (1) is going to the dogs, and (2) must have Protection to save it. Even if (1) be true, (2) does not necessarily follow. But in fact the *Economist* of 21st March 1931 was able to tell us that in 1929 we had 800,000 more workers in active employment than in the pre-war boom year of 1913, in spite of progressive displacement of labour by rationalization; and that 'Britain, exposed as she is to the full force of

---

[1] Stated by Lord Privy Seal in House of Commons, 16th April 1931.
[2] *Economist*, 11th April 1931, p. 783.

world depression, has weathered a year of storm (1930) better than many of her rivals, her level of productivity having fallen far less than those of Germany or the United States.'

If another world war is one of the possibilities of the future – and who can say that it is not? – Protectionists in all countries are justified in claiming this possibility as an argument in their favour. The Free Trade doctrine pre-supposes a world at work and all, or most of, the nations busy in supplying one another's needs. When the chief nations turn aside from this business to that of mutual slaughter and destruction, then even those that are not actually engaged in the conflict are likely to be thrown back on their own resources and to be damaged if they have relied too much on supplying their needs from their neighbours' workshops.

During the last war, with the leading industrial nations putting every available ounce of energy into equipping their fighting forces and with all the other nations working hard to supply them with the where-withal, the countries which had confined themselves to the primary industry of agriculture were almost forced to start factories to make their own clothes and boots because they could not buy them from their former sources of supply.

We who had, under Free Trade, specialized on manufacturing industry, because of our natural advantages in that direction, and had left our farmers to struggle as best they could against the competition of the virgin soils of Argentina and North America, came near to being starved into defeat by Admiral Tirpitz and his U-boats and his floating mines. Our sailors saved us, though some of our digestions have never quite recovered from the effects of the stuff that had to be sold to us as 'war bread'; but, as the Duke of Wellington said of the Battle of Waterloo, it was a 'devilish nice thing.' It is easy to answer that no tariff or other devices could enable us to feed our population. Science may do wonders in that direction in the course of the next half-century, and even now many people who ought to know think that, if our agriculture were given a better chance, we might do much more towards feeding ourselves without causing any appreciable rise in the price of food. If this be so, a food supply which depends on command of the sea is a weakness to be remedied as far as possible, if it cannot be abolished. If Germany had left her farmers as bare and unprotected as we left ours, would she have stood out as stoutly as she did against our blockade?

From which it appears that all Free Traders in all countries and all who object in England to taxes on food or any other form of assistance to farming, should be earnest supporters, by work and subscription, of the League of Nations Union.

This argument, then, from the danger of another world war, shows us that those who prefer Free Trade, with its tendency to make the nations specialize on what they do best, are in fact gambling on peace. This may be a fair gamble, for a century had passed between the last two world wars, and the results of the last one may have been disastrous enough for all parties to leave a lasting impression on the minds of those who rule us and of the voters who elect them. It may, therefore, be safe to argue that the balance of advantage is still, from this point of view, on the side of Free Trade; and the immense wealth acquired by England in the century before the last Great War and thrown into the scales when it came, may be cited in favour of this claim.

CHAPTER XV

SPECIALIZATION OR SELF-SUFFICIENCY?

Specialization for an Individual – And for a Nation – Advantages of Diversification of Activities – And of Trade in the Home Market – New Factors in the Problem – Pros and Cons – Should we try a Blend?

Is specialization, whether for individuals or for nations, so desirable that it should be carried to extremes, even if it be the most profitable system? Profit is not the sole end of life, and Adam Smith told us that 'defence is of much more importance than opulence.'[1] Is there not also something besides defence that is more important – namely, versatility and wide range of practical interests?

If you and I think of nothing but doing our special jobs as well as ever we can, we may – though even that is very doubtful – do our jobs better than if we mix our work on them with other activities. But we shall not have lived so well, or got so much out of life for ourselves; and we shall probably have been much less pleasant to our neighbours – and being pleasant to our neighbours not only helps them and us, but promotes the creation of wealth. What more infernal bore can it be our unfortunate fate to meet than the man whose only interest is in his 'shop'? And what

[1] *Wealth of Nations*, Book IV, Chapter II.

chance is there that such a man will set about his work with that consideration for others and sympathy with the desires and claims of those who are not so fortunately endowed as he is, that is even more necessary to progress than intelligence and skill? There is already enough intelligence and skill in the world to make us all rich if they were applied in a good temper by all who possess them. Is this good temper likely to be supplied by those who work in blinkers with their noses glued to one item of one job, or by those who, by exercising many faculties and activities, keep every part of their minds and bodies taut and vigorous?

Comparisons between individuals and nations must not be pressed too far, but they do throw light on the matter. Mr. Godoletz, whose *Free Trade or Protection?* has already been quoted on page 230, uses such a comparison as an argument for Free Trade. He imagines two hypothetical countries, one, Atlantis, rich in minerals but poor in soil, the other, Franconia, rich in soil and poor in minerals, and argues that Atlantis should specialize in manufacturing and Franconia in agriculture, produce double the quantity of goods that they require and exchange their surplus halves with one another; and then continues: 'If our two above countries should decide to impose duties high enough to exclude the other's products, each country will be forced to produce both classes of goods at home, and each being inefficient at one of them will enjoy less goods in the aggregate. In other words, the income of each country will be diminished. Such a policy would resemble the conduct of a man who earns £10 a week at a City job and who, wishing to prune his trees, instead of employing a professional gardener at a cost of £3, stays a week at home in order to do the job himself. He would then economize £3 on the gardener's wages and lose his earnings of £10 in the City. So far from increasing his wealth, he will suffer a net loss of £7. So stated, the case for universal Free Trade is incontestable.'

Undoubtedly, as far as easily earned profits are concerned. But how much has Mr. Godoletz's City worker gained to set against the loss of £7 that he has suffered? He has had a week of work in fresh air and used muscles and faculties that do not come into play when he is busy on his ledgers. By that week's work he is more a real man and less a calculating machine. Moreover by doing that spell of manual work he has given himself a more real understanding of what manual work means to those who earn their living by it, and a practical experience of the dirt and exposure and effort that it involves. If he has a proper love for his garden and his trees, he will enjoy his week's work and wish he could have many more such weeks; but he will recognize that those who do this work for low pay in all weathers, and all the year round, have firm ground to stand on, when they draw comparisons between the £3 a week that they get for it with the £10 that he earns in the warmed and cleaned and sheltered City.

For the nations the case for variety in occupation is much stronger. A man, to earn his living, must concentrate on his job in his working hours. If a brainworker, he is well advised to indulge in games and hobbies which give him manual work to do in his leisure, because his brain and his general health of mind and body will be all the better for the varied activity. But it would certainly be absurd for the City worker, as described by Mr. Godoletz, to try, under present conditions, to be a half-timer in the City and a half-timer as a jobbing gardener. But in the case of a nation with its multitude of inhabitants, with a multiplicity of skilled faculties, it is a different matter. Atlantis and Franconia are richer by concentrating, one on manufactures and the other on farming; but have the statesmen who have guided their destinies in this direction really done the best thing for them? Would not they enjoy a fuller and rounder and nobler life as nations if Atlantis, at some cost to herself in the price of food, did a certain amount of farming, and if Franconia paid a little more for slightly inferior articles of manufacture? And need this higher cost and lower efficiency endure for all time?

All these things are a question of degree and of the balance of advantage and disadvantage. For the ruler of a chiefly agricultural country to 'want to see the tall chimneys smoke' was a natural and reasonable ambition – and is more so now that tall chimneys consume, or ought to consume, their own smoke – as long as he did not make his country pay too much for it. For a nation to want its inhabitants to do as many different kinds of work as possible is a desire that can easily be defended on grounds that are by no means as short-sighted and stupid as many Free Traders would have us believe. And the disadvantages attached to the early efforts of manufacturing industry are not necessarily perpetual. Brazil, as we saw on page 215, may – owing to her high tariff – be paying more than she need for cotton goods that are not as good as those that she might buy from countries that are more experienced in manufacture; but with great possibilities of cotton supply on the spot and with plenty of water power handy, there is no reason why she should not follow America's example and build up a great position both as grower of materials and maker of finished goods.

In fact, as has already been stated, Protection for 'infant industries' is admitted as necessary and sound by some distinguished exponents of Free Trade. Though practical experience shows that when once imposed, tariff duties designed to shelter their infantile struggles are apt to remain long after they have attained to vigorous maturity.

If a chiefly agricultural state can thus show some good reasons for fostering its manufacturing industries, if it can be done without too great a cost to the community, it is still easier to show that many advantages may be gained by a chiefly industrial country, if it decides to foster its farming activities. Almost every country has plenty of soil and the worst of soil can be enriched by modern fertilizers and science; and even when Kropotkin wrote, some thirty years ago, he was able to say that 'in the hands of man there are no infertile soils,' that the most fertile soils are not in the prairies of America or in the Russian steppes; but 'in the peat bogs of Ireland, on the sand dunes of the northern sea-coast of France, on the craggy mountains of the Rhine, where they have been made by man's hands.'[1]

[1] *Fields, Factories, and Workshops*, Chapter 3.

253

There is no need to lay stress on the advantages to a nation's health and physique of having a high proportion of its population at work in the fields and in the open air and sunshine. It is true that as towns are rebuilt and slum areas cleared and as factory conditions improve, the need to have the race recruited by a lusty band of open-air workers is lessened; and it may also be true that plenty of country villages are insanitary sinks of disease, and that the common tendency of dwellers in the country to marry their neighbours for many generations has been bad for the health of the stock. A neglect of agriculture may also have picturesque advantages and may be one of the reasons why foreign visitors to England tell us that our country looks like one big park. A hunting friend of mine also once told me that 'one good thing your rotten Free Trade has done – it's kept down the ploughed fields and given us plenty of nice pasture to gallop over.'

But when all this is said, a policy which encourages a country's population to work in factories and offices rather than in fields, may be good for its pocket – for all down the ages the country worker has been fleeced by the quick-witted townsman – but it is not one that many of us would wish to see carried to its logical conclusion. Atlantis, as imagined by Mr. Godoletz, concentrating entirely on manufactures and selling half its products abroad, would find itself in a tight corner if the buyer determined to manufacture for itself, and might well wish that it had cultivated at once its land and its home market. By giving its farmers a better chance, it would have developed a body of home buyers of its manufactures, and would have freed, to that extent, its industrialists from dependence on the fiscal whims of other countries; to say nothing of the effect on the national health and sanity of keeping part of its citizens at work in sunshine and fresh air and free from the noise and hustle and racket of modern life in towns.

Free Traders tell us that if a country checks imports by tariff duties or other protective methods, it is bound to check its exports, because other countries cannot buy goods and services from it unless it buys goods and services from them. In so far as imports are checked this argument is evidently true. But Protectionists can counter it by contending that Protection need not ultimately check imports, but rather promote them by encouraging home industry and so making the country richer and a larger consumer of foreign goods – that if, for example, England reduced her imports of manufactured goods and of food that she can grow at home, and if – it is a large but not impossible if – her manufacturing and agricultural activity were thereby stimulated and the productive power of her whole population were increased, its consumptive power would also grow. The result would be that its demands for foreign goods would be increased, and it would import goods of a different character, possibly to a value equal to that kept out by the tariff, and these goods would have to be paid for by some kind of an export. The example of America, as a large importer of manufactures, in spite of a stiff tariff, may be cited as a case in point.

But if this did not happen, the reduction of imports and corresponding reduction of exports might be fully balanced by greater activity in the home market and in the exchange of home-made goods. The Free Trade argument which says that goods imported are not given to a country but have to be paid for by some sort of an export is certainly true; though, as was shown in Chapter XIII, the export need not necessarily consist of goods. But what is true of imported goods is also true of goods made at home. They are not made to be given away but to be sold; and they cannot be sold unless somebody has provided the necessary money by selling goods or services. Free Traders sometimes lay too much stress on foreign trade as a test of prosperity. We know that England must, under present conditions, export that she may live. But it might be possible for her to export less and live as well or better, by developing her home market and widening the range of her own production.

To a Sheffield cutler, it makes no difference whether he sells goods to China or to Cheshire. If imports are checked and China's power to buy Sheffield goods is consequently lessened, while Cheshire's power to do so is increased by the Protection which has kept out the imports, then Sheffield will, or may, be just as busy as before. Because the movements of goods across the frontiers are more easily noted and measured than those which happen within a country, they sometimes are given a position of overwhelming importance, that they do not quite deserve, by statisticians and others who discuss trade questions.

On the score of international amity and intercourse, it may be a finer ideal to trade with as many nations as possible and to have business relations and connexions all over the world; and this policy has some business advantages in times of partial depression, when one customer's prosperity may balance another's poverty. But these advantages may be bought too dear; and it is quite possible, in theory, for a country that is well supplied with natural resources to attain to a high state of material comfort by the exchange of its own products among its own citizens, without any foreign trade at all. Its horizon and its interests might be narrow, but within that narrow circle it could contain countless talents and versatilities of its own; and it might lead a careless and comfortable life, without any thought of the varying fortunes and fiscal vagaries of its neighbours, which complicate business so much for those who depend for their living on international trade.

Another assumption as to which we have to be cautious is one that Protectionists are fond of making when they argue, that if the home market is reserved for an industry, its export trade will go on just as merrily as before, so that the added home trade will be a net addition. As, for example, when it is claimed that if the British iron and steel trade is protected and the great bulk of the imported iron and steel products are kept out, the British industry will increase its output by the amount of the excluded imports and yet suffer no loss in its exports.

It is very much to the point when the Free Trader inquires what is going to happen to the steel products shut out of the British market? It seems likely that they will be directed to neutral markets, making competition in them all the more severe and so making it more difficult for the British exporter to maintain his sales abroad. In other words, he runs the risk of gaining the home market at the expense of his foreign business and so finding that all the benefits hoped for from an increased scale of production and consequent reduction of overhead charges[1] for each article produced have vanished.

'To-day,' says the *Economist's* ably argued *Case for Free Trade*,[2] 'Great Britain makes roughly 8,500,000 tons of steel, imports 3,000,000 tons and exports 4,250,000 tons. Under Protection she might import only 1,000,000 tons; but her exports would probably fall by at least 2,000,000 and her total output would remain stable at roughly 8,500,000 tons. Her lost 2,000,000 tons of exports would be divided between Germany, France and Belgium, who would have to find markets for that tonnage in order to maintain their own output at their present figures; and during the period of readjustment the struggle in terms of prices would be calamitous. Moreover . . . the policy of trade restriction must hamper seriously the activity of our merchant shipping and hence lead to a contraction in British shipbuilders' demands for iron and steel.'

One is sometimes asked whether anything has happened lately to weaken the Free Trade convictions that have so long guided England's fiscal policy. I think that the war and the peace are both new factors in the problem. The war forced many of our customers to make things that we used to supply and encouraged

---

[1] See *ante*, p. 231.
[2] Reprinted in pamphlet form from the *Economist*, 13th April 1929.

them to protect their manufacturers against ours when we wanted to resume business on the old lines; and the peace created a number of new States and consequently of new trade barriers that have increased our industries' difficulties in selling abroad. Again, the mechanization of industry, immensely stimulated by the war, has made the technical skill of the British worker less effective in competition. And the development of big industrial units, needing a big market to keep their plant fully at work, has been noted as a new argument on the Protectionist side.

Moreover, for half a century and more, we have been supplying the rest of the world with capital, machinery and workers to equip it for industry. After doing so can we expect to sell manufactured goods abroad as easily as we did? At a point the cumulative effect of this process was bound, in the absence of an immense growth in consumption, to oblige us to give more attention to the cultivation of the home market.

Free Traders play a strong card when they remind us that shipping and shipbuilding, two industries in which we have long been eminent, are damaged by any obstacle to the free movement of goods across the seas. But even here there is a little item on the other side of the account – if Protectionists are right in saying that their policy would stimulate industry and increase employment, shipping and shipbuilding would be relieved from a certain amount of taxation.

Free Trade, again, is alleged to secure for us the goodwill of other countries. Such goodwill is a priceless asset, but do we get it by leaving our markets open? And how much of it should we lose if we gave our home industries a moderate amount of Protection? Could all our Protectionist neighbours really feel that they had a grievance against us, if we offered them the sincerest flattery of imitation?

And so on and so on. One could go on putting pros and cons until the crack of doom, and come back finally to the conclusion with which I started, that Protection and Free Trade are not nearly such important matters, from a business point of view, as they are generally supposed to be. In spite of rampant Protection and its immense increase since the war owing to the creation of new States all anxious to keep out one another's goods, international exchange of goods and services grows steadily; because all nations want to sell abroad and they cannot sell unless they buy something, or lend other nations the money to buy with. (In 1929 and 1930 this exchange was very roughly jolted by a combination of disastrous influences that will have to be examined later.) The country that has the stiffest tariff, the United States, is also one of the greatest importers of manufactured goods, and it also sends, year by year, flocks of its citizens to spend money, estimated as we saw [1] at £132,000,000 for 1929, in other countries – an 'invisible' import of services in the form of hotel accommodation and amenities of travel.

The strongest arguments on both sides seem to me to be: for Free Trade, the tendency of Protection to make politics muddier, and the objection that free men feel to being told what to buy by a Government; and for Protection, the depressing effect on producers

[1] *Ante*, p. 205.

of the feeling that they are not given a fair chance, because of foreign competition, possibly fostered by conditions that would not be tolerated in their own country. In times of acute depression this feeling of discouragement has quite incalculable effects in checking enterprise and delaying recovery.

It thus comes finally to a question of taste, and of the sort of ideal that we cherish of our country's position in the comity of nations. Do we want it to be a great international trader with friends and customers and business connexions in every country of the globe?

Or do we want, in the homely Scottish phrase, to 'gie our ain fish-guts to our ain seamews,' and confine our trade to our own countrymen, buying at home as much as we can, even at some slight monetary loss if necessary, and so making our own country as far as possible a self-sufficient unit, with all its talents and capacities exercised and some of them, if this is found necessary, artificially fostered?

Or should we prefer the policy of Mr. Facing-Both-Ways and try a blend? It ought to be possible, without joining in the general race for high tariffs, to give a better chance to our farmers, to our organizers of industry and to the shareholders who have lately shared little but its risks.

CHAPTER XVI

BIG AREAS AND EMPIRE TRADE

The United States of Europe – To Fight America's Domination? –
Freeing of Europe from Versailles Barriers – British Empire Co-
operation – The Case for it – The Difficulties – Tariff or Import
Boards – Business Agreements.

SIDE by side with the uprising of new tariff barriers
and the raising still higher of existing tariff barriers,
and the general growth of what is called economic
nationalism – the desire of the nations to make and
grow things for themselves rather than buy and sell
with one another – there has appeared, in Europe, an
idea of Europe for the Europeans in business, and
there has reappeared in the British Empire and in
Great Britain the notion, actively urged by Mr. Joseph
Chamberlain in the early years of this century, of a
revival of the old system by which trade within the
British Empire was to a certain extent restricted to its
own members by means of tariff arrangements.

In Europe the dream of a United States of Europe
has for some years been discussed not only by political
visionaries but by hard-headed business men. They
have been impressed by the immense and quickly
created wealth of the United States of America, and
have rightly found one of the reasons for America's
prosperity in her huge tract of country free from any

262

restriction on the movement of goods within it. Also many of them have been alarmed by the great power which is given to America by her wealth and by the big debts that most of the chief countries owe her, in consequence of the financial help that she gave to Europe during and after the war.

This threat of domination by a rich and industrially powerful people is not really as terrifying as it seems to many who shudder at it. A rich people can only dominate its poorer neighbours through its wealth by lending them money; and when debtor and creditor speak together in the gate, the position of the debtor is in many ways the stronger and more comfortable. He has had the money; and the creditor, whether he likes it or not, has to take care of him and nurse him kindly or he will not be able to pay the interest and the sinking fund for the redemption of the debt.

In the same way a people that is a great producer of food, materials and goods can only dominate its neighbours who are less bountifully endowed by selling its produce to them, and can only do so if it buys something from them, because otherwise they will not be able to pay for its produce unless it lends them the money to pay for it with – a process which cannot be long continued without reducing itself to absurdity. For American investors, by subscribing to European loans, to provide Europe with the power to buy goods from American farmers and manufacturers may be good for all concerned for a time. But it cannot go on indefinitely. The day comes when the investors want their money back; and then either America has to take European goods or services in payment (possibly sending its tourists to consume them on the spot), or has to find another group of investors to lend Europe the money to pay the first.

This idea of domination by loans and selling power, then, need not greatly terrify those who fear it; for if it is carried too far it produces a state of things that is more comfortable for the dominatee than for the dominator. And another side of it, which makes Europe fear America because America has acquired about half the gold in the world, is also a matter that need not make us on this side of the world shake too cravenly in our shoes. The gold standard is a convenient mechanism that helps international trade and keeps all the currencies of the chief countries on a common basis;[1] but if any country attempted to dominate its neighbours by cornering the world's gold stock, it ought not to pass the wit of man to find ways and means of doing without gold and inventing other methods of international payment. So here again the alleged dominator's supposed ambition would be checked by his actual interest. He would discover that he can only dominate by keeping those with whom he has business relations in as flourishing and comfortable a state as possible. If he wants to lend money he must keep his clients solvent; if he wants to sell goods he must enable his customers to pay; and if he has a passion for gold-hoarding he must leave others enough gold to work with, or gold will cease to be a means of international payment.

Nevertheless, though the fear of dominaiton by America may easily be exaggerated, there is much

[1] See Chapter XVIII, pp. 294, 295.

more solid foundation for the view that Europe, if she could wipe out her nationalistic jealousies and form herself into a great customs union with free or freer trade within and a tariff ring against the rest of the world, would be able to undo much of the harm that has been inflicted on her trade and prosperity by the Treaty of Versailles, which ended one war and began another of a different kind, by covering Europe with a chess-board of little new States, each wanting to keep out one another's goods.

That such a union would be possible does not seem at all likely in the present state of international bitterness and jealousy. But unlikely things do happen sometimes. With her area of 2,000,000 square miles, rich in soil and minerals, and over 300,000,000 of inhabitants,[1] many of them highly skilled in industry and enjoying the priceless heritage of an old-standing civilization and culture, Europe, if she broke down the internal trade barriers, might gain immense power for dealing with any business rival; and the movement towards European union seemed to have been quickened, in the spring of 1931, by the sudden announcement, by Germany and Austria, of their intention to arrange a customs union, involving a common tariff and mutual free trade.[2]

'A month ago,' said *The Times* in a leading article on 27th April 1931, 'the two German-speaking countries tried to steal a march on the rest by arranging secretly to effect their economic unification; and their furtive approach to a legitimate goal has at least had

[1] These figures exclude the British Isles and Russia in Europe.
[2] *Economist*, 28th March 1931.

the result of spurring on those who were advancing perhaps a little leisurely in the same direction. M. Benesh' . . . [Foreign Minister of Czechoslovakia] 'in a long and lucid examination of the situation created by their action last week, refused to adopt a merely negative attitude. A constructive plan, elaborated in common at Geneva by the interested States, is in his opinion not outside the bounds of practical politics. The Austro-German compact had shown the States of Europe as by a stroke of lightning, he said, the dangers to which they were exposed; and he advocated first of all joint action by the agricultural countries of South-eastern Europe to enable them to market their surplus grain. An agreement must follow, he urged, between the industrial States in regard to output and distribution of products. He was quite hopeful . . . that European countries would soon agree to a lowering of customs duties and a gradual stabilization of industrial prices; and he thought that agreement could also be reached on certain principles of social legislation, including the shortening of hours of labour. The final goal, he said, must be the constitution of an economic unit of Europe.'

With the British Empire, if economic union of the kind that has lately been proposed were carried out, there would be no lowering of internal barriers, but a raising of obstructions against the entry of goods from outside. The Dominions, which already have high barriers against the world at large and slightly less high against Great Britain and one another with regard to any articles that they themselves produce, would raise the barriers still higher against non-Empire goods, thus giving a greater advantage to goods produced within the Empire; and Great Britain would be expected to put a tariff on food, materials and manufactures produced outside the Empire, so as to reciprocate the advantage granted to her by the preferential tariffs of the Dominions.

To all who are proud of the British Empire as a great civilizing power that has carried the torch of order and justice to the uttermost ends of the earth, this ideal of closer co-operation in business between its parts must carry a strong appeal. Its advantages have lately been stated by the late Lord Melchett in his *Imperial Economic Unity*, by Lord Beaverbrook in his pamphlets on Empire Free Trade, by Dr. Stephen Leacock (giving the point of view of the Dominions) in his *Economic Prosperity in the British Empire*, by Mr. L. S. Amery in his *Empire and Prosperity*, and many other writers.

Briefly summarized, they may be stated as follows:

(1) The preferences given to British trade by the Dominion tariffs have been a substantial benefit to British industry. The Dominions are ready to extend the system, but they want a more substantial return in the form of a British tariff against non-Empire goods, including food-stuffs. The electioneering cry that 'your food will cost you more' is maintained to be baseless in view of the immense possibilities of production within the Empire.

(2) All the world is putting up tariffs against Britain and taking advantage of the British market. The Dominions alone, while putting up tariffs

against us, put still higher ones against our competitors and so give us an advantage. It is surely sound business to encourage our best trade friends by giving them a better *quid pro quo* than the preference that we already grant on the few articles of import on which we impose duties on entry.

(3) In the late war the assistance rendered by our kinsmen from the Dominions was of immense value in providing us with magnificent fighting material. If such a crisis should occur again it would be to our advantage that the rest of the Empire should have been, in the meantime, enriched in wealth and population; to this end it is better that we should concentrate our trade and capital and emigration on the Empire, instead of enriching all the world, and especially America, as we did in the half-century before the war, with our money, our market and our men and women.

(4) The dwellers in the Dominions are our kinsmen, talking our language, and maintaining a similar standard of life. It is better to keep our trade in the family, and keep out the goods produced by nations which have a lower standard, paying lower wages and working longer hours.

(5) If the Big Trade Areas idea grows and becomes practicable, if to America's Big Area are added a United States of Europe and possible customs unions in the Far East and Latin America, and Russia, perhaps, transformed under iron discipline into a great producer of farm and factory products, where is England going to stand if she has not, in the meantime, in co-operation with the

Dominions, welded the Empire into the biggest and strongest and richest area of all?

It is small wonder that arguments such as these stir the blood and cheers of popular audiences, and when put forward with the due patriotic and Imperialist appeal, make anything that can be said against them look pitifully sordid. But though sentiment is immensely important in business, the sentiment that cheers at public meetings is not quite the same sentiment as quickens the activities of the average worker when seated at his office desk. He wants to know how much there is of practical possibility in the idea of Empire co-operation, and how far it could be carried without damaging those British interests that have been so prosperously developed in the past with non-Empire countries and with non-Empire customers.

Looking into the matter from this merely business aspect, he notes that though the Dominions are earnestly desirous of closer trade relations within the Empire they frankly put their own interests first. Mr. Bennett, the Canadian Prime Minister, made this very clear at the session of the Imperial Conference held in London on 8th October 1930. 'I stand,' he said, 'four-square behind the policy of Canada first,' and while he offered to the Mother Country and to all other parts of the Empire a preference in the Canadian market in exchange for a like preference in theirs, based on the addition of a 10 per cent. increase in prevailing general tariffs or upon tariffs yet to be created, he was careful to add that 'the basis of the proposal is the adequate protection to industries now existent or yet to be established.'[1]

In other words, any industries that the Dominions have established or are ever going to establish are to be so protected by the Dominion tariffs that British industry cannot compete with them; for what else can 'adequate protection' mean? In the matter of goods that are allowed to come in, British industry is to have preference, but if Canada wants to make anything for herself her market is to be closed. In return for this Britain is invited to tax her people's bread, with the prospect, which is quite reasonably probable, that it will not really cost them any more; and also with the probability, which almost amounts to certainty, that these arrangements will be to the disadvantage of the great world-wide trade that she has built up with countries outside the Empire.

Looked at with the cold and sceptical eye of business, the bargain seems a little one-sided, especially as it is likely that when the world pulls itself out of the present mire of depression, industrial development will go ahead rapidly in Canada and the other Dominions; with the result that more and more articles will be produced there under the 'adequate protection' that will keep British goods out. Mr. Bennett was equally frank on the subject of 'Empire Free Trade,' a phrase that has been very emphatically repeated in England but was very emphatically repudiated by the avowed policy of the Dominions. 'It follows,' he said, 'that this proposed preference should not be considered as a step towards Empire Free Trade. In our opinion

[1] *The Times*, 9th October 1930.

Empire Free Trade is neither desirable nor possible, for it would defeat the very purpose we are striving to achieve.'

If the example of the United States of America, with their immense area free from all internal customs barriers or other hindrances to trade, is to be followed by the Big Areas to be created in Europe and elsewhere, the principles on which the spokesmen of the British Dominions proposed to found a British Zollverein were very wide of the mark. Their idea was a Big Area with growing tariffs raised by each of the component parts against one another and especially against this poor old Mother Country, as (at present) the most efficient maker of manufactured goods.

And apart from this purely business aspect of the matter, there is the question whether tariff arrangements, or other devices for artificially stimulating inter-Imperial trade, are more likely to tighten the bonds of kinship than to loosen them owing to possible friction.

Trade is undoubtedly a great civilizer and a potent help to amity between peoples when it flows freely under the guidance of mutual advantage to buyer and seller. But when Governments meet to haggle and bargain about the terms on which goods are to be admitted into one another's territory, it is likely that one or other, or both, will feel that it has been bested, and both are likely to be told so by the Opposition Press, which will be believed by a certain number of people, and these things do not further international amity. When two peoples are akin this danger is perhaps increased, for both sides are likely to feel that the other fellow might have shown better feeling. In private life, business relations with one's kinsmen are notoriously a cause of family friction. Anyone who has a tea merchant or a coal merchant among his relations and buys the family article is fortunate if he does not feel annoyed when he pays his bill or pokes his fire or drinks his tea. Whether he goes on with the arrangement and grumbles, or changes his source of supply, the consequence is not helpful to family good feeling.

This kind of difficulty need not arise in the case of inter-Empire trade, but the Dominions are intensely, and naturally, jealous of their fiscal autonomy and any suggestion that any of them have made mistakes in trying to develop certain industries and would be better advised if they left them to other parts of the Empire might be seriously resented. Some of the Empire builders appear to allow too little weight to this question of the susceptibilities of the inhabitants of its different parts.

In fact, this question of closer Imperial co-operation is full of difficulties that cannot easily be solved if it is to be treated by the process of shouted assertions and deftly selected figures that is usually applied to business when it becomes a matter of politics. The Dominions as well as Great Britain have built up considerable trade connexions with non-Empire countries, and there is an immense network of interests that may be seriously injured if politicians and professors are turned loose among them. To make our rich and friendly Empire richer and more friendly is a splendid ambition, but if the ambition is pushed with more enthusiasm than intelligence the result may be that the Empire will find itself poorer and with its internal jealousies strengthened.

These jealousies are already quite strong enough. One of the results of the high tariff of the Dominions is that British firms, unable to export British goods over the tariff wall, establish factories in the Dominions within it. This process is welcomed by the Governments as tending to expand and consolidate the local industries, but it is not so popular with the local manufacturers. The *Economist* of 20th December 1930 had a letter from its Ottawa correspondent which stated that 'there is said to be some apprehension in woollen circles lest a number of British woollen firms establish plants in Canada – one Yorkshire firm has already acquired a factory in Perth County, Ontario – and try to secure a share of the local protectionist preserve.'

Inter-Imperial goodwill is a lusty and vigorous sapling, but it cannot have been strengthened by the news, announced in *The Times* of 2nd June 1931 that, under an Order in Council gazetted at Wellington, practically the whole range of Canadian exports to New Zealand were to be deprived of the advantage of the British preferential rates and placed on the general tariff list from that date. It was explained that this action had been taken owing to the complete failure to reach a satisfactory understanding with Canada about reciprocal tariffs, negotiations about which had been proceeding since Canada heavily increased the duty on New Zealand butter in 1930.

Would these dangers and difficulties be lessened if,

instead of trying to promote Imperial co-operation by tariffs, its champions adopted the system – attractive to those who like Governments to exercise active control over trade – of import boards, bulk purchases and licences?

By this system the Government hands over to specially selected committees the whole business of buying a certain article from foreign countries, and it is suggested that these committees, by giving the bulk or the whole of British custom to Empire producers, might make Imperial preference more effective than any tariff arrangements, and at the same time avoid all the objections that are associated, in the minds of many, with any attempt to regulate trade by duties.

Mr. Amery urges weighty objections against this proposal. 'The various alternative schemes,' he says,[1] 'such as bulk purchases or import boards, all suffer from the fact that they involve, on the one side, a far greater interference with the liberty of the ordinary citizen, and check the healthy tendency to experiment in new wares by subjecting it to all the delay, vexation and favouritism arising from the need for special applications for licences to import, while on the other side, they imply a far more drastic interference, and directly by the Government, with the trade of friendly nations. It is one thing to tell a friendly nation that, in the interest of our own producers, we are imposing a duty against the outside world at large. . . It is quite another thing to tell them that the heavy hand of our Executive Government is suddenly going to forbid them selling anything to us, or more than some arbitrarily fixed

[1] *Empire and Prosperity*, p. 45.

fraction of what they have sold hitherto. The one method is impersonal and elastic; the other brutally rigid and in appearance directly aimed at them. There can be no doubt which method is more likely to lead to international complications – or for that matter to inter-Imperial complications, when it comes to deciding how a bulk purchase scheme is to be allocated between various Dominions.'

Moreover, Mr. Amery contends that a tariff automatically produces revenue (which is only true in so far as it does not keep goods out), and that this revenue in our case, will be largely, if not wholly, paid by the 'large bodies of foreign producers who rely mainly upon our market for their existence,' while most of the alternative schemes either cost much more or involve possibilities of heavy losses. Nevertheless, he thinks that in the case of certain commodities such a method as that of a quota may be preferable to that of a duty. As applied to wheat, the quota system usually means in effect that every loaf sold must contain a certain proportion of home- and British-grown wheat; for sugar and certain raw materials, which are included by Mr. Amery as susceptible to treatment by quota, the system would presumably be worked by giving the various Empire countries a proportionate share of the British market. Which, again, might produce a certain amount of friction. The preferential tariff certainly seems to be the simpler system, and it is quite complicated enough.

But when all these difficulties are recognized, the fact remains that Imperial co-operation appeals to the patriotic sentiment of most of us; and it seems likely that definite efforts to further it will be part of our practical history in the next half-century. What form they will take remains to be seen; but it is at least possible that in Imperial trade, as well as in international, the big business combinations, working by agreements between business groups, will produce more effective results, with less chance of friction, than any attempts at control exercised by Governments.

But whatever is done towards stimulating inter-Imperial trade in the British Empire, and towards promoting European unity with a Zollverein, and establishing Big Areas of trade in other parts of the world, the example of the United States, with their huge volume of external commerce, indicates that, in spite of artificial restrictions, the tendency of all the nations to trade with one another will be maintained and will grow, as the increasing wealth of the world enables men and women to satisfy new and ever-varying desires for material comfort and enjoyment. But this growth of wealth and trade is only possible if nations and classes and individuals show a reasonable amount of good temper and good sense in their mutual relations.

CHAPTER XVII

A MACHINE OUT OF GEAR

A Crisis of Plenty – Too Many Good Things – And Too Cheap –
The War's Stimulus to Production – The Fall in Prices – Its Bad
Effects – On Debtors and Organizers – And on the Rest of Us –
The Remedy of Cheap Money.

In the foregoing chapters we have seen in broad outline
how the pool of world wealth is filled by the work – our
own or that of those from whom we have inherited –
that we put into it and how claims to help ourselves
out of it are awarded to all of us different kinds of
workers and contributors. And we have also reviewed
the pros and cons of the problem of freer or more
restricted trade between nations, or between groups of
nations possibly to be organized into big trade areas.
And now, we can find a good deal of instruction
concerning mankind's power to produce wealth, from
the present partial breakdown of the system by which
it does this job.

There ought to be a pleasant and steady increase in
the material comfort of all the nations, proceeding
from the progress of science and discovery and the
greater skill with which, owing to the spread of education, appliances and inventions can be used. Instead
of which we find world-wide depression, dwindling
prices of commodities, the credit of many nations

277

seriously shaken, stock markets first complaining of idleness and neglect and then reeling under a tidal wave of selling, unemployment figures running into millions in America, Germany and England, and we are told that all these things are happening because the raw materials of all the good things that we want are too plentiful or too cheap.

'Too silly for words' would be the natural comment on our position made by a detached observer in Mars, who was watching the exhibition that this planet has made of itself, in the matter of its business arrangements, during the last two years. 'There are those funny little men and women on their funny little ant-heap, growing good food and fine materials so cleverly and well, and digging up useful metals so cunningly and fast, and manufacturing all kinds of things that delight the hearts of men and women so plentifully and cheaply that they cannot use nearly all that they make; and so their markets are glutted and they are worried because there is not enough work to do, and they are all more or less poor and miserable and anxious and destitute in the midst of plenty, because the good things of life are too cheap and abundant!'

Small wonder that the many critics of our present business arrangements are loud in hailing their present breakdown as evidence of their inherent rottenness. There never was a time when it was easier to demonstrate by obvious and practical facts that there is something very seriously amiss with a system that breaks down through its own success. If anyone would show us a better system that can be counted on with any certainty to lead us into a less ridiculous quagmire we should most of us be ready enough to work for its introduction. But when the critics are given power they do not attempt to replace our present system with a new one, because power and responsibility quickly prove to them that any such attempt is much more likely to do harm than good.

In Russia a new system is on trial, concerning the results of which it is difficult to arrive at truth. But at least it seems to be safe to say of it that it has not yet succeeded in providing the country in which it is being tried with any approach to the material comfort that has been secured elsewhere even for the poorest classes; and that it has involved a degree of effort, and a surrender of personal liberty, that people that have been used to the fleshpots and freedom of the capitalist system would find it difficult to endure.

In other countries there is plenty of growling and discontent and criticism and apprehension about what may be going to happen next; and a great variety of solutions is ventilated for the world's present difficulties; which solutions correspond to the great variety of reasons to which the difficulties are attributed by different kinds of critics. Some of these reasons and their attendant solutions we shall have to consider. The interesting point about them all is that they do not imply any really fundamental alteration in our present business system. It is true that a Minister in the House of Commons, defending the Labour Government against criticisms of its failure to solve the problem of unemployment, said that the present crisis was due to capitalism; and if he merely meant that it had happened in a world which was based, in its business arrangements, on capitalism, he was certainly right. But whether capitalism (as roughly defined in Chapter IX) was responsible for the crisis, or whether it happened because forces outside capitalism had interfered with the free working of the system, we may be able to see more clearly as we go on.

In spite of such criticism, however, it is interesting to note that in these years of distress the general tendency of opinion in many countries, as far as it can be detected, has been rather in the direction of what may be described, according to the taste of the observer, as conservative or reactionary, than towards any drastic reshaping of our business life. It seems to be recognized, except in Russia, that the rights of property, in spite of the handicaps and anomalies that they involve, are the only basis on which the world, as it is now, can work.

Political indications seem, on the whole, to show that mankind in general is very angry with its rulers, and holds them rather than capitalism responsible for the present distress and for the absurdity of a crisis due to too much plenty. Perhaps we shall find that one reason why capitalism has not been working well is because too much attempt at restriction and control has been forced on it from outside and inside.

If, then, we incline to the view that it is better to try to improve our present system than to turn it upside down before we have got one ready that we are quite certain will be able to take its place, a study of the causes that have led to our present distresses may help us in our search for improvement.

We shall find that most of them come back, directly

and indirectly, to the World War, which was due to
instincts and jealousies that are very much older than
capitalism. Business is not organized to meet great
shocks such as it, which turned most of the most
important nations of the earth from producers into
destroyers, dislocating the whole course of orderly
progress in making and growing good things, diverting
their activities into making weapons for wiping one
another out and into supplying food and equipment
for the millions of the best men of the human race,
who were suffering unspeakable discomfort and horrors,
and many of them dying horrible deaths, in carrying
out this grisly job.

So one thing is very clear and simple – if we want to
avoid the kind of crisis that at present puzzles and
terrifies us, we must not have another world war. We
can credit the last one with a great stimulus to production, but we must also debit it with a much greater
dislocation of the machinery of distribution and
consumption.

One of its results was an immense demand for food
and materials. The armies were better fed and
equipped than armies had ever been before, and better
than most of their members had ever been fed and
clothed in peace-time. There was also a considerable
destruction of food and materials owing to the German
submarine campaign. Consequently, the producing
countries that were outside the war area put more
and more ground under crops and devoted more energy
and cleverness than ever before to making Mother
Earth more fruitful by means of improved fertilizers and
the application of machinery to agriculture.

At the same time, the industrial peoples were inventing new machines and devising new processes and doing everything that they could, under the stimulus of patriotism and profits, to improve their power to work up the increased store of materials into finished goods. Many of these goods were of a kind only wanted in war-time, but the adaptability of machinery to different uses had also been greatly increased by the war effort; and so, when the war was over, mankind found itself, in spite of war's destruction, with a far greater capacity than ever before for growing and making all the good things that we want.

What a chance for a great increase in material comfort, and perhaps even for a great advance towards a higher and nobler civilization, with poverty and destitution abolished, and contentment and co-operation spread like rich manure over the surface of the earth! The chance could not be taken at once, because some of the richest countries were seriously impoverished, tempers were still bad and nerves had not yet recovered from the war strain, and we clearly had to take a long time to work through and out of the results of the war-time dislocation. But the chance is still there, though we have been blinded to it by the bogey of over-production.

Over - production! Too many good things! This seems a queer bogey to be frightened of when there are very few dwellers on this earth who have got all the good things that they want. If it were the other way round, and the world were faced with the danger of scarcity and famine, then there would be more than good reason for being terrified. But when it is merely a question of a kink in our business arrangements which prevents the supply of goods, ready and that might be made ready for use, getting into the hands of the millions of people who want them, surely all the clever folk who rule us, and manage our business for us, ought to be able to straighten out that kink.

Unfortunately more than cleverness is necessary, if, as I think we shall find, bad temper and bitterness, between nations and between classes, are at least as responsible for the kink as ignorance and misunderstanding. Charles Kinglsey's poetical advice to a young lady, to 'be good, sweet nymph, and let who will be clever,' might very aptly be given to the world of to-day. The Artful Dodgers have shown plenty of cleverness, but science and knowledge have gone ahead much faster than kindliness and good feeling, and they are what are most wanted at the moment. What the world needs is some modern Peter the Hermit who will teach and preach in favour of decent behaviour. But it sounds so dull.

Touching this over-production, however, it was a very real fact, if falling prices are a proof of it. The general level of commodity prices, as measured by the *Economist's* index number, which puts the prices of all the chief articles of commerce together and brings out a total figure to indicate their average price, fell from 100 as the average for 1924, to 59·4 at the end of 1930,[1] and a large number of staple articles at this latter date were being sold in the world's markets at prices that did not cover, or only barely covered, the cost of growing them or digging them out of the earth: wheat,

---

[1] *Economist*, 10th January 1931.

cotton, sugar, rubber, copper, tin, oil are examples familiar to all who study such matters in the newspapers.

'Very nice for the people who want them,' you may naturally answer. 'We can all have more of everything and soon use up any surplus stocks.' But unfortunately this simple solution does not work easily. When we go into the shops to buy, we find that the extreme cheapness of materials is very far from being reflected in the prices of finished goods, and this 'lag' which makes retail prices so sluggish in following the fall in wholesale, is one of the many matters that we want to see mended.

Moreover, falling prices have bad effects on business, and especially on the mind of the business organizer – the man who, as we saw in Chapter VII, must above all others be kept happy and confident, because he is the one who gives the necessary push to the whole machine of production.

Nearly all businesses have to keep a stock of materials, half-finished goods and finished goods. As prices fall, these articles all lose value and the holders suffer loss; and so they buy as little as possible, and, what is still worse for the general temper and sentiment of the business world, they are less inclined to expand manufacture and enterprise. 'What is the use,' they think, 'of cheap materials if by the time we have worked them up into saleable goods, materials are going to be still cheaper, so that Smith across the road, who had the sense to wait, will be able to sell the public a cheaper article than I can?' And so, when prices are falling there is a general tendency to go slow, and very often there are definite agreements among growers and manufacturers to restrict output, which often, as recent experience has shown, break down and make matters worse.

And there is another disadvantage about falling prices, namely, that they give an unfair benefit to creditors and all holders of fixed interest securities, and make it more difficult for employers to pay wages and salaries, and to meet the interest on debt, which is a charge upon most active enterprises, which habitually borrow money from bankers or from the public, or both. A manufacturer who is turning out ready-made great-coats at £2 and has to reduce the price to 30s. has to sell so many more coats before he can pay what he owes to his cloth merchant for cloth, and to pay the interest on the money that he has borrowed by an issue of debentures secured on his factory. His wages bill is no lower, unless he finds himself obliged to reduce the number of his hands; and if he points out to his workers that, owing to the fall in the cost of living they are getting higher 'real wages' because the wages go so much further, and that they ought in reason to submit to a reduction in money wages, which would leave them no worse off than they had been originally, the wage-earners are likely to jib. They will say, with a good deal of truth, that wages are always the first things to be attacked, that they are seldom raised when trade is good unless the wage-earners have insisted on a rise, and that if wages are to be reduced all round there will be a decrease in general purchasing power, less goods will be wanted, and trade will be worse than ever. The employers may also argue, with a great deal of truth, that the lowering of wages would

285

lower retail prices, and so quicken the sale of goods and make everybody better off, including the wage-earners, who would find it easier to get work. But, unfortunately, past experience has made the wage-earners view such arguments with suspicion.

As for the debenture holder who has lent the manufacturer money for a term of years at a fixed rate of interest, he will reply, if it be suggested that he should accept a lower rate of interest because the fall in the cost of living makes the money that he receives go further, that when prices rise he does not get a higher rate of interest, that prices have been rising, more or less and with fluctuations, ever since 1896, and that it is high time that the holder of fixed interest securities should have a turn of luck; and, moreover, that a contract is a contract and if once you are going to begin to vary contracts, because their terms have proved inconvenient to the borrower, there is an end of all business stability. And he will add that he is in quite a different position to the wage-earners, who can secure higher wages whenever trade is good and prices rise, whereas he has made his bargain for a long term, has to stand the racket when rising prices reduce the buying power of his income and so is fully entitled to any advantage that falling prices may give him, when the wheel of fortune turns that way.

And then there is taxation, payable in pounds, or other kinds of money, that are continually, owing to the fall in prices, more difficult to earn. Government debt-holders want their interest, and Government expenditure in times of bad trade is likely to rise in countries which make provision for the unemployed.

The tax-gatherer is more clamorous, and harder to satisfy.

And so in time of falling prices the first loss and difficulty involved by them falls on the employers who manage their own businesses and finance them with their own capital *plus* a certain amount of borrowed money; and in the case of joint stock companies, on the shareholders who have risked their money by supplying the ordinary capital,[1] and on the managers and managing directors if, as is common, they receive a commission on the turn-over or profits of the business. And so the organizers are dispirited and business confidence withers.

This lack of confidence, due to falling prices, very soon hits all the rest of us. If falling prices only affected the profits of organizers and shareholders the rest of us might view them with indifference, consoling ourselves with the thought that these risk-takers fare sumptuously when fortune is favouring the world with big banquets and so can well afford to tighten their belts when the meals are more meagre. But this tiresome belt-tightening process catches us all in its grip. Wage and salary earners may not be cut down in income, but the number of those who are able to earn is pretty certain to be reduced. Unemployment benefit softens the blow for displaced wage-earners, but most of those who get it would prefer to be at work. Doctors, lawyers, writers, artists, all have to stint. Their fees may be still the same, but they will not earn so many. Newspapers get fewer advertisements and so have less to spend on 'copy.' Booksellers and pub-

---

[1] See *ante*, pp. 109, 161.

lishers have their shelves stuffed with unsaleable literature. We cannot afford to be ill expensively or to go to law behind the shield of a crack K.C., or to be painted by the artist whom fashion has stamped with its approval. Only those producers flourish who provide us with cheap necessaries and cheap amusement.

All these uncomfortable facts have lately been brought home to most of us – I have just lost a job with a weekly newspaper that has helped me during more than five years to boil my family pot. And this disease of bad business due to falling prices is world-wide. We saw in Chapter XIII how hard Australia had been hit by the fall in wheat and wool, which made it difficult for her to meet the interest on her debt held abroad. The same problem afflicted Argentina, Brazil, Chili, India – all countries that sell food and materials abroad to provide the money owed to debt-holders. The debt charge does not vary. It is expressed in dollars or pounds or other foreign currencies; and when wheat, coffee, copper, cotton and all other materials fetch less in dollars and pounds the weight of debt on these primary producers grows heavier. Consequently they cannot buy so much, and the industrial manufacturing countries lose part of their custom and cannot sell their manufactures and there is more and more depression and unemployment and the vicious circle gets viciouser and viciouser.

Somebody, you will say, must be making something out of it, and this is true. In all these business kinks there is nearly always a compensating advantage for somebody, and there is generally an inherent remedy which, if left to itself and given time enough, will tend to straighten out the kink. We have seen that those wage and salary earners who keep their jobs and their rates of pay, benefit from the fall in the cost of living as it slowly comes down, and that the *rentier*, the pensioner and the annuitant and all holders of fixed-rate charges and long term debts score for the same reason. It may also be true that retailers and shopkeepers make more by continually buying cheaper and bringing prices down more slowly to their customers; but on the other hand they are hit by the fall in the value of their stock-in-trade and also probably by a smaller turn-over and sluggish business.

It has also been claimed for falling prices that they spur the clever and intelligent organizer to improve his methods and cheapen production, and perhaps this may be so. But is it better that he should be kicked along by a spur that disheartens him, undermines his pluck, and spoils his temper, or pushed into his collar by the expectation of a good feed of oats? I think we shall get better work out of him if we administer the latter medicine. Thus the balance of disadvantage behind falling prices seems greatly on the whole to outweigh the advantages, not only in the case of those whom falling prices obviously and directly hit, but also in that of the whole community – for even the *rentier*, if prices fall far and fast enough, will find that his interest is in jeopardy, because his debtors will be coming nearer and nearer to the point at which they simply cannot pay it.

As to the compensating remedy which business nearly always provides when any of its parts get out of gear, that which falling prices used to carry with them was decreased production and increased consumption. As prices fell, in days when there was real competition, those producers whose cost of production was highest were driven out of business. Nowadays we have to a great extent abandoned this system, which had obvious disadvantages, for one which seems to suffer from still more serious drawbacks. Schemes and arrangements, with and without State aid behind them, encourage the weak producers to go on producing, while, for example, a Farm Board in America accumulates a stock of 200,000,000 bushels of wheat; and at the same time the manufacturers, merchants and retailers with their rings and amalgamations and agreements keep up the price of finished goods and so increased consumption – the other end of the remedy – does not get a fair chance, as we consumers know.

But falling prices still bring with them another remedy, and that is cheap money. Because when raw materials are cheap and trade is moving at a sluggish trickle, there is less demand for money to carry stocks of goods and to finance their distribution. Cheap money, the power of being able to borrow at low rates of interest, helps to cheer business men up, and some very clever people say that this is the only remedy and one that can be relied on with perfect confidence, given time enough, to cure our present difficulties.

They also contend that scarce and dear money and the muddle into which the world's monetary arrangements have fallen in recent times have been the cause of the fall in prices and of all the bad consequences that have followed it. General over-production, they tell us, is in economic theory impossible. If all kinds of goods are made more plentiful, the larger quantities of goods can easily be exchanged for one another, and without any fall in prices, if the supply of money is at the same time increased. But the Quantity Theory of Money[1] tells us that if the supply of money is not increased as fast as that of goods, then the relatively small quantity of money will rise in value, which means that prices of goods will fall, letting loose all the evil brood of mischiefs that live on falling prices.

Scarce and dear money, in the opinion of these critics, has inflicted on the world all the evils from which its trade is now suffering, owing to the foolish policy of those responsible for some of the world's chief central banks. These gentlemen, by accumulating unnecessarily large stocks of gold, are said to have deprived the rest of the world of the power of expanding credit to the extent required to keep pace with the expansion of the production of goods. This accusation we must examine in the next chapter.

[1] See *ante*, Chapter V, p. 80.

CHAPTER XVIII

THE GOLD MUDDLE

Money and Gold – Advantages of the Gold Standard – Inconveniences arising from its Mishandling – Mr. Keynes on Central Bank Policy – Sir H. Strakosch on Mal-distribution – America and France – Were their Central Banks Responsible? – Gold and Public Opinion.

IT was shown in the last chapter that the world is now in a state of great distress because it is producing more goods than it can consume; also that there is high economic authority for the belief that scarcity of money is at the bottom of the mischief: though this scarcity has been produced not by any actual lack of gold, but by its 'mal-distribution' owing to the absorption of inordinate stocks by certain countries.

At the back of this belief is the Quantity Theory of Money, which was roughly explained on page 80. It tells us that unless the supply of money keeps pace with the supply of goods prices must fall. As has been shown, the war greatly stimulated the production of goods, but according to the Quantity Theory there need not have been any fall in prices if money had been multiplied as fast as goods.

In dealing, in Chapter V, with the functions of the bankers, we found that they create money for us by making advances and investments, and that their power to do so is based on the possession of a certain amount of 'legal tender' money, such as Bank of England notes in this country, and of a certain amount of balance – money on deposit – at the central bank of the country. These legal tender notes and balances in the central bank's books are created for the commercial banks – which make advances to the general public – by the central banks; and the latter's power to issue notes and make advances is in most countries regulated by law in proportion to the amount of gold that is held by them.

In England, as was shown in Chapter V, we have a system that differs in detail from that of other countries. But the practical effect is the same as elsewhere – that the amount of the central bank's stock of gold has an important influence on the extent to which the commercial banks can supply the business community with credit, which carries with it the right to draw the cheques which are the chief money of commerce.

It seems at first sight a very stupid arrangement that the supply of money, which we have seen to be so important to business stability, should depend on that of a metal that has to be dug out of the earth at the cost of much labour, expense and risk, and then kept in the vaults of central banks. And this system is certainly one of the things that are likely to be improved out of existence if ever the world becomes really civilized.

As things are, it has great advantages. Experience has shown that unless some such check is imposed on the creation of money, there is a great temptation to Governments to pay their way by printing notes, or making their banks print notes, instead of by collecting taxes from the citizens over whom they rule; and so the door is open to inflation,[1] and a rise in prices, which if it goes far enough deprives a country's money of all value and produces business chaos and general misery.

Against this danger the gold standard protects those who use it; and besides this negative advantage it also confers a great benefit on international trade by linking together the moneys of all the chief countries and preventing violent fluctuations in rates of exchange. We saw in Chapter XIII how, when a country has been buying more than it has been selling, or, by too much lending abroad or by any other means, has been giving other countries more claims against itself than it has been creating in the course of trade and business against them, the rate of exchange between it and other countries moves to what is called 'gold point' and gold begins to leave the country. When gold is taken for shipment to an extent that seems undesirable to the central bank, it corrects the position by a rise in bank rate, which means, in effect, that the price paid for loans by all borrowers in the country is raised; or by taking other measures (such as selling bills or securities) for making credit scarcer and dearer. In normal times there is always a mass of floating money which goes from one centre to another as it is attracted by the rates of interest current; and when any country raises its bank rate or by other measures offers higher terms to the international moneylenders,

------

[1] See *ante*, p. 80.

they will send money to it and so turn the exchange in its favour and stop the drain on its gold stock. At the same time the higher price of credit tends to make manufacturers and merchants sell goods at lower prices, and so the country becomes a good one to buy in and a bad one to sell in; and this also helps to turn the exchanges in its favour.

In this way rates of exchange between all the countries that are on the gold standard are kept within the limits of the gold points, and so anyone who buys and sells abroad knows approximately how much any foreign money that he has to pay or receive will cost him to provide, or be worth when he has brought it home. And this knowledge is of incalculable benefit to the smooth course of international trade.

With these advantages on its side, the business world is generally ready to ignore any absurdities and anachronisms involved by the gold standard, as long as it does its work well; but it has many critics, ranging from very clever theorists who think that we ought to have some cleverer system, to business men who think that they ought to get credit more easily and believe that the gold standard cramps their bankers' ability to grant it to them.

Criticism has been especially rife and incisive in the last few years, though it has been directed less to the gold standard itself, than to the manner in which it has been handled by the world's banking authorities.

In his speech at the meeting of the National Mutual Life Assurance Society on 29th January 1930, Mr. J. M. Keynes, its chairman, who is everywhere acknowledged as a leading authority on monetary theory, laid the whole blame for the recent fall in prices, which has dealt a terrible blow upon business, at the door of the world's banking governors. He said that the fall in the wholesale prices of raw materials had taken on the character of a world-wide disaster; that the storm centres were then to be found, not in Great Britain nor in the United States, but in the great producers of raw materials overseas – Australia, South America, Asia and Central Europe.

'Between 1921 and 1924,' he continued, 'the reaction from the great post-war inflation was practically completed, but since 1924 our wholesale index number has fallen by a further 20 per cent. This rate of fall, lasting over a period of four or five years, otherwise than as a reaction from an immediately preceding inflation, is, I believe, unparalleled in modern economic history. The consequences have already reached the dimensions of a first-class disaster. Nor is it by any means certain that a further movement in the same direction is going to be avoided.'[1]

How right Mr. Keynes was in this forecast is shown by the subsequent fall, of 22 per cent., that has been shown by the *Economist* Index Number in the course of the year 1930.[2] He went on to say: 'I believe that these events, so inimical to the wealth and happiness of the whole world, are avoidable and remediable. But they are to be attributed to the want of collective wisdom on the part of the central banking authorities of the world taken together, and are not now wholly remediable by the isolated action of any single country.

[1] *The Times* report, 30th January 1930.
[2] *Economist*, 10th January 1931.

The internecine struggle for gold stocks must cease and the market rates for money in the leading financial centres of the world must be reduced to a really low figure – which presents no difficulties if they all move together – in the neighbourhood of, say, 3 per cent. and must remain there for some time, before it is reasonable to expect a recovery of enterprise and confidence throughout the world, and the general enjoyment of that measure of prosperity which the ever-increasing achievements of scientific and business technique would make possible, if only the government, or want of government, in international monetary affairs would at last permit.'

Here we have it, 'plain as way to parish church,' from one of the world's leading authorities on money, that it is only the mismanagement of international monetary affairs that stands between the world and prosperity.

This view is endorsed, with a wealth of facts and figures and detailed arguments, by Sir Henry Strakosch in his memorandum on *Gold and the Price Level*, published as a supplement to the *Economist* of 5th July 1930. This document should be studied by all who wish to read a full and scientific exposition of this difficult gold question. Here its main arguments can only be briefly summarized.

Sir Henry tells us that an increase of production, extending over the whole range of commodities in an orderly and symmetrical fashion, cannot lead to 'over-production,' because it simply makes available to the population a greater amount of all the goods that it consumes. If all commodities are increased in volume

by 3 per cent., then all the producers will have
3 per cent. more to exchange with one another, the
general standard of life will be raised, and 'no disturbance in the exchange of the greater output need, or
does, arise, provided there are available media of
exchange in the form of money of all kinds to an
amount that corresponds to the increased volume of
exchanges that this greater production necessitates. If
it is available the general level of commodity prices
will remain stable.'

This seems clear and evident, if the Quantity Theory
of Money be accepted; and if Sir Henry's assumption
of 'orderly and symmetrical' increase in production is
correct; but has the recent increase in production been
orderly and symmetrical? If the figures of the Index
Numbers are studied it will be found that there has
been a considerable difference in the extent of the fall
even in different classes of raw materials; and it may
be that the unevenness in production that this fact
implies may have been a cause of business dislocation.
And there is no cure for this unevenness until we can
not only ration all consumers, but rationalize Nature
and regulate the vagaries of the seasons. Moreover,
Sir Henry ignores the dislocating effect of the much
faster fall in prices of raw materials than in those of
finished goods; the importance of this lack of harmony
in decline will be seen in the next chapter.

He goes on to show that there is a super-abundance
in nearly three-quarters of the various kinds of raw
materials that the world needs, and that there is 'an
anxiety of the producers of each of these materials to
exchange them for others, and yet they are not ex-

changed. We are, in these circumstances, entitled to conclude that these exchanges failed to be made, not because goods generally were in excessive supply, but because the process of exchange was in some way impeded. And if – as is the case – there are no observable impediments of a physical or moral character, the theory of "over-production" fails, and we are driven for an adequate explanation to the only remaining factor affecting the process of exchange, viz. the adequacy of the amount of money that is available to effect these exchanges.'

But is Sir Henry right in asserting that there were no observable impediments, physical or moral, to the exchange of the world's bigger output? It may be respectfully suggested that such impediments were found in political unrest and bitterness in Europe, civil war in China, the almost complete exclusion of Russia from the world's commerce, the drying up of the international capital market owing to lack of confidence and the attractions of the Wall Street boom, and the tariffs and trade barriers to which Sir Henry himself seems to refer when he says later that the free flow of commerce was 'impeded by barriers of the most diverse kind, and with it the flow of gold.'

'This,' he continues, 'coupled with an ill-directed monetary policy pursued by some of the Gold Standard countries accounts for the persistence of the maldistribution of the world's gold reserves and their partial sterilization.'

Since, as we have seen, the supply of money must keep pace with the output of goods if prices are to be kept steady, and since the output of goods is estimated to increase at a rate of 3 per cent. per annum, it follows that the gold stocks of the central banks must also increase at this rate, and must be distributed generally among them. If any countries take all the new gold that is available and also draw on the stocks of other countries, mal-distribution takes place and also 'sterilization'; because the gold so absorbed is added to stocks that are already sufficient or excessive and so does not perform its function of widening the foundation for credit expansion.

And this is what has been happening. A table given by Sir Henry setting forth the gold holdings per head of the population in the gold-using countries showed that whereas Great Britain's gold reserve per head was £3·3, that of the United States was on an average about £6·7, and that of France £6·1 in 1928 and £8 in 1929.

France and America thus had very adequate gold stocks, but these stocks have lately been still further increased. Sir Henry tells us that 'the deficiency of supply of monetary gold in relation to the assumed requirements of 3 per cent. per annum was moderate in the three years to the end of 1928, and so was the fall of the general level of commodity prices during that period. But when we come to the year 1929, we find a deficiency of well over 100 per cent. of requirements, accompanied by a sharp fall of prices which continues into the present year (1930). Not only was the whole of the new gold that had become available for monetary purposes in 1929 absorbed by the U.S.A. and France, but the two countries have, in addition, managed to deplete the reserves of some of the other Gold Standard countries to the extent of £14,000,000, after due allowance has been made for the release of £36,000,000 by the Argentine. Together they have in this manner sterilized gold to the value of £110,000,000 and deprived the Gold Standard world of the possibility of augmenting the amount of currency and credit that was needed for the exchange of its increased production. That sufficiently explains the catastrophic fall of the general level of commodity prices in 1929 and the beginning of this year'; (and, as we now know, to the end of it). 'It also,' Sir Henry adds, 'suggests that co-operative action for the purpose of co-ordinating the demand for gold by the central banks of the principal Gold Standard countries, which the Geneva Conference so strongly advocated, was either absent or ill-directed.'

Such, in brief outline, is the charge brought against the banking authorities of America and France of having caused the price fall, which as we have seen, has had such dire results. But before we condemn them to be gibbeted by the business opinion of the world, it seems worth while to look a little further into the problem and ask why these disconcerting gold movements happened and whether the Federal Reserve Board of the United States and the Bank of France were wholly responsible for them.

Why did all that gold go to America and France in 1929? America had made a gallant effort, in 1927, to redistribute some of the immense mass of gold that she had acquired (and can hardly be blamed for acquiring) during the war, in payment for goods sold to the European belligerents. She made New York a cheap centre to borrow in by a reduction in its bank rate, with the result that by the end of June 1928 America's gold stock had declined by £116,000,000 from the level of May 1927.

Unfortunately the cheapening of money there had other consequences, illustrating the limits on the power of bankers (as shown in Chapter V[1]) to rule over the course of business with the despotic power that is sometimes attributed to them. Bankers may cheapen credit and expand it (if they can find borrowers), but they can never be quite sure what the public will do with the new credit created. It may go into purchases of goods and so help to steady or raise their prices; but it may also – and here is a weakness in the Quantity Theory of Money – go into purchases of things that do not come into the Index Numbers, such as securities or 'real estate' – houses and land.

What happened in America, as most of us remember, was that the public was encouraged by cheaper money to go even more whole-heartedly into the biggest Stock Exchange speculation that the world has ever seen or dreamt of. Flushed with the spectacle of their own unparalleled prosperity and with a sincere conviction that it had come to stay, they saw no limits to the profits that their industries were going to earn some day or (consequently) to the prices at which shares in it were some day going to stand; and they backed this view with furious enthusiasm.

Could the Federal Reserve authorities have stopped this amazing outburst? Many have blamed them for not putting the bank rate up more quickly in 1928, but it

[1] See *ante*, p. 88.

is doubtful whether any increase in money rates would have checked the public as long as prices of shares were soaring; and raising rates in New York would only have helped to bring back gold. As it was, all the impoverished world was pouring money into America to earn high rates by financing the gamble, and so gold was pouring back across the Atlantic. When the boom collapsed, this flow continued, because America would neither buy nor lend.

If anybody was to blame it was the American public and still more the brokers and tipsters and the financial authorities who led it to believe that being 'a bull of the United States,' at any price, was the sure way to fortune; and also the American Government, with the public again behind it, which held up a stiff tariff against all the world, when all the world was their debtor; the debtor, with his power to send goods in payment thus hampered, had to send some gold. For these and many other reasons that might be mentioned, it seems to me unfair to charge the Federal Reserve banks with having, by lack of co-operation in econo-mising gold, produced the movement of gold to America in 1929 and 1930.

In the case of France also there were influences, over which the Bank of France had no control, that sucked gold into its vaults. In 1926 the French franc, which used before the war to be valued at 25·22 to the pound, was seriously depreciated, so that at one time it cost 250 francs to buy a pound. Frenchmen accused foreign speculators of having caused this depreciation by selling francs; but it seems to have been largely due to the nervousness of Frenchmen about their own money, and the haste with which, in their 'flight from the franc,' they sold securities abroad or anything else that they could sell and bought dollars, pounds and other foreign money and so turned the exchanges against France. But foreign speculators certainly took part in the operation; and when M. Poincaré restored confidence in the franc by masterly financial reforms, France caught these foreign speculators short and fairly skinned them, as the franc was doubled in value and stabilized at 124 to the pound. The profit made at the expense of these operators increased the funds in foreign centres that Frenchmen had placed there in fleeing from the franc; and these foreign balances have been accumulating steadily at compound interest for many years, because the balance of international payments has been in favour of France; and France, once a great provider of international capital, has not been taking any substantial part in after-war loan operations, but has been leaving her money on deposit abroad or investing it temporarily in foreign bills of exchange or other short-dated obligations.

This change in French investment habit may be traced to the disillusionment of the French investor owing to his huge losses on the milliards of francs that he poured into Russia, under the influence of political sentiment, before the war, and many other bad investments that he made, which did not even provide him with a political ally.

These losses have shaken the confidence of the French investor in foreign long-term loans. And this want of confidence, in one form or another, which is one of the by-products of the war and of war temper, I believe to be the most important cause of the world's present distresses. It made Frenchmen stack up big balances abroad and then, when money was wanted in France owing to increased trade activity, it had to be brought home in the form of gold because it was only by taking gold to the Bank of France that the French commercial community could increase the circulation of Bank of France notes.

Because the French money market is amazingly primitive in its arrangements; and the Bank of France has not nearly as much power as the Federal Reserve banks of the United States, or the Bank of England, to expand credit by discounts and advances, and it is an astonishing fact that in this enlightened country – so highly civilized in many respects – the central bank is forbidden by law to hold investments.

This being so the power of the Bank of France to co-operate in the economy of gold is very limited. You may say that it is scandalous that France should continue in these days to work with an antediluvian monetary system. Perhaps it is, but here, again, it is possible that lack of confidence, in another form, is at the bottom of the mischief and encourages the French to pile up gold to their own loss and to the detriment of the world's business.

For France is naturally apprehensive as to what may happen in Continental politics – a fact which should not be forgotten by critics of her financial and political actions. And there be many that say, that France is in no hurry to reform her medieval monetary system, since it brings gold to her shores which, if unprofitable as an investment, may be very useful some day if Continental war should come again.

If we could restore confidence – in peace and in political and financial stability – in other words, if we could be sure that the nations and their inhabitants were going to behave decently and sensibly – we should not hear much more about the internecine scramble for gold. France and America would be lending freely abroad and the international capital market would be well supplied with lenders, goods would be moving.

In the meantime it seems to be clear that all our troubles have not been entirely due to bad policy on the part of central banks; because the gold movements for which they have been blamed were largely forced on them by influences that they could not control, chief among which were unbounded optimism, followed by deep depression, in America and unrest and lack of confidence elsewhere.

Nevertheless, in so far as European bankers have, by scrambling for gold, made matters worse, they have been helping the downward tendency of commodity prices, and so strengthening that domination by America, of which they are so much afraid. We all owe money to America and we have to find dollars to pay it in; and as the price of goods and services falls, we have to sell more and more goods and services to America – in the teeth of her tariff, her shipping subsidies and all her other devices for making business with her difficult – in order to provide those dollars. It is true that we pay her less for her wheat and cotton and automobiles; but her exports are not much more than a drop in her brimming commercial bucket, while Europe's debt to her, in Europe's impoverished state, is a very real item; and for Europe to increase its weight by a faulty gold policy is, like so many other features of the present muddle, a tragical absurdity.

It is therefore very necessary that sane sentiment on the subject of gold should be preached to European central banks and also to the public for which they work. Because a central bank cannot go far ahead of its public and of the public abroad, in this matter, for fear its courage should be mistaken for weakness.

We in England can say with pride that our central bank, as has been recognized by foreign experts, set the world an example of sound sense in 1929 when it let its gold stock fall below £130,000,000, although for quite inadequate reasons which need not here be discussed, the figure of £150,000,000 had been set up as a sort of fetish by many people in the City.

There are far too many people who look on a big stock of gold as a sign of banking strength, whereas in fact it is, if accumulated deliberately, a sign of weakness, funk, bad banking, and bad service to the community. A strong bank is one that has the confidence of its customers and so can safely work with a small reserve of cash. That is the principle on which English banking has worked and so has gone on strengthening itself. But even so, with the Bank of England's gold stock, after a year of drain to France, Germany and other countries, nearly up to the £150,000,000 level at the end of 1930, many people in the City were inclined to begin to shake in their shoes when they heard that still more gold was going to France (where the Bank of France had nearly £430,000,000) and people abroad were said to be wondering whether the pound sterling could stand the strain. All this is rather absurd at this stage of our alleged civilization. In 1929, when Wall Street was booming and crashing and bank rates were jumping and the Bank of England, as usual, was bearing the brunt of the world's financial vagaries, the worst that happened to its gold stock, in that year of unparalleled nightmare, was that it lost £23,000,000 of its gold during the first nine months and recovered about £16,000,000 of its losses during the final quarter.[1] Does this look as if a stock of £150,000,000 – or even £100,000,000 – is really necessary as a minimum? Does not it rather seem that public opinion, both at home and abroad, should support and applaud a policy of lower gold stocks all round in the financially strong countries, so that those that are weak may enjoy more of such comfort as comes from larger stores of yellow ingots?

A League of Nations Committee, composed of highly distinguished experts, has been studying the question of the probable future scarcity of gold owing to the gradual exhaustion of the gold mines and suggesting that, in order to protect mankind against the consequent scarcity of money and credit, the nations should agree to alter the legal ratios of gold to liabilities that the central banks are obliged to keep.[2] Since these ratios

[1] Commercial History of 1929. Supplement to the *Economist* of 15th February 1930.
[2] Interim Report of the Gold Delegation of the Financial Committee of the Council of the League of Nations, Official No. A. 29, 1930, 11. Geneva, September 1930.

are based on nothing but custom and convention and have been handed down from a time when international banking was at an infantile stage of development, this suggestion seems highly sensible. It is true that immense difficulties and interminable discussions are usually involved when any business or monetary question has to be settled by gatherings representative of the statesmen of many countries. This is all the more reason for applying any possible ginger to the minds of the statesmen who will have to make the move, if the expected scarcity of gold is really as imminent as distinguished authorities tell us.

Professor Cassel, a Swedish economist who has done much to lighten our monetary darkness during and since the war, made an even more radical suggestion in the course of an address delivered at the end of May 1931 to the Institute of Bankers in London. He proposed immediately to abolish all laws regulating the gold reserves of the central banks. In the present state of public opinion on the subject of banking and money in many countries, this proposal seems most unlikely to be adopted. Moreover, neither it nor the League of Nations Committee's suggestion of all-round reduction of legal ratios would have solved our present difficulties in so far as they are due to accumulations of gold by America and France far in excess of legal requirements.

Reform, or according to Professor Cassel, abolition of laws regulating gold stocks, might, however, be useful in bringing central bankers to a saner view concerning banking strength, and it might also help to produce a sounder public opinion on this point in the minds of business men, and to kill that bogey that terrifies them whenever gold shows signs of leaving their countries. That such fears should be current in America, as was lately reported by financial correspondents, at a time when the Federal Reserve system's gold stock represented over 80 per cent. of its note and deposit liabilities, showed that public opinion there needs a good deal of education on this point.

We have to get it into the heads of business men that gold for purposes of coinage and circulation is a luxury that the world cannot now afford; it is only wanted as a reserve by central banks to be shipped as a corrective for an adverse rate of exchange, so preventing wide fluctuations in the exchange market. For this purpose, as was shown by the experience of the Bank of England in 1929, far smaller amounts are necessary than custom, convention, and a false view of a big gold stock as a sign of banking strength, now impel some central banks to hold; and a change of sentiment on this point, in the minds of central bankers and their publics, would help to put gold in its right place as a useful servant (until we have found a better one) and topple it off the pedestal on which it stands as a bogey and a master.

Some day, perhaps, if well-meaning people are not too anxious to make it run before it can walk, the Bank for International Settlements will give practical help in this problem of gold holdings and gold movements. Established in 1930 to handle German reparation payments, it may grow into a useful and efficient central bank for central banks and carry out, by transfers in its books, adjustments that are now effected by lugging lumps of gold about the world.

But we shall have to be a good deal more civilized before such nice arrangements as these can work. And even if we had them now, and America and France's gold stocks were held in the form of entries in the B.I.S.'s ledgers at Basle, there would still be 'mal-distribution,' not of gold but of book entries. The real solution of the gold muddle is redistribution of the metal by international exchange of goods and services, quickened by loan operations carried out by the countries that have, whether by their fault or not, stacked up the gold. If America and France would lower their tariffs and open their pockets to borrowers who want capital, their action would work more quickly and effectively and genuinely than any best-meant co-operation by central banks. Their central banks have done their best by reductions in Bank rate (New York, Chrismas Eve 1930, Paris, 2nd January 1931); and on 7th May 1931 the New York Federal Reserve Bank beat another world record, by being the first central bank that ever quoted such a low official rate as $1\frac{1}{2}$ per cent. But the rest of the world wants a freer market in America and France for goods and for long-term loans. To this last request they may very naturally reply, 'Why should we lend you money when you continually quarrel and snarl and indulge in revolutions?' And so we come back again to the question of confidence and decent behaviour.

And if we in England talked less about gold and its terrors and thought more about getting our cost of production down, so that we can sell our goods abroad, we should quickly lay that gold bogey. 'The depression in trade,' aptly observed the City Editor of *The Times* on 3rd January 1931, 'is largely due to the fact that British goods cost too much. Prices of manufactured goods to consumers have fallen a great deal less than primary products; consequently producers of primary products cannot afford to pay 50 per cent. (or more) over the pre-war level for goods while they themselves receive not more than before the war, and in some cases a great deal less. This unsymmetrical relation of prices creates a vicious circle, since the purchasing power of producers whose products normally exchange for each other is reduced and the reduction tends to become greater, partly because costs per unit rise with a smaller output and partly because confidence in the ability to sell output is weakened, thus discouraging enterprise. If more attention were paid to the simple truth that British goods cost too much, and less to the supposed power of the monetary magician's wand, it would be possible to take a more hopeful view of British trade prospects.'

CHAPTER XIX

OTHER CAUSES OF COLLAPSE

Too Much Wheat? – Retail Prices – An Old Problem – Greatly Accentuated – Effect on Primary Producers – Tariffs as a Cause – Check to Flow of International Capital – Unemployment – Should Mechanization be checked? – Closing of Russian and Chinese Markets – Bad Temper – Currency Readjustment – Silver.

IN the last chapter I ventured to question the doctrine put forward by eminent economists that mismanagement of monetary affairs by the world's banking authorities was the sole cause of the recent collapse in prices. And, in so doing, found several influences that underlay and had assisted, if not wholly caused, the mal-distribution of gold and so may more truly be regarded as the origin, or part of the origin, of our recent troubles.

These influences were: (1) more and higher tariffs, largely due to the war; (2) political animosities and unrest, also largely due to the war, causing lack of confidence which led to (3) a reduction of the flow of international capital; and (4) the American boom which sucked money into America which was very much wanted elsewhere. And the City Editor of *The Times*, in his little homily to British industry with which the last chapter ended, pointed to another world-wide influence: (5) the relatively slow fall in the prices of

313

manufactured goods. This list of causes may be supplemented by one furnished by the International Chamber of Commerce, at a meeting held in Paris at the beginning of December 1930.

It began with over-production in relation to population. This seems to imply that there is really more of certain articles than the world wants. Is this true? We are nearer this point in the case of wheat than in that of any other commodity. As the general standard of life is raised those who have more to spend eat less bread and more meat. Even so, if half of what we are told about privation in Russia is true, Russia ought to be eating the wheat that she is selling abroad; and if all the Oriental folk who are said to want to eat wheat rather than rice could get it and pay for it, that alleged surplus of wheat production would soon look different. At an International Wheat Conference, held in Rome at the end of March 1931, the chiefs of the Australian, Canadian and British delegations agreed that any surplus production of wheat would disappear by the normal action of economic law.[1]

Second on the International Chamber's list came one that has already been mentioned – the relatively slow decline in retail prices as compared with those of raw materials. Why has the cost of living come down so much more slowly than the index number that marks the course of commodity prices? If it had been otherwise, and if living were as cheap as commodity prices would seem to make possible, we should all have so much more to spend that our increased demand would soon sweep the glutted markets bare and start

[1] *The Times*, 30th March 1931.

314

that recovery in prices that would mean so much to business confidence. The alleged scarcity of money would not stop this process; because the lower all-round level of prices would enable a smaller quantity of money to do the work required.

We saw in Chapter VIII in dealing with the functions and expensiveness of the salesman, that according to Mr. Dibblee, who published his book on the *Laws of Supply and Demand* in 1912, that even in those pre-war days it was roughly true that it cost more to sell most articles than to make them.[1] This being so, the relatively high cost of retail articles is only an accentuation of an old evil. But this accentuation may have made all the difference between active consumption and glutted markets. How this evil has lately grown, may be shown by a striking example given by Mr. F. W. Hirst in his recently published book, *Wall Street and Lombard Street*.[2] 'If,' he writes, 'I had to review the position in a sentence or two, I would say: The real economic mischiefs are, first, the barriers and restrictions which prevent exporting growers from finding the best market for their produce; and, secondly, the obstinate refusal, in many cases, of retail prices to follow at a reasonable interval the downward course of wholesale prices. Of this I can give a remarkable example from conditions in the autumn of 1930. Among my friends are a sisal grower and a farmer. The sisal grower is losing heavily because he can now only sell the products of his Kenya plantation at the ruinous price of about £20 per ton, whereas a year

[1] See *ante*, p 133.
[2] Published by the Macmillan Company, New York.

ago he was selling at over £40 a ton and making a fair profit. My farmer friend complains that binding twine made out of sisal hemp still costs him £60 a ton, as it did last year, owing to a close ring of manufacturers and merchants who hold up the price.'

This may be an extreme example, but it is not far from being borne out by the general experience of consumers. For the gap between wholesale prices and the cost of living has grown enormously in the last few years. In the *Economist* of 10th January 1931 an article entitled 'Back to Pre-War Prices,' showed that whereas 'in 1924 it was fair to say that there was at least no great disparity between wholesale prices and the cost of living in relation to their pre-war equilibrium . . . by the end of 1925 a considerable disequilibrium had developed, and this grew wider until the autumn of 1929, when a further enormous widening of the gap between the two index numbers, with all its attendant economic difficulties, took place.' A chart published with the article shows the two figures starting in 1924 at 100; by the end of 1930 wholesale prices had tumbled headlong to just below 60, while the cost of living had wobbled along much more easily and was slightly below 90 at the end of the period.

If the cost of living index number can be taken as a fair measure of the retail prices of those articles and services that are necessary to life – and it is as good a measure as we can get – we see at once how serious these movements have been for the unfortunate 'primary producers' who provide the commodities included in the wholesale index. They have seen 40 per cent. knocked off the prices of the stuff that they produce, while the things that they buy have fallen by only 10 per cent. For though the *Economist's* figures applied only to Great Britain they can be taken as a rough indication of what has been happening elsewhere. Since world trade consists chiefly of the exchange of farm and mining produce for manufactured goods, it is easy to see that the facts just set forth must have inflicted a terribly severe jolt upon world trade. The farmers, with 40 per cent. knocked off the value of what they sell, and charged prices only 10 per cent. lower for what they buy, have inevitably been able to buy much less, and have had much more difficulty in meeting interest charges on any debts that they owed.

Not only so but those countries, such as Australia, Argentina, Brazil, etc., whose financial position and power to meet their debt charges depends on the prices fetched by commodities exported by their citizens,[1] have had great difficulty in maintaining their solvency and have had their credit seriously impaired, owing to the same process. The fall in export prices made it difficult for them to find the pounds, dollars and other foreign moneys that they needed to meet their overseas debts, and the diminished buying power of their citizens reduced that part of their revenues that was derived from import duties. Both as customers and debtors the primary producers were thus weakened and the industrialists who wanted to sell them goods and the creditors who were anxious about their interest and dividends were all in the same uncomfortable and unseaworthy boat.

[1] See *ante*, p. 214.

So if we can see why these things happened and can get them right and see that they do not happen again we shall have gone far towards setting the world on its legs again.

One cause of the relatively great fall in agricultural prices was the policy of the agricultural countries in putting up import duties on manufactured goods in order to stimulate manufacturing industries at home; they thus inflicted depression on the industrial countries and made them less prosperous and ready consumers for agricultural produce. This cause has been at work from some years. Professor Henry Clay, in an address on World Prices and Trade Barriers, delivered in May 1928, quoted the Final Report of the League of Nations Geneva Conference of 1927 to the effect that 'the economic depression in agriculture is characterized by the disequilibrium which had arisen between the prices of agricultural products and those of manufactured products: as a result agriculturalists in a great number of countries no longer receive a sufficient return for their labour and on their capital.'

But, as Professor Clay shows, the chief agricultural countries have been the leaders in the 'policy of obstructing trade, to which, through its influence on their industrial customers, the losses of agriculturalists can be traced. . . . The countries which are most interested in good prices for agricultural exports have done most by their tariff policy to prevent their most important export markets from paying good prices.' And so the farmer is doubly hit by the tariff policy of the agricultural countries. 'Inside the tariff barrier the protection tends to raise the price which the farmer has to pay for what he buys; outside the barrier it tends to reduce the price that he can get for what he has to sell.'

And the industrial countries are also doubly hit by the reduced purchasing power of their customers – they earn less, and also, owing to reduced turnover, they are unable to lower cost of production. 'The nationalist policy,' says Professor Clay, 'of Governments all over the world has aggravated the excess capacity of the munitions industries by subsidizing and protecting new iron and steel, engineering and chemical industries in countries that used to draw their supplies from Europe in exchange for agricultural products. And so, too, with the textile and other manufacturing industries. The older industrial areas, which by their purchasing determine world prices for the staple agricultural products, are unable to get down their costs, because they are unable to work at full capacity owing to the protective tariffs and other barriers that obstruct their entry to their former markets.'

Such was the state of affairs in the earlier years of the period covered by the *Economist* chart. From 1924 to 1928 the widening of the gap was gradual but considerable. In 1929 and 1930 it was enormous. Can we find any new financial feature to account for it? I think we can in the very serious reduction of foreign lending by the two countries, America and England, which have been most active in this business since the war. As we shall see, the British effort in this field which has been feeble ever since the war as compared with its ante-war figure, dropped considerably in 1929; while America, which had been doing yeoman's service in her new rôle of international lender by supplying impoverished and backward countries with buying power, turned off the tap with a reduction of nearly £160,000,000.

How could world trade expect to stand up against this abrupt check to the flow of borrowed buying power, happening when the effect of tariffs was already warping the exchange of goods between the nations?

If we have thus narrowed down the causes of world depression to these two chief influences, we have to go back a step further and ask what produced the influences, and what chance there is of stopping or reducing them. In the matter of tariffs it is easy enough to see why they grew. We have already seen in Chapter XIV that the desire to keep out other people's goods is general throughout the world, though always offset to a certain extent by man and woman's natural craving for something new and strange and distinctive. And we also saw reasons why the natural tendency towards Protection was greatly furthered first by the war, which forced many nations which bought goods abroad to try to make them themselves because their old sources of supply were cut off, and then by the peace, which broke up customs-free areas into the new Succession States, each anxious to keep out one another's goods.

It is not so easy to see whether there is any chance of reducing tariff walls. Geneva and the International Chamber of Commerce work hard at telling the nations that they are strangling the growth of international trade. But the nations go on putting up tariff walls and when 1930 brought severe depression, Canada, Australia and other countries tried to cure it by keeping out foreign goods, so making foreign markets still more difficult to sell in, and there was a strong movement in England, which affected members of all political parties, towards Protection.

On the other hand there is said to be a tendency towards reaction in favour of a more moderate tariff in America. As to the strength of this reaction it is idle to guess. All that can be said is, that if the interests of American producers who want to sell abroad were strong enough to cause a substantial lowering of America's tariff, the effect, both on trade and on sentiment abroad, would be great and good.

It is also easy to see why the international capital market dwindled and dried up. Before the war the chief foreign lenders were England, France and Germany; for America was then still, on balance, a borrower. After the war England was saving less owing to higher taxation, especially on the big incomes, and the general desire to 'have a good time' to-day and let the future take care of itself; and she was also placing a much larger proportion of her savings at home.

Look at the record of new issues in London, taken from the *Economist* of 27th December 1930, from the point of view of their destination in £ millions:

	1913	1928	1929	1930
For U.K.	36	264	198	170·6
Overseas	160·5	105	87·2	97·1
Total	196·5	369	285·2	267·7

France, disgusted by the loss of the milliards of francs that she had lent to Russia, was piling up balances

x

abroad but not investing them, but leaving them on deposit or putting them into bills of exchange and other short-dated securities. Germany was borrowing to meet her reparations charge and for other purposes. America, a world creditor at the end of the war, was also a world lender on a handsome scale for some years, until she began to concentrate her financial attention on the biggest speculative boom that ever staggered humanity, in her own railroad, industrial and public utility shares. Under this influence, according to the *New York Commercial Chronicle* of 10th January 1931, the capital issues in the United States for foreign investment fell from $1,576,500,000 in 1928 to $780,000,000 in 1929 – a decline of nearly $800,000,000, or £160,000,000.

At the same time not only was American money largely kept at home, but funds poured in from impoverished Europe, attracted by the rates – 8 per cent., 12 per cent., on one occasion even 20 per cent. – that speculators in Wall Street were ready to pay – for what did the price of money matter when share prices were going up like rockets? Small wonder that the already dwindled capital market dried up.

In the meantime its dwindling had as usual set up a vicious circle. The diminished borrowing power of the debtor countries diminished their buying power, helped to make trade worse and bring down the prices of their products, and so impaired their credit and made them less than ever able to borrow; and now that the American boom is over and the international capital market might wake up again if there were more confidence, investors are talking of 'safety first' and wondering which of the many countries that would like to borrow can be relied on to meet the service of any debts that they may contract.

And with bad times comes bad temper, of which there was already more than enough, and a series of revolutions and violent changes of political sentiment has increased the shyness of the capital market – 'Germany,' says Mr. A. M. Samuel, M.P., in an article in the *Investor's Chronicle* of 14th February 1931, 'was rehabilitating herself as credit-worthy; Herr Hitler's threat of repudiation injured German credit. Before that threat the world paid 90 for the German $5\frac{1}{2}$ per cent. Reparations Loan: the post-Hitler price is about 75.'

Since then the Continental atmosphere has grown more stormy, owing to the failure of the Franco-Italian naval negotiations, suspicions aroused by the proposed Austro-German customs union, and other causes; during the first half of 1931 international loan issuing has been pretty nearly dead, and finally there was a run on Germany in June and July.

Such is the state into which the international capital market has been reduced by high Protection in most countries, the American boom, and above all, lack of confidence, which has kept the French investor's pocket so tightly buttoned. The consequence has been a severe accentuation of the trade depression which has itself been a cause of the lack of confidence. 'We have always known,' said Mr. Keynes in his speech at the meeting of the National Mutual Life Assurance Society, on 28th January 1931, 'that the whole course of international trade and finance depends on a steady flow of lending, equal to the amount of their surplus resources, from the creditor countries as a whole to the debtor countries as a whole.'

In the meantime Governments, or farmers' associations with official assistance behind them, have been trying to help farmers by providing them with credit to enable them to hold up prices and at the same time the farmers have been officially implored to reduce production or to diversify production by sowing less wheat and more of other crops. These contradictory measures – encouraging farmers to grow wheat by artificially holding up the price and at the same time urging them to grow less – have naturally had little effect either way. The price has not been maintained, and the area under wheat has been little if at all reduced. The position has become so unmanageable that we see the dreams of State Socialists coming true and Governments dealing with one another in huge quantities of wheat. On 30th December 1930 it was announced by Mr. Bennett, Prime Minister of Canada, that he had persuaded the French Government, in order to promote the adjustment of Franco-Canadian trade in wheat, which had been almost killed by repeated rises in the French tariff, to buy between 7,000,000 and 9,500,000 bushles of the Canadian 1930 wheat crop.[1] *The Times* Washington correspondent, in a message published in its issue of 30th March 1931, stated that the United States Federal Farm Board 'holds at least 200,000,000 bushels already; it will hold much more before 1st June, and the future is a vast uncertainty.'

[1] *Economist*, 3rd January 1931, p. 13.

Unemployment was another cause of general depression on the International Chamber's list. Whether it be a cause or an effect it is, as every one knows, at the present time (1930-31) on a scale unprecedented in human memory; and we saw in Chapter X that much of it is due to the mechanization of agriculture and of manufacture which has enabled much more work to be done with far fewer hands. In countries such as Britain and Germany, where provision for the unemployed has been systematically established, the effect of this unemployment on the purchasing power of the wage-earning class has been effectively lightened. (It was noted that the circulation of Bank of England notes for purposes of Christmas shopping at the end of 1930 was as great as in the previous year in spite of increased unemployment and the reduction in retail prices.) But unemployment among the salary earners, who also have been affected by adding machines and other forms of mechanization and also by the general depression, has no cushion of unemployment relief to fall back on; and the relief given to wage-earners, sound in principle as it is, though amazingly ill-administered,[1] is a heavy burden on those who live on industry, as organizers or shareholders and on those wage-earners who are still at work.

Here again it is clear that business as now organized is making (whether by its own fault or other people's) a cause of depression and distress out of what ought to be a highly beneficial and profitable fact. Having been provided with machines which enable us to do much more work with much less effort, we ought, if

---

[1] See *ante*, pp. 183, 184.

things were properly managed, to be leading easier and more comfortable lives and nevertheless enjoying a larger supply of good things. Machinery has released millions of people and set them free to do other work, and instead of being able to give them other work to do or to share out the work that is being done so that we can all enjoy more leisure, we bewail the fate that has produced this great release of human energy.

In fact we go further and begin to wonder whether it would not be better to stop machinery from doing its work so well, because we cannot afford to have such a good and efficient servant. This suggestion, amazing as it seems, has been put forward by a distinguished official of the International Labour Office of the League of Nations, Mr. H. B. Butler, who lately returned to Geneva after a visit to the United States and Canada, to study unemployment problems there. He had been so much struck by the large extent to which unemployment was due to mechanization, that in a statement published in *The Times* of 6th January 1931 he suggested that the problem, whether mechanization cannot increase too fast in relation to the consuming power of the markets and to unemployment, seemed to be a question which might have to be treated on an international scale. Meaning, presumably, that an international conference might profitably discuss a general agreement for the restriction of the use of machinery. It does not do much credit to those who are responsible, as organizers and political rulers, for the state of our business arrangements, when we have to admit that Mr. Butler may be quite right, in present conditions, to bring forward this proposal which looks like putting back the clock; it reminds one of a suggestion made about a hundred years ago by Robert Owen, that it would be better to give up the use of the plough and go back to spade work in agriculture.

The charge against machinery that it deprives manual workers of a livelihood is a very old story. Just a hundred years ago, in fact, 'the Game Laws helped the Corn Laws to keep food scarce, and it only needed the introduction of threshing-machines and a couple of bad harvests to drive the farm hands over a considerable part of the south and east of England to open insurrection. Night after night, in the winter months of 1830, "Captain Swing" lit the sky with blazing ricks; half-starved labourers earning seven to nine shillings a week smashed machines and demanded money and a rise of wages with threats of violence. After the Yeomanry had easily suppressed this outbreak of despair, after the wages raised under duress had been reduced, there followed the vengeance of the law. Though no single life had been taken nor anyone even been seriously wounded, yet to atone for the damage to property and public order nine labourers were hanged and 457 transported. . . . The Whig Government approved the sentences.'[1]

Such were the views in those days of labourers on mechanization and technological unemployment and such was the answer of the authorities. Now 'the whirligig of time brings in its revenges,' and an international conference is suggested for the purpose of, in effect, endorsing the action of those labourers, not in

[1] *History of England, 1815-1918,* by J. R. M. Butler, p. 49.

smashing machines, but in being strongly opposed to their introduction.

At the time their attitude was thought to be due to misguided ignorance. Machinery, it was argued, was going to increase production, stimulate trade and cause in the long run a greatly increased demand for manual labour, which would get a better share of the bigger supply of good things that machinery was going to produce.

As it turned out, this argument proved to be correct; and before the process of mechanization is frowned on by the collective wisdom of the world it seems worth while to consider whether, if production and trade are given a reasonable chance, the same thing might not happen again. In the meantime there can be no question that technological unemployment, due to failure to absorb labour displaced by mechanization, is a very real cause of the general depression. The buying power of those displaced is reduced, and when it is supported by the State, or by the contributions of those still at work, it is a burden on industry.

The next two causes enumerated by the International Chamber – the closing, partial or complete, of some of the world's most important markets, and political unrest – we may take together, because they are largely two aspects of the same influence – bad temper, misunderstanding and suspicion. This influence I believe to be by far the most potent in checking trade and production. Without good temper at home and abroad, and the expectation that goes with it, that business is not going to be interrupted by wars and industrial disputes, we cannot have that confidence which is the mainspring of enterprise. Actual civil war has been seriously interfering with the development of what might be an enormously busy and profitable market in China, with its 450,000,000 of people. Russia, in the hands of people who think that other countries are ruled by capitalist bandits who ought to be abolished, is regarded by the rulers of other countries with an almost equally malevolent eye. She is accused of enslaving her population and her exports are branded as dumped goods, produced by convict labour. Whatever justification there may be for Russia's opinions about the rest of the world and its opinions about her, they do not help trade and prosperity. Dissatisfaction and suspicion, partly the effect and partly the cause of trade depression, have caused political unrest culminating in actual revolution in many countries of Latin America and in Spain, and much sabre rattling among our Latin neighbours in Europe. Signor Mussolini, in a recent speech discussing the financial position of Italy, stated that her military expenditure had grown from 650,000,000 lire (about £26,000,000[1]) to about five milliards (about £53,000,000[1]) at the present day, of which over two milliards had been added since 1922. But he 'defied anybody to say that this expenditure was not absolutely necessary at a moment when all the world was arming to the uttermost while at the same time it bleated about peace.'[2]

When the political atmosphere is thus charged with electricity to the tune of thunderous mutterings, it is

---

[1] Taking the pre-war at 25 and the present lira at 93 to the pound.
[2] *The Times*, 19th December 1930.

no wonder that capital is shy and the international market for securities in all the chief Stock Exchanges has been queasy and unreceptive. Inside the various countries bad temper and misunderstanding embitter the relations between employers and employed, in spite of vigorous and more or less successful efforts to improve them. Many wage-earners and wage-earners' leaders believe that the employers are actuated by mere greed, when they contend that industry, in view of present conditions, cannot stand the current rate of wages; and many employers and other critics accuse the wage-earners of mere greed, when they do not see why wages should be attacked before all other methods of lowering production costs have been tried.

If we had confidence and good feeling and were all trying to get things right instead of making ugly faces at one another and nasty insinuations about one another's motives, capital would be moving freely to the countries that need equipment and improved transport, goods would be moving in spite of tariffs and gold would be getting redistributed; America, instead of regarding (with some reason) Europe's evils as due to the incurably quarrelsome temper of our Continental neighbours, might be more ready to listen to Europe's plea that she cannot pay her debts if America keeps such a high tariff against her goods; and capital and labour might be making a quicker approach to the very practical ideal put before them by the late Lord Melchett, of co-operation to secure the prosperity that both want and neither can get without the other.

Then there is the 'slow readjustment,' as the International Chamber expresses it, 'of national to the international situation owing to the varied bases chosen for monetary stabilization.' We in England, for instance, screwed our pound up in 1925 to its old pre-war parity with gold, while other countries, such as France, Belgium and Italy, 'stabilized' their francs and lire more or less in accordance with the depreciation that the war had wrought in them, owing to excessive creations of paper money. All these variations upset the relation between prices in one country and another and so made trade difficult. Did we, by bringing the pound sterling back to its old parity with gold, sacrifice our industry to considerations of financial prestige? This problem is too technical to be discussed at length here. Mr. A. Loveday, chief of the Intelligence Service of the League of Nations, has dealt with it (and many others) in a very interesting book called *Britain and World Trade*.[1] His investigations showed that 'the exports of all the European countries, except the United Kingdom, which by a process of deflation have re-established the pre-war value of their currencies continued to expand after stabilization had been effected, in the face of the competition of neighbouring states with debased currencies.' In other words, a change in the value of a country's money will not make any but a temporary difference to its power to sell goods abroad, if it makes the necessary adjustments. 'Deflation,' says Mr. Loveday, 'was more detrimental in England than elsewhere, because other countries made the necessary adjustments to their whole machinery of production and we did not.'

[1] Published by Messrs. Longmans, Green & Co.

331

Nevertheless, those who argue that we were too hasty in returning to the old gold value of the pound, or even that we should have been well advised never to have returned to it at all, can still retort that their withers are unwrung by Mr. Loveday's facts. They are entitled to urge that our monetary authorities ought to have known that, owing to the influence of our trade unions, it would be difficult to readjust wages; that owing to the slowness and backwardness of some of our industrial organizers it would be difficult to effect other reductions in costs of production by reconstruction and improved methods; and that our scale of taxation was much heavier than in any other country, and was difficult to reduce owing to the tendency of all political parties to give public money away with both hands; and that therefore they ought to have waited until trade was more settled before inflicting on our industries this added problem of readjustment to a higher exchange value of our currency, which made us a good country to sell to and a bad one to buy from.

On the other hand, there is the fact – at least I think it is a fact – that Britain's greatest asset of all is the prestige of the Englishman as a man who keeps his word. Foreigners had lent us money, or left money in our keeping, during the war, and we owed them British pounds. It was to our advantage that these pounds should as soon as possible be restored to the pre-war gold parity, so that our creditors should not think that we had swindled them by writing down the value of the debt.

'Thy silver is become dross,' says the prophet Isaiah. Silver, that used to share with gold the task of providing the richest countries with money, and to fluctuate around a value of 5s. per ounce, has been pushed out of this proud position by her rival, as nation after nation has adopted the gold standard, and touched 12d. per ounce early in 1931, having touched 28⅞d. in May 1928. Immense hoards of it are held in India and it is more or less the basis of the chaotic currency with which China trades; and so the International Chamber was justified in saying that this fall has 'further reduced the purchasing power of one-third of the world's population.'

In *The Times* of 9th January 1931 a telegram from its Shanghai correspondent reported a growing feeling there 'that foreign Governments interested in Far Eastern trade will have to consider measures to stabilize silver, and, failing action for this object, that there is a risk that the market for foreign products in China in particular will collapse altogether.'

And the Bimetallists are busy again – people who want to cure scarcity of gold and over-plenty of silver by running the two metals in double harness. Theoretically, their proposal is attractive, but I think it is too complicated for public consumption, and that they are barking up a dead tree.

Mr. Brownell, Chairman of the American Smelting Company, has put forward a suggestion that seems more practical. He says, according to a Reuter telegram in the papers of 20th January 1931, that the fall in the price is not due to over-production, but to sales of silver formerly used as money, and that the problem would be solved if the Governments of the United States, Great Britain, including India, France, including Indo-China, and any others that might join, would agree to withhold sales at any price below a certain level. Is there any chance of such an agreement?

Another item in the International Chamber's list was high taxation. But this must wait for the next chapter. The conclusions reached in this one were eloquently summed up, and expanded, in a passage in the address, already referred to on page 309, given by Professor Cassel. He said that the present generation has been guilty of a whole series of the most appalling faults, mistakes and violations of fundamental economic principles. The greatest of these was the war itself. Having finished the war we have proceeded to claim war debts and reparations without being willing to accept payment, to cut up the world's markets into watertight compartments, to prohibit the international movement of men, to hinder the free movement of capital, and to prevent by valorization schemes a natural adjustment of the prices of certain commodities. Within our different countries we have developed monopolies both of enterprise and of labour, doing all that we can to restrict internal freedom of movement, and we have created systems of unemployment doles calculated to increase the immobility of labour in a very dangerous way and to ruin public finances. At the same time some people have started so-called radical movements aiming at the revolution of the whole economic system, the only effect of which has been to destroy the confidence and spirit of enterprise on which our whole economic life is founded.

In spite of all these things, the Professor continued,

the world enjoyed from the restoration of the gold standard up to the middle of 1929 a period of prosperity and progress. Something must have happened then that altered the situation and produced the present violent crisis. This something was, in his opinion, the extraordinary fall in prices, which he considered to be a monetary phenomenon and proposed to remedy, as already recorded, by abolishing the laws that regulate the gold stocks of central banks.

But was the fall in prices caused by scarcity of money? Money was no scarcer at the end of 1929 than it was in the middle of the year. The real change in the business position that happened in the latter half of 1929 was the conversion of the American public from wild optimism to acute depression which has gone on growing more acute.

The effects on the international capital market, first of the American boom which sucked in money from all the world to finance it, and then of the collapse, which made the confidence of investors ooze, like Bob Acres' courage, out of their finger-tips, have already been noted. But the collapse had a still more direct effect on prices by checking the American demand for commodities. 'In the case of American cotton,' says Professor J. A. Todd in his book on the *Fall in Prices*,[1] 'there is no doubt that the huge consumption in the United States up till last year was a big factor in the world position, and the restriction of that consumption in 1930 was largely responsible for the fall. In the motor trade it is well known that America's demand has fallen off very seriously since the crash. It seems

[1] Published by the Oxford Press.

reasonable to assume, therefore, that motors and cotton, which may be taken as representative of luxuries and necessaries respectively, are typical of a general restriction of consumption in all sections of the United States and in all commodities.'

And when America tightens her belt and cuts down consumption, the effect on world consumption of food and materials is immense. For we are told by Dr. Carl Snyder, statistician to the Federal Reserve Bank of New York, that her 'total trade is possibly greater, measured in money transactions, than that of all the rest of the world put together.'[1]

This new factor of the American market collapse, added to the cumulative effect of all the mistakes and faults enumerated by Professor Cassel as having been committed by the present generation, seems to be a much more practical cause of lack of confidence and low prices than scarcity of money, especially at a time in which money had not become any scarcer but had been made more plentiful, being no longer in keen demand for financing a bull campaign.

[1] See his address to the American Academy of Political Science at its annual meeting, 22nd November 1929.

CHAPTER XX

TAXATION

The Price of Government – And Security – These Benefits Especially Important to the Rich – Hence Greater Proportion of Incomes paid by Rich in Taxes – Through Direct Taxes – Vices of Estate Duties – " Robin Hood " Taxation – Is it carried to Excess?

TAXATION is the price that we pay for the inestimable benefit (when we get it) of good Government and security at home and peace abroad if possible, and if not, a vigorous defence of the national interests if unjustly threatened. When Government is bad, taxation is the price that we pay for allowing our affairs to be in the hands of those who mismanage them.

Peace and security at home are provided, almost entirely, not by any effort of Government but by the decent and considerate behaviour of the great majority of the citizens of all civilized countries. If we all wanted to rob and murder and cheat, no Government could stop our doing so. We keep order ourselves because we nearly all want to live on kindly and reasonable terms with our neighbours. But the Government does an immense service for us by providing a police and a machinery of justice, to check the activities of the small minority that wants to make a nuisance of itself.

These services rendered by the Government are the only commodity that we have to pay for whether we

Y 337

want to or not. Other things we need only pay for if we buy them. Government, which benefits us all if it is good, and always thinks it is good and nearly always is better than none, says, very reasonably, that as we all benefit by it we all ought to pay and must pay.

It is true that in a country like England where there is little or no taxation of the necessaries of life, and the chief weight of taxation falls on the very rich, it is nearly possible to avoid paying for Government if our income is small enough to escape the income tax, if we drink no alcohol and smoke no tobacco, consume no sugar and never go to a theatre or cinema and never travel in a motor bus or railway train. But there are very few who live thus austerely.

From the business point of view the chief advantage that we get from good Government is the security that it gives us in earning our incomes and owning our property. If besides earning and owning we had also to protect our income and property against thieves, the more we earned and owned the more we should have to spend on guarding them; and in an increasing ratio, because the bigger our possessions the more tempting they would be to those who find stealing easier and more pleasant than working, and the more open they would be to attack and depredation.

This is one justification for the principle that has long been the basis of England's fiscal system, that the richer our citizens become, the higher the proportion of their income that they should hand over to the Treasury to be spent on public purposes. Another justification of this principle is the fact that as we saw

338

in Chapter VII,[1] money has what economists call a Marginal Utility; that is to say, the more we have of it the less use it is to us. Consequently, if we take for the purposes of the State a larger proportion of a rich man's income, it inflicts no personal hardship on him, as compared with the privation imposed by a small amount of taxation on the poor.

One who has £50,000 a year and has to pay £25,000 to the tax-gatherer is still left with £25,000, a very ample income to satisfy all reasonable needs. But one who has £100 a year and has to pay £10 to the tax-gatherer is forced to stint himself in purchases of the necessaries of life. In other words, by means of this principle of graduation – taxing in a higher proportion those who have the larger incomes – we lay the burden of taxation on the shoulders best able to bear it.

But this principle can only be applied through what are called the 'direct' taxes, such as income tax and estate duties, that are paid directly by the tax-payer to the inland revenue officials. Indirect taxes, such as those on tobacco or beer, are collected originally from the tobacco manufacturers and brewers, who get them back from the public as it pays for its smokes and drinks, and pays more for them because of the tax, which the consuming public thus pays indirectly, and often without knowing it. It thinks it is buying beer whereas it is really buying beer and Government.

In this case the principle of graduation – suiting the burden to the shoulder that bears it – cannot be applied. A packet of cigarettes bought by a millionaire has paid the same duty as a similar packet bought by

[1] See *ante*, p. 126.

a housemaid. And since the principle of graduation is clearly just, there has been a growing tendency, at least in England, to get more and more of our revenue by means of direct taxes. An ideal system of taxation would seem to be one which would supply all the expenses of Government by means of direct taxation, equitably graduated and paid in fair proportions by every member of the community that receives an income.

This ideal is, or is said to be, impossible to achieve, because of the difficulty and expense of collecting the very small sums that those who have the small incomes would pay; and so a certain amount of indirect taxation is still levied, though its proportion to the total revenue collected has declined rapidly during the past century. In 1841-2 it provided 73 per cent. of a total tax revenue.[1] In 1930-1, according to the estimates of Mr. Snowden's Budget of 1930, the proportion was to be 36·4 per cent.

Indirect taxation is justified by the report of the Colwyn Committee on the ground that it is the most effective way of levying a contribution to national expenditure from the mass of wage-earners, and it adds that 'there is great force in the argument which connects taxation with representation.' Which means to say that those who have votes and so are responsible, through their representatives, for the spending of the nation's revenue, should also be responsible for providing at least some part of it.

In the days when our ancestors fought for the right to tax themselves, instead of being taxed according to the whims of a monarch, their watchword was 'No

---

[1] *British Budgets, 1887-1913*, by Sir Bernard Mallet, p. 105.

taxation without representation.' Now that we all have votes, and so representation in Parliament, it is evidently right that we should pay our fair share of taxation. It is nowadays a case of 'No representation without taxation'; for, to quote the Colwyn Committee again, 'it would be a bad state of affairs if a large majority of citizens were themselves to make no actual contribution, and were to enjoy benefits provided entirely by the taxation of the few.'

We have not come to that point yet, but it is a question whether we have not come dangerously near to it. For Mr. Snowden's Budget of 1930 provided for a total revenue of over £441,000,000 to be collected from the direct taxpayers – £260,000,000 in income tax, £64,500,000 in supertax, £83,000,000 in estate duties, £27,000,000 in stamps (a duty on transfers of property and securities), £4,000,000 from motor duties, and £2,500,000 from oddments of the old war-time Excess Profits Duty, the Corporation Profits Tax, and the Land Tax.

These £441,000,000 (out of a total revenue from taxes of £694,000,000) are paid by 2,250,000 people, out of a population of about 45,000,000. Increases in taxation announced by Mr. Snowden came to £46,500,000, and it is noteworthy that all the increases were so arranged as to fall on the larger incomes – an increase of 6d. in the pound on the income tax was balanced by a revision of the system of graduation, so as to protect small incomes, whether earned or from investments, from additional liability; and the only increase in indirect taxation – 3s. per barrel on beer – was explained by the Chancellor to be too small to justify any alteration in retail prices, and so fell wholly on the brewers, who, as he was able to inform the House, had promised him that the strength of the beer sold would be maintained.

Income tax was raised (with the already mentioned safeguard for small incomes) to 4s. 6d. in the pound, surtax – an additional income tax paid by those with incomes of £2000 and upwards – was raised, on any excess of income over £50,000, from 6s. to 7s. 6d. in the pound. Estate duties levied on the property of those who have died 'worth' over £2,000,000 were raised from 40 to 50 per cent., the existing scale being amended all the way up from £120,000 upwards.

These estate duties are mouthfuls bitten by the State out of property left by people who die. Since the power to hand on what we own to our heirs, without attack or depredation by robbers, is secured to us by the existence of police and Government, some toll on it, as it passes from deceased owner to heir, is evidently equitable. But estate duties are, in some ways, a particularly vicious form of taxation. Firstly, because they are a tax on capital, and to take a lump of capital and spend it for current purposes is bad business for a nation, just as it is for an individual. It is true that in the case of a nation the savings of the citizens make good the hole that the Government's bad finance has created, but the fact remains that to the extent that money raised by estate duties has been spent for current purposes the nation's capital fund has grown less fast than it would have otherwise.

In so far as the money so raised is used for debt redemption, there is no diminution of the nation's capital fund. In the Budget of 1930 estate duties were estimated to produce £83,000,000 and £55,500,000 of the revenue were to be used in debt redemption; so that nearly £30,000,000 of the sum taken from capital account was, according to the original plan, to be dissipated on purposes of current expenditure. What actually happened was that the estate duties produced £82,500,000 and the net sum available for debt redemption was, according to the calculations of the *Economist*,[1] £1,250,000, and the nation's capital fund was thus squandered to the extent of over £80,000,000.

Estate duties suffer from another fault, as a form of taxation, in that they are necessarily based on valuations, which are in fact guesses at the value of the property left. If a man dies with property believed to be worth a million his estate pays a certain rate of duty. But except in the case of a few securities that are freely dealt in every day, it is impossible to be sure about the real value of anything until one gets a price for it by actual sale. The guesses about the price at which an estate should be assessed may be unfair to the tax-payer or to the tax-gatherer, but they are pretty sure to be unfair to one party or the other. Whereas income tax, being based on actual receipts, involves no error of this kind.

Another serious drawback to this form of taxation is the capriciousness of its incidence, because it is imposed at the death of property owners; with the result that it recurs, not at regular intervals, as a fair tax should, but at the whim of all the accidents and chances that determine how long we shall live. One

[1] See its issue of 2nd May 1931, p. 930.

343

estate may escape it for ninety years, while another
may be disembowelled by it two or three times in a
decade.

It is thus not nearly as equitable as a carefully
graduated income tax, but it is justified in practice on
the ground that a certain number of income tax payers
are known, or believed, to evade part of their liability
by concealing the extent of their incomes. The only
time when these tax cheaters can be made to stand and
deliver in full, is when they die and their wills are proved
and their estates are transferred to their heirs and
assigns. And so because of the dishonesty of a few, a
bad and unscientific tax has to be imposed on all
property owners. Just as, because a few rascals like to
cheat railway companies when they can, we all of us
are bothered every day to show our season tickets.

Combined together, these direct taxes press with
quite terrific severity on the very rich and make a big
hole in the spending power and saving power of the
moderately wealthy.

In answer to a question asked in the House of
Commons in May 1930 the Chancellor gave figures
showing how much would be paid by holders of various
incomes in income tax and surtax and in insurance
premiums to provide against estate duties. The possessor of an income of £50,000 derived wholly from
investment, would pay in income tax £11,132, in
surtax £14,506, and in insurance premiums £25,349,
making a total of £50,987, and leaving him with less
than nothing to spend![1]

To which many people who regard the existence of

[1] *Economist*, 24th May 1930.

these huge fortunes as a social evil, will say that there is no reason why the owner of the income should expect to be able to leave such a mass of money when he dies; and that if he chooses to try and do so his insurance premiums are a form of saving which increases the country's capital fund. Though this latter contention is not true of that part of the estate duty revenue that is spent by the State for current purposes.

On the more moderate incomes the pressure of direct taxation is less severe but still very heavy in England as compared with that imposed in other countries or at earlier dates in our history. As to other countries, the difference between their taxation and our own was shown by the figures quoted on page 55.

As to our own pre-war taxation a holder of an income of £5000 paid, in 1913-14, £292 in income tax, and probably considered himself a martyr to the extortion of the tax-gatherer. In 1930-1 he would pay £1007 in income tax and £306 in surtax – £1313 in all against less than £300 before the war.

'The income tax and supertax,' says Dr. Bowley, 'are steeply graded, with numerous allowances on small incomes; so that the rate is very moderate for a married man with less than £1000 a year. The effect is to diminish very markedly the great inequality of incomes, so far as this is due to great wealth. At the same time the death-duties cut continually at the amassing of wealth.'[1]

These effects will be welcomed by all who think that big accumulations of money in the hands of individuals

[1] *Economic Consequences of the Great War*, p. 139.

345

are a bad thing for the community; and in so far as the money so collected is spent in making life easier for the poor this process is welcomed as a wholly unmixed blessing by the bold spirits of the Labour Party in Britain.

Miss Susan Lawrence, M.P., presiding at a Conference of the party in October 1930, rejoiced that the work of the Government was 'Robin Hood legislation' – taking from the rich and giving to the poor. 'Any child can understand that,' she added.[1] But not only any child, but the tax-payers also understand it very clearly, and when they think that the process is being carried out, to a length and at a pace that industry cannot stand, it exasperates and dispirits them.

It was stated at the beginning of this chapter that since the rich have more to lose, it is fair that they should pay more for the security that good Government gives them. But when the Government takes their money, not in order to provide security, but in order to endow the poorer classes with pensions, unemployment relief carried out on questionable lines, education, and health service, and so on, the fairness of the proceeding is not quite so evident to those who have to pay. A detached observer may consider that these objects are at least as desirable as security, but it is natural that the rich should doubt whether all those things should be done at their expense, especially when they can show that these huge drafts on their capital and incomes are a heavy burden on industry and so are ultimately bad for those who are meant to benefit by the expenditure on social services. They begin to

[1] *Morning Post*, 7th October 1930.

question both the equity and the efficiency, in the national interest, of Robin Hood legislation when carried beyond a certain point.

Those who are in favour of this redistribution of wealth by means of taxation can retort that it is to the national interest that our society should be founded on a healthy, intelligent, and contented population, that wise expenditure by the Government is necessary to secure this, and that the necessary funds can only be got by taxing those who have the money. If we accept these arguments, and so favour a certain amount of redistribution of wealth by taxation, we still have to be careful to see that it is not carried to a point at which it tends to check the filling of the pool of wealth.

This it is likely to do, if it weakens the effort of the organizers, whose importance to the brisk working of the whole machine of wealth-making was shown in Chapter VII.[1] As things are, under our present business arrangements, we can only increase the contents of the pool of wealth with the help of the people who are paid highly, in one way or another, for planning and managing the arrangements by which capital – their own or that of shareholders who entrust it to them – is set to work to make wealth for us all with the assistance of manual labour and machinery. The qualities of the successful organizer – confidence, energy and readiness to take responsibility – are rare. He has to be paid highly and if he feels that the State takes too much back from him, on the Robin Hood principle, he will cease his effort towards expansion and drive which is so useful to all the rest of us who

[1] See *ante*, p. 128.

lack the necessary qualities for making this essential effort.

Some day, perhaps, as already suggested on page 129, the wage-earners will produce their own organizers and provide them with the necessary capital. But until this happens we have to take the highly paid organizer, because he is the only man who is there to do the job, and we have to leave him what he thinks a fair reward or he will not bother to work away with that necessary effort and strain that his task, with all its anxieties and responsibilities, demands.

And this is especially so in times of difficulty and depression and falling prices such as was 1930. We saw in Chapter XVII[1] how many are the wet blankets that falling prices throw over the head of the organizer. His profits are cut, but the wages and salaries that he pays do not come down if those who earn them can help it, and his interest charges on money borrowed for long periods are not reduced. If at such a time he is not only taxed as usual but is asked to pay more taxes, to help his poorer neighbours, who are benefiting by the fall in prices which is causing him loss, he may surely be excused if he feels inclined to throw up the sponge.

How much reason he may have for doing so was shown by a letter signed 'Tantallon,' published in *The Times* of 3rd May 1930, from the head of a private limited company owned by himself and his family, and described as a 'progressive manufacturing concern'; it has, since the war, started or built two additional factories and each was then employing about or over

[1] See *ante*, p. 284 *et seq.*

one thousand people. He found, on consulting his accountants, that 'if our business continues its present progress for the next five years and makes an additional average annual profit of £30,000, my estate would at the end of that time and on the same basis of valuation be involved in additional Estate Duty of £148,000, even though the total increased profit, after income tax, had only left me £116,500. Which means that, by forging ahead, adding new plant and giving large additional employment, my estate would in the event of my death at the end of five years be the poorer by £31,750, apart from the sums I should have to pay in surtax.' Small wonder that he goes on to observe that 'it will take a very heroic spirit to continue pioneering under these conditions! My own case,' he adds, 'I know is typical of many concerns in Lancashire and elsewhere, where new equipment and new enterprise are made impossible because of the estate duties.' In fact, this Robin Hood taxation, however necessary we may think a certain amount of it to be, is a many-pointed weapon which has to be used carefully because it has an awkward habit of cutting the wrong man.

These rich folk whom it mulcts are deprived by it of money which they either spend, so giving employment, or subscribe to hospitals and other charities, thereby helping their poorer neighbours, or save and invest at home or abroad, thereby either supplying industry with capital much needed for reconstruction, or supplying foreign borrowers with the means of buying our goods, and so giving employment to sorely depressed export trades. Consequently any money that is taken away from them by taxation, in a well-meant effort to benefit the poorer members of the community, is taken away from the very people whom it is meant to help.

If the money so taken is not excessive in amount and is wisely spent, it may do more good than harm; but the system has to be handled carefully. Finally, taxation that is thought to be oppressive is paid slowly, grudgingly and not at all if it can be legitimately evaded, to say nothing of the extent to which this feeling of extortion stimulates the efforts, already referred to, of the tax cheaters.

When M. Clemenceau was in England in 1921 he stayed with Dr. Farnell, the Vice-Chancellor of Oxford University, and in talking about certain criticisms of England that had appeared in the French press, exclaimed: 'Never mind about that: there are two things that every Frenchman at the bottom of his heart admires about England: first, you raised an army of some two million men by the voluntary system. No other nation in the world has ever done that or could do it. Secondly, you bear the most crushing income tax in the world and make honest returns for it, for the Chancellor of the Exchequer often gets more than he reckoned on. No other nation would bear it or would declare it.'[1]

This willingness to pay on the part of the great mass of the direct tax-payers of England is a priceless national asset. But when taxation is stiff and thought to be oppressive even those who are willing to pay what is due find themselves obliged to be extremely careful not to pay a penny more than they can help, and to

[1] From a letter to *The Times*, 27th November 1929.

pay experts in these matters to take charge for them of their relations with the inland revenue officials.

One other justification, that is often put forward, for the high level of direct taxation in England, needs to be considered – namely that since direct taxes produce £441,000,000, and interest and redemption of national debt absorb £360,000,000, and since the national debt is held mainly by the rich, therefore most of the money taken from the direct tax-payers is merely handed over to be paid back to them.

This specious argument seems to me to be fallacious. In the first place the national debt is not, I think, held mostly by the rich, though that is a matter about which no one can be certain. In the second place even if it were it would make no difference to the fallacy. For if the national debt had not been raised, its holders would presumably have invested their money in other directions – such as home industry, foreign railways, foreign bonds, etc. – from which they would have derived an equal and perhaps greater income, without being taxed in order to provide it. As it is a certain amount of their own tax money is paid back to them in interest. By the other system they would have got interest and profits not out of their own pockets but somebody else's.

On the whole, then, we may conclude that the International Chamber was right, at least with regard to England, in including high taxation as a cause of bad trade, and that its effects by damping the spirits of the organizers and drying up the sources of charity and capital have adverse effects on those whom the advocates of Robin Hood legislation want to help.

On this subject the Colwyn Committee throws interesting light, in its report on National Debt and Taxation. While justly condemning the old distribution of taxation, which laid nearly the whole burden on the necessaries of life, it admits that 'under it industry advanced enormously, and the standard of living improved for the whole community more than in any comparable period.'[1]

What we want now is another enormous advance in industry and another great improvement in the standard of living for the whole community, especially that part of it whose standard needs improvement. We cannot get those things if we take all the heart out of those who have to plan and lead the movement. In the words of that much-quoted passage from the Report on Taxation issued by the General Federation of Trade Unions in March 1930, 'It is foolish to expect that the social improvements for many millions can continuously be paid for by exactions from the wealth of a few thousands.'

Nevertheless, even if we conclude that our taxation has been based too much on the Robin Hood principle, it does not necessarily follow that we are, as a nation, overtaxed, but only that our taxation has been ill arranged. It was shown on page 340 how fast the proportion that direct taxation provides of our revenue has grown in the past century. If we reversed that process and relieved direct taxation, in view of its adverse effects on the community, by getting more revenue from indirect taxation, whether by import duties or excise duties or both, then we could raise

[1] *Colwyn Report*, p. 241.

more money from those who are benefiting by the fall in the cost of living and so would hardly feel the pinch, if at all – especially if a Consumers' Council were successfully controlling the extent of intermediate profits made by dealers and middlemen and retailers.

TOO MUCH ROBIN HOOD

CHAPTER XXI

REPARATIONS AND WAR DEBTS

The Indemnity Principle – Its Soundness – Its Practical Disadvantages – To All Parties – Ally Debts – England's Position – Her Settlement with America – Unreasonable Criticisms – Revision 'in the Air.'

THAT a victorious nation or group of nations should fine the vanquished at the end of a war is a practice recognized by custom. The justice of it can only be unquestioned if not only the conquerors, but all neutral observers are convinced that the vanquished began the war and began it without due cause. But the principle is generally recognized and was carried out by Germany when she imposed an indemnity of £200,000,000 – then thought to be a staggering sum – on France in 1871.

Sir Norman Angell in his well-known work, *The Great Illusion*, showed reasons for thinking that the receipt of this huge sum had done Germany more harm than good. His arguments were not universally accepted but he went a long way towards showing that war does not pay even the victor; and many people who endorsed his view thought that since war did not pay, there would not be any more war. But Mr. H. G. Wells aptly pointed out that men do plenty of things, such as falling in love, which do not pay. When nations are in a sufficiently bad temper or are convinced that their honour or rights are threatened, the thought of possible monetary loss has never yet stopped them from fighting.

Nevertheless it may have some effect in the early stages of a quarrel; and if the possibility of having to pay a huge amount, if vanquished, may have any effect in making nations think twice about going to war, it is worth while to maintain the principle, that the conquered must pay.

From the business point of view, however, the payment of indemnities on the modern scale is a nuisance to all concerned, because of the disturbance that they involve to the ordinary course of trade; and there can be no doubt that those people are right who contend that the German indemnity payments have been one of the causes of trade difficulties in recent years.

These payments involve disturbance because they are not made in discharge of an ordinary debt. Normally, when a country has to make payments abroad, it is either because it has been buying goods and services from other countries, or because it has borrowed from other countries money which has enabled it to equip itself with machinery, or with railways, harbours and other means of transport, which help it to produce goods more easily for export and for home consumption.

But when a country is told by its conquerors that it has to pay so much a year by way of fine for having lost a war, there has been no such preceding benefit to make the payment easy – on the contrary the payment is enforced at a time when, from the nature of the case, the paying country has been exhausted by war and dispirited by conquest.

355

'*Væ victis!*' you may say with Brennus the Gaul. 'It is the risk that those take who go to war; and this risk has to be kept real, as a reminder to those inclined to be warlike. Germany is only taking the medicine that she administered to France in '71, and would have made the Allies swallow in enormous doses if she, and not they, had dictated terms after 1918.' All which is quite true, but now let us look at the other side of the picture and see how the payment of war indemnity affects the countries that receive it.

Under the Young Plan of 1929 Germany had to pay until 1965 a yearly sum that averages about £100,000,000 a year over the period, and for 1930-1 was £85,500,000; after 1965 the payment was to fall to £80,000,000 and remain near that point till 1985, when it drops to about £45,000,000, ceasing altogether in 1988. France, as the country that suffered most, was to take the chief share, followed by the British Empire, Italy and Belgium and the other Allies. For 1931, for example, France was to have £42,000,000, the British Empire £18,000,000, Italy £9,500,000, Belgium £5,000,000, and others smaller sums.[1]

At first sight it would seem that these arrangements ought to be quite comfortable for the creditors. France, Italy, Belgium and England, receiving these sums from Germany, are enabled to that extent to meet the expense of Government (or of their debts to America) without calling on their tax-payers. If the German payments are sent directly to the creditors in the form of goods, the populations of the creditor countries have all the more goods to consume. Or again if the process

[1] *Economist*, 3rd August 1929.

is roundabout and Germany sends textiles to Argentina and tells Argentina to pay the money to the creditors, then Argentina sends us wheat and meat in payment. These goods come in for nothing and are sold, in effect, for the receiving Government which uses the money to relieve the tax-payer. Could anything be pleasanter?

But it often happens in business affairs that arrangements that look pleasant have awkward consequences. Just as a great increase in man's power to make and grow things has made man look ridiculous by reducing him to poverty and distress when he ought to be growing fat and happy; just as machinery, which ought to make life easier, gives us an unemployment problem because we have not found out how to make the necessary adjustments; so getting things for nothing, which to an individual or family is so comfortable a cause of well-being if a sensible use is made of it, may be a cause of real inconvenience to a nation, or at least to certain sections of it.

As tax-payers we in England were all relieved to the extent of something like £20,000,000 a year that we should, if it were not for the war indemnity, have to pay to America. But to the extent of the whole £100,000,000 a year that Germany had to pay to all her war creditors, Germany was less able to buy British and other foreign goods; and so those British industries that used to send goods to Germany were hampered by the impoverishment of a good customer; and at the same time all the trades that compete with Germany in neutral markets were hampered by the need imposed on her to sell goods abroad in order to make the indemnity payments.

Inter-Ally debts incurred for the purpose of carrying on the war have much the same effects on payer and receiver, as a war indemnity. The money was lent not to fertilize the borrowers' land and industry, but to be shot away in shells or eaten by men who were busy on the work of destruction; and the payment of the interest, while relieving the tax-payers of the creditor countries, is likely to make it more difficult for some of their industrialists and workers to earn profits and wages.

From all which we are forced to the obviously absurd but partially true conclusion that it does not pay a nation to be paid a debt. It ought not to be true, but there is some truth in it, and this is only so because we have not yet begun to try to solve the problem of making use of benefits that relieve us of the need for working – such as improved methods that make goods plentiful and receipts on account of reparations. Any man or family that is enabled to supply its needs with less work either by working more easily and well, or by receiving an addition to its income by debt payments, either enjoys more leisure and lives more comfortably or continues its rate of work and grows rich more rapidly. But when such things happen to a nation it is apt to find that the benefit to tax-payers is balanced, perhaps more than balanced, by loss inflicted on industry. And so the cry goes up, 'Keep out these goods that compete with ours unfairly, and lower our standard of life.' When this policy is carried out, the debtor is justified in asking how he is to pay if the creditors refuse to receive goods in payment. It is a difficult tangle, and shows once again that the effect of war from a business point of view is an unmitigated nuisance.

It is all the more difficult because the chief creditor in this case, the United States, is strictly Protectionist and keeps other people's goods out as far as possible. And so Americans have to come to Europe and spend there the money that Europe owes to them, as we saw in Chapter XII, from a study of America's trade balance.[1] Nevertheless, even America is beginning to find that getting goods, whether imported or supplied abroad, for nothing, raises difficulties for its export trade. To the extent that money has to come from Europe to America in payment of war debts, Europe is less able to buy America's automobiles, typewriters, harvesting machinery, wheat and cotton; and those who make or grow these goods are said to be inclined to listen to those who tell them that a revision of the reparations and war debt problems would enable them to do better business.

Nevertheless, it is easy to exaggerate the effects of these payments on world trade and prosperity. Partly owing to the monstrous promises that were held out at the end of 1918 by the Coalition Government in England and other bodies that ought to have known better, about the huge sums that were to be extracted from Germany, the notion that Germany cannot possibly pay what is asked of her has become an article of almost passionate conviction in the minds of some people. No one could possibly know how much an industrious and scientific people could pay, if all the world were busy and friendly and ready and able to buy goods across the frontier, and if international trade were allowed to grow as it might if the nations

[1] See *ante*, p. 205.

could learn to be sensible and good tempered. But ever since an indemnity has been talked of, the assumption has been popular in some quarters, that whatever its amount might be, it was more than Germany could pay.

Under this influence the Dawes Reparations Settlement, which Germany was punctually and successfully carrying out, though largely by means of borrowing abroad, was replaced by the Young Plan, which reduced the annual payment from £125,000,000 to an average of £100,000,000 as noted above. Under existing conditions, with all the world impoverished by plenty, and putting up high tariffs against imports, Germany's task has certainly been made much more difficult; and the fall in prices which makes it harder for all debtors to pay their debts, because they have to sell more goods or services in order to do so,[1] adds to this difficulty, though not so much as it seems to do at first sight. Because Germany imports, as does England, food and materials and exports manufactured goods; and the prices of food and materials have fallen much more heavily than those of finished articles. If German cotton and woollen goods fetch less than they did two years ago she buys her raw cotton and wool to much greater advantage, so that the fall in prices is by no means all dead loss to her as a manufacturing debtor.

If we look at Germany's obligation side by side with the total of world trade, it looks much less formidable. World trade, as estimated by the Economic and Financial Section of the League of Nations, amounted to $66,708,000,000, or £13,341,500,000 in 1928, having increased by $1,660,000,000, or £332,000,000

[1] See *ante*, p. 214.

over the previous year's.[1] So that the mere increase in one year would have absorbed Germany's average payment three times over.

As far as England is concerned, this question of reparations and war debts has no direct effect, though the quickened competition of Germany in neutral markets may be awkward for some of our industries. What we collect from Germany and our Allies we hand over to America, keeping a small margin. A great deal of nonsense has been and is talked about this matter of our debt to America; and Mr. Baldwin has been and is most unjustly accused of having laid an intolerable burden on us by the settlement that he made in 1923 with our American creditor. Mr. Bonar Law is reported to have said that it would cripple us for two generations;[2] and too many people in England believe that the Americans are bleeding us white by exacting payment of what was due, which by the way they did not do.

In answer to a question in the House of Commons, the Chancellor of the Exchequer stated at the end of January 1931 that during the financial year 1931-32 England should collect on account of reparations and war debts £33,350,000 from Germany and from our Ally debtors, and the amount payable to America would be £32,864,000;[3] so that this intolerable burden in fact weighs rather less than nothing. As to the statement that Mr. Baldwin might have made a much better settlement if he had haggled, there is plenty of

[1] Memorandum on Production and Trade, 1923-1928-9, Geneva, June 1930.
[2] See *The Dupe as Hero*, by Logistes, p. 12.
[3] *The Times*, 30th January 1931.

evidence to the contrary – for example a letter in *The
Times* of 20th January 1931 from Sir Robert Horne,
who was in America at the time when the settlement
was made. But the composition that we made was not
a bad one from the point of view of a debtor accustomed
to pay debts in full. We owed the Americans more than
£900,000,000, payable on demand, with interest at
5 per cent., and they reduced the rate of interest to
3 per cent. till 1932 and 3½ per cent. thereafter – a
pretty handsome concession.

It is true that they made compositions with France
and Italy which were much more generous; but they
worked on the principle of settling in accordance with
the debtors' capacity to pay. It is possible that they
underestimated the capacity of Italy and France, but
if so that mistake makes no difference to the equity of
their arrangement with us, which left us, as shown, in
the position of brokers between our debtors and creditors, passing on what we receive and retaining a small
margin in consideration of payments made in the past.

All this question of war debts has been embittered by
stupid exaggerations and misunderstandings. Many
Englishmen think that the Americans have been too
greedy because they lent money to us which we passed
on to our Allies and with which they bought America's
goods and foodstuffs at enormous prices; and that
America ought to have wiped out the debt incurred in
a cause for which we and they were fighting. And
many more Frenchmen think the same about America
and are still more bitter against England because she
made a separate settlement with America instead of
waiting for a grand general debt composition.

All this bitterness seems to me to be entirely stupid. It is absurd to pretend that America was as closely interested in the result of the war as we were: if they charged us high prices we and Europe had made the prices high by going to war and flooding the world with paper money; and when the American Army came across it is safe to assume that it was charged full prices for any goods and services supplied by England and France.

As to the French grievance against us – that we settled without waiting for them – we had no choice. The Americans, knowing that we were in a position to settle, and that France, with her devastated area to mend, was not, called on us to come and settle like honest debtors. It was at that time very necessary that something should be done to recall the world to common sense in business matters and to remind it that contracts must be carried out, if business is to be possible and mankind is to be fed. Our debts settlement was one of the influences that helped to restore the world to a certain degree of sanity.

And when the Americans, in considering hints from the Continent, that all debts between brothers in arms should be cancelled, wonder whether any generosity of that kind, if carried out by them, would not only encourage European nations to waste the money so saved on preparations for another war, they have a good deal of reason on their side.

It is certainly true that America is open to plenty of criticism concerning the uses that she has made of her war-created wealth. She has led the world in the race to build up the most obstructive tariff walls, to blow up the most monstrous bubble of speculation, and to burst it with the most resounding and disastrous explosion, followed by deep and long-drawn depression, which still (in 1931) infects other countries with its shivering palsy. These were natural ebullitions on the part of a race of enthusiasts intoxicated by a sudden access of power and opulence, and it might easily be argued that the sudden transfer of wealth and money power to America, through the war, and the bad use that she has made of them, are the most important cause of the present crisis. But even if this be so, we come back to the war as the real cause of the trouble; for if America had won her power – as she would have if there had been no war – slowly and gradually and through ordinary developments of trade and finance, she would have learnt, in the process of winning it, how to use it for her own benefit and other peoples'.

But in the matter of war debts, she has treated her brothers in arms with at least as much generosity as was good for them.

Nevertheless, revision of reparations and of war debts is in the air. The German Government issued on 6th June 1931 a manifesto urging that 'the economic situation of the Reich inevitably compels the relief of Germany from the intolerable reparations obligation';[1] and in other countries it is more and more generally recognized that, as shown in the earlier part of this chapter, they warp the natural course of trade in a way that is bad both for debtors and for creditors.

Some people who are anxious about the security of contracts and argue, very truly, that if bargains are

[1] *The Times*, 8th June 1931.

364

not carried out the whole basis of business is undermined, deplore this tendency. But if revision is carried out it will have at least two satisfactory results. It will clear obstacles out of the way of trade recovery, and it will also make it much more difficult for any country that is at war to borrow from its neighbours.

And if, as has been hinted as possible, the United States make European disarmament a condition of war debt revision, we can add another advantage to the list.

Postscript. – Since this chapter was sent to be printed the question of revision has been brought to the very front of the stage by Mr. Hoover's announcement, on 20th June 1931, of the American Government's proposal for the postponement, during one year, of all payments, both of interest and principal, on inter-Governmental debts.

This complete reversal of American policy had, apparently, been caused by the very serious position to which Germany had been reduced and the very serious effects that it was having and threatening on American banking and trade. The shock to the confidence of investors in Germany, produced by the Hitler election of September 1930, has already been noted on p. 323. It was followed by a flight from the mark on the part of Germans and by rapid withdrawals of credit from Germany by foreign, especially French and American, banks and money-lenders. French withdrawals were quickened by irritation caused by Austro-German customs proposal (see *ante*, p. 265), the pocket-battleship and other political influences. The 'run on Germany' was thus largely political in origin, but it inevitably awoke financial fears which made its effects more terrifying. In a statement reported in *The Times* of 8th July, Herr Dietrich, the German Finance Minister, said that the losses suffered by the German economic system since the extremist elections of last September had amounted to between £150,000,000 and £200,000,000 worth of foreign exchange – more than double the Reparations charge for a year. (Incidentally, the fact that Germany was able to pay Reparations and meet such a run, in a time of acute trade depression, seems to confirm the contention of those who consider that the Reparations charge, by itself, need not have been too heavy in normal times.)

Mr. Hoover's proposal was rightly hailed as a statesmanlike measure of relief; but objections and hesitations, very natural from the French point of view, on the part of France prevented its immediate adoption; and so the run on Germany went on and the French bankers, who also had domestic troubles to alarm them, began to be anxious about their balances in London, which, they believed, London had lent to Germany, whom they themselves had helped to reduce to the verge of bankruptcy; and so they and other Continental operators took £30,000,000 in gold from the Bank of England in two weeks.

This incident shows once more how political bitterness and bad feeling are at the root of most of the world's present troubles. It had one satisfactory result, the action of the Bank of France and the Federal Reserve Bank of New York in arranging a £50,000,000 credit for the Bank of England.

CHAPTER XXII

IF WE HAD PEACE AND GOOD TEMPER

Hopes and Fears – Business Advantages on the Side of Sanity – A World Despot – Saving on Armaments – Cleaning up the World – An Easier Life – Freer Trade – Universal Money – Levelling up the Standard.

FROM what we have seen already it is clear that the future is bright with brilliant hopes, clouded by dire and disgusting possibilities.

If all the nations and all the people who compose them could be induced to behave reasonably and with due consideration for one another's difficulties, what a series of record scores we could make in this wealth-creating game, and how much fuller we could fill that pool out of which we all draw, to the limit of the money that we earn or receive, what we need in goods and services!

Instead of which the nations snarl and growl at one another across the frontiers and put all possible difficulties in the way of goods and people that want to cross them. I can remember the time when one could travel over Europe (except Russia) without needing a passport. Now I am not even allowed to go out of my own country without the permission of somebody in Whitehall, granted only after I have wasted hours in being photographed and filling up exasperating forms.

Behind the scenes, we are told, scientists are busy perfecting weapons of destruction and poison gases that will wipe out whole populations when next the world displays its intelligence and skill in the art of mutual slaughter; and the front of the stage is crowded with chatterers accusing the wage-earners of being greedy because they want a better share of life's benefits, and the employers and managers of being bloodsuckers because they want to earn a profit for themselves and the shareholders for whom they work, and the capitalists of being extortionate parasites because they want to receive some payment for the use of their property. And all this chatter induces a few of each class to believe what is said about the others, and consequently to bicker and quarrel, making everybody's share smaller. Whereas if they all recognized that the other fellow's point of view is reasonable and got together to try and make a bigger and better cake to be cut up among them, there would be more than enough for everybody.

Here then we have the two dangers that may hold up material progress – international bad temper that may, if violent enough, wreck our whole civilization; and bad temper between the dividers of the dividend that may, if bitter enough, give us a dwindling and meagre dividend to be shared.

Success in avoiding these dangers can only be secured by getting a sufficient number of the men and women of the world into a reasonable frame of mind, supplying them with the necessary information and advice, to be furnished by economists who have no theoretical or political axe to grind, and can say what they mean in plain language, and then telling the Governments to get to work and do things, or, more often, to stand aside and not meddle. But where could we find such economists? I can think only of three (and one of them is dubious) who are according to specification. And how long will it take before the gift of seeing the other fellow's point of view will be general enough to make material progress easy?

In the meantime there is plenty of reason for hope, because the possibilities are so alluring and the advantages to all of making use of them are so obvious. We have seen that most of the evils that have lately beset us have been owing to an immense increase in the power of mankind to make and grow the good things which we want, combined with the failure to absorb and distribute the stocks of goods that science and organization have let loose upon us. We have proved the power of the world to provide its inhabitants with a much higher degree of comfort; and it is to every-body's advantage, from a strictly business point of view, that this increased power of production, instead of causing dislocation and distress, should be matched by the necessary increase in consumption, so that the wheels of commerce and exchange should all spin merrily and harmoniously.

We saw also that the modern system of mass produc-tion – turning out an immense quantity of goods and articles very cheaply – needs for its success a general public with plenty of money in its pocket so that the mass-produced stuff can be sold quickly. This means to say that it is to the interest of Big Business – that is, those who control finance and industry – that those who do the dull mechanical and book-keeping work, the wage-earners and the small salary earners, shall be able to have an increasing share of the world's buying power – in other words, that the inequalities of wealth which are such an ugly blot on our civilization as it is, shall be gradually ironed out by a growth in the buying power of the least fortunate.

It was also clear that what is perhaps the most terrible of our recent evils – the number of people in all the chief countries who want to work and cannot find work to do – is partly due to the efficiency of machinery. Both in agriculture and in industry the mechanical slave has been working so well for us that the human hand-worker and even the human calculator have found that they were not so much wanted. And this change, that ought to have lightened human labour and made life easier and more comfortable, has blighted our business life with the problem of unemployment. Here again we have turned a blessing into a curse because we do not know how to use it. But there must be a way round.

Thinking about what might happen if something impossible befell is generally an unprofitable pastime, but it sometimes helps to clear one's mind. Let us consider for a minute how the world's business would be affected if the whole of it were ruled by a benevolent despot. He would, of course, abolish all the armies and navies and air forces that the nations now maintain, and have a small well-equipped police to keep the peace on land and sea and above the clouds.

Mr. Hoover, in an address delivered to the International Chamber of Commerce in May 1931, told the

370

world that it was then spending nearly £1,000,000,000 a year on armaments. Giving our supposed despot a good round sum to spend on his police, we should still secure a saving of something like £500,000,000 or £600,000,000 a year, which could be applied by the nations to the general work of reconstruction that is so necessary for them all – cleaning out slums, rebuilding a large part of nearly every town that stands anywhere, making new railways, harbours, roads, giving light, water and drainage to country villages, and generally furbishing up town and country; together with this spring-cleaning job that so clamorously needs doing but is not done because it might not pay anybody to do it, the nations could set about giving the young generation a chance of growing up better than their fathers and mothers, by giving them a real education, mental, bodily, and manual, and especially in the art, which they would learn chiefly from one another, of living healthily, happily and pleasantly together.

These are only preliminary indications of what might be done if we could afford it. There are plenty of other things to follow; but these two general measures, and the immense amount of work and equipment that they would involve, show us that we need not continue to be haunted by the ridiculous fear that there is not enough work to do to keep every one busy who can work, in spite of the activity of the mechanical slave.

But if we are wrong about this, and there is not really enough work to do to keep us busy, is this a position that ought to terrify us? Ought not it to encourage us to throw up our hats in thanksgiving and begin to lead civilized lives in which we have more leisure to amuse ourselves and 'fleet the time carelessly'?

And here we get into a virtuous circle because a general shortening of working hours would mean a great increase in the demand for goods and services. The less we all work the more work we shall want and the more easily we shall drive that unemployment bogey off the map. For it is while we are at leisure that we are active consumers and set other people to work to meet our demands for the innumerable things that we need for amusement.

Viewed as a world problem, unemployment can best be cured by shortening hours of work all round and teaching us how to make good use of leisure, an art of which we are most of us amazingly ignorant.

'But what is the use,' the practical critic naturally inquires, 'of dreaming these Utopian dreams when there is no chance of a benevolent world despot?'

And quite rightly. Nevertheless there is a chance that the millions of money and horse-power expended on armaments may be greatly reduced as mankind becomes more civilized. Locarno and the Kellogg Pact and all the other efforts of statesmen to arrive at more reasonable ways of settling international difficulties have meant something; and a still more hopeful sign is the fact that war is becoming more and more a job for what schoolboys call 'smugs.'

Good soldiering in the future will no longer be the amusement of the strong and handsome heroes so gloriously drawn for us by Lever and Ouida, the 'careless clean-built Army men,' who sport and flirt in Kipling's pages, but the very serious occupation of highbrow mathematicians and scientists commanding highly-skilled mechanics. Every cavalry regiment that is mechanized into a tank corps makes an army less attractive, in the eyes of a population that has a healthy prejudice in favour of athletic magnificence.

When war was a test of physical courage and endurance there was much to be said for it as a means of settling disputes. For victory then went to those peoples that contained the largest number of fine, strong, brave men. Now that it is to be decided by skill in the laboratory war loses all its sentimental and most of its practical appeal, and may be put on the scrap heap sooner than we think.

Other consequences of the union of the world under one beneficent ruler – if I may be allowed to waste a page or two more on this phantasy – would be (1) a general reduction, if not abolition, of trade barriers between the nations now converted into provinces, and (2) a universal money issued by a world central bank. There would also be (3) the advantage that legal regulation of hours of labour and wages could be applied all round.

Import duties would not necessarily be abolished, for the provinces would need revenue, and it was shown in Chapter XIV that such duties have advantages, both to Governments and to taxpayers, over other forms of taxation.[1] For this purpose, the more goods that come in the more revenue is collected; and duties would be arranged at such a level that goods would come in freely – instead of being designed as they often are now to keep goods out. This change

---

[1] See *ante*, p. 237.

would have to be carried out very slowly and gradually, for it would involve, perhaps, a good deal of shifting of industry, such as has lately been seen in America, where cotton manufacturing has been moving from New England to the south. Such movements cause local distress; and though they are more than compensated by the general advantage, they must happen slowly so as to give time for the necessary adjustments. The consequence would be that goods would be made and grown where the natural conditions are most favourable and the skill of the population is most advantageous. There would be little or no interference with their free exchange and their quantity and quality would be immensely increased and improved. 'How,' it may be asked, 'would it fare with those parts of the world which did not possess these natural advantages? Would not universal freer trade be bad for them because they could not compete?'

The worst that could happen to them would be that they would be no better off than they are now, because, being unable to sell abroad, they would not be able to partake of the big freer trade feast. In this case it seems probable that in the better conditions of international intercourse and travel that would prevail, their inhabitants would tend to migrate to more favoured spots. But nearly every district has some quality that makes it good to live in or at least to visit; and so those parts of the world that have least advantages for growing and making things would be attractive to those who like a peaceful open country and would come there to spend the wealth earned where wealth is most easily got, and so to create a demand for services that can only be rendered on the spot. For instance, the rural parts of England, still unable to compete with the wheat of Canada and the wool of Australia, would be kept full and busy and made more beautiful than ever, as a park and pleasure ground and garden for those who draw wealth from industry at home and agriculture abroad; and as a supplier of prime English beef and South Down mutton, and fresh fruit and vegetables, to many who now have to be content with chilled meat and tinned foods.

With a universal money there would no longer be the nuisance of difficulties inflicted on trade by the efforts of central banks to maintain gold stocks, under the delusion that a huge heap of gold is a sign of financial strength; it would be much easier for a single central authority to do all that can be done, by regulating the supply of money, to keep the price-level steady;[1] and the abolition of war, and the complete confidence in which business would consequently work, would eliminate one of the risks that entitle the capitalist to a high rate for the use of his money. For we are assuming, of course, that there is no doubt about the strength and staying power of the despot. Money would thus be plentiful and cheap and all debts – war debts, public debts and private debts – would quickly be either paid off or converted to lower rates of interest. Solon's *seisachtheia*[2] – throwing off of burdens – would happen, not as a revolutionary measure, but in the course of ordinary business.

Of the third consequence of a world despotism – the

---

[1] See *ante*, p. 88 *et seq.*, 292 *et seq.*
[2] See Grote's *History of Greece*, Part II, Chapter XI.

all-round application of regulations of hours and wages –
the effect would be that the efforts of the workers in
certain countries to improve their lot would not be
continually hampered by backward conditions elsewhere. No benevolent despot would tolerate the
exploitation of the backward races in the interest of
exaggerated profit for 'advanced' exploiters. And here
again a virtuous circle would be established, because a
general increase in wages and leisure would quicken
the demand for goods and services.

But this question of the different standards prevalent
in different countries is so difficult and real that it is
high time to wake up. The dream in which we have
indulged has shown us how much better off we should
be if we had better international temper, less costly
armaments, freer trade and more co-operation in
money matters.

CHAPTER XXIII

ENGLAND'S SPECIAL PROBLEMS

Fiscal Policy – Should She lend Capital Abroad? – Cheapening Manufactured Goods – By All - round Sacrifice – England's Strength – Her Industrial Difficulties – The Weight of Taxation – The Maintenance of the Standard – America's Example – The Full Use of Machinery.

So much for what the world might do for itself if it learnt to keep its temper. Now let us try to think what England might do to help herself round a bad corner and to restore the prosperity of other countries which have helped her to prosper in the past.

Apart from the question of good temper, which she can only promote by showing it, the chief causes of the world's, and her, present distresses have been shown to be: (1) stiff tariffs; (2) a diminished flow of international capital; and (3) the relative dearness of manufactured and retail goods as compared with raw materials. But she has her own special problems in (4) the relatively high standard of life of her wage-earners; and (5) the terrific weight of direct taxation which, as was shown in Chapter XX, sucks capital out of industry and the heart out of its organizers.

If, out of the welter of political chaos and the discredit into which Parliamentary Government has fallen, we could produce a real ruler with the confidence of all parties and classes, what could he do for us?

Looking first at the world problems, he would see that nothing that he can do about his own country's fiscal policy would have much effect in checking the tendency (now said to be wilting) of the world in general to raise tariff walls. Free Traders would tell him that any reaction on England's part towards Protection would have quite fatal effects in confirming other countries in a disastrous delusion. Protectionists would tell him that the one hope for freer trade between the nations would be a determination shown by England to protect her home market and refuse to be any longer the dumping ground of the world. Allowing these contrary counsels to cancel one another out, he would be guided in this matter by what he believed to be best for his own country. As to which, he would reserve his opinion until he had looked at other aspects of the problem.

In the matter of the international capital market his responsibility would be much graver, for England, except in the few after-war years, when America took the lead as foreign lender, has for a century been the chief lender to other countries. Would he do his best to keep the outward flow of British capital at an attenuated trickle, or would he advise us to help our export industries by lending freely abroad?

Here again he would have a multiplicity of counsels to choose from. He could cite Mr. Keynes in favour of either course. If he acted on the sentence quoted on page 323, he would tell us, that since the whole course of trade depends on a steady flow of lending, and since

England depends on the course of trade for prosperity, one thing that we can all do to help our country is to save and lend abroad. But if he looked further into Mr. Keynes' speech he would find him talking about the 'ultra-cautious attitude of your own board towards foreign bonds,' and saying that 'from our own individual standpoint it is a wise and necessary precaution. Yet from another point of view it is absolutely the opposite of what is needed to put things right. For *someone* must lend to these countries if a catastrophe is to be avoided. Nevertheless our own policy coincides, I think, with the interests of this country. For it is not any holding back on our part which has caused the trouble. Indeed, quite the contrary. London's difficulties have been due to her efforts – experienced and considerate creditor that she is – to save the position by carrying more of the responsibilities of the creditor countries as a whole than properly belongs to her. Now we, too, are feeling that we must sit back until someone else takes up the running.'[1]

One can imagine our ruler thinking that it was not by sitting back and waiting for someone else that England built up her great and beneficent strength as a world lender, and that London's difficulties are less important than those of our export trades, hampered by the lessened flow of our lending abroad. Nevertheless he would feel terribly puzzled. Will America or France take up the running, and if not will not the catastrophe that Mr. Keynes foresees have dire effects on England, both as world trader and general creditor?

On the whole our ruler might most probably think

[1] *The Times*, 29th January 1931.

Mr. Keynes' demonstration of the necessity of lending abroad more convincing than his suggestion that we should suspend it and would urge us, and help us by any fiscal changes that would make saving easier, to save and lend abroad.

Touching the slower decline in the prices of manufactured goods than in those of food and materials, he would see that this lopsided movement can be corrected either by getting food and material prices up, or bringing down those of manufactured articles. Since large sums have been lent to the primary producers on the basis of higher prices for their goods, it would evidently be fairer to them, and safer for their creditors, if we could work a recovery in the index number of commodity prices. If, for example, wheat and wool could be brought back to the level of 1924 or thereabouts, Australia's difficulties would be greatly lightened and her creditors would feel more comfortable. This recovery in wholesale prices in the world market can only be secured by a general restoration of confidence and activity. England can do something towards this by freer lending; but another important thing that she can do to help both herself and world trade, is to stimulate her own activity as producer and consumer, so that she offers a better market for food and materials.

How is this to be done? By a general sacrifice and a general cutting down of wages, salaries, unemployment benefits, fees and taxes, so that cost of production is lowered and manufactured goods can be sold cheaper? In this way, at least, part of the hardship inflicted on primary producers who have to sell cheap and buy relatively dear, would be reduced. And this is a method by which many advisers would recommend our ruler to approach the problem. Or would he see that in this way lie great difficulties because the wage-earners would bitterly resent what they would believe to be an attack on the standard of life, to win which they have struggled successfully for a century? He might be convinced that their real standard would be improved, through lower wages accompanied by greater all-round cheapness; but would he convince them?

Moreover, he might well think that an all-round sacrifice is not a good way of clearing glutted markets and curing a crisis due to plenty. But what of all those critical voices, foreign and domestic, who would tell him that England is living on her accumulated fat and must stint if she is not to starve?

On this point Mr. Keynes would reassure him, with a definitely stated opinion (given in a broadcast address on unemployment early in January 1931, and printed in the *Listener* of 14th January) that 'we are not inefficient, we are not poor, we are not living on our capital.' On the contrary 'our labour and our plant are enormously more productive than they used to be,' and so 'our national income is going up quite quickly.' And then he gives a few figures – productive output per head probably increased by 10 per cent. since 1924, and by 20 per cent. since pre-war; national income (apart from changes in the value of money) even as recently as 1929 increasing by as much as £100,000,000 a year (though not, of course, quite so good to-day), having been improving at this rate for a good many years; and at the same time 'we have been quietly carrying through almost a revolution in the distribution of incomes in the direction of equality.'

Mr. Keynes' conviction, that England is still quite alive industrially, was endorsed by Sir Walter Layton, editor of the *Economist*, in an article in the *Revue de Paris* of 1st April 1931, summarized in *The Times* of 31st March. He mentioned that 'our rising standard of living had not in 1929 shown itself to be higher than we could afford, since it was accompanied by increased productivity and an increasing volume of employment.' He also showed that in the collapse of 1930, which he described as a 'transitory phase,' Great Britain, in spite of her dependence on markets which were specially depressed, met the storm with surprising success, being less battered by it than Germany or America.

Let us pass a hearty vote of thanks to these two great economists for giving us these words of cheer at a time when so many, at home and abroad, are preaching funeral sermons over the alleged corpse of England and her industry. But in opposition to Mr. Keynes and Sir Walter, our ruler would hear the voices of industrial leaders in that antiphonal anthem that chairman after chairman at company meetings intones – British wages twice as high as some on the Continent, and considerably higher than most, British rates and taxes the highest in the world, the falling cost of living putting higher real incomes into the pocket of wage-earners, salary-earners and creditors at the expense of employers and shareholders, profits dwindling, ruthless foreign competition in neutral markets and in our unprotected market at home, enterprise fleeced to the skin and shivering in the blast.

He would hear also Sir Robert Horne, an ex-Chancellor of the Exchequer, saying at an Economy Campaign meeting[1] that within the past twelve years the Inland Revenue have collected in the shape of income tax from the public companies of this country approximately £600,000,000 out of moneys put to reserve; that these reserves are the funds which industry requires for providing adequate depreciation of the companies' property and for keeping equipment up to date, buying modern machinery, and launching into all the developments which a progressive business must take up if it is not to stagnate and die; and that the last increase of 6d. in the income tax extracts £6,000,000 more per annum from these precious funds.

From another corner of the choir he would hear Messrs. Maxton and Kirkwood very ably arguing that the way to cure the 'curse of plenty' is a statutory minimum wage to be provided by issues of paper notes. Mr. Maxton gave us a practical example of the effects of ill-distributed buying power. 'Recently,' he said in the House of Commons on 6th February 1931, 'I was visiting some mining villages in Wales. In one house I went into the wash-house, and the people apologized for the fact that there was no wash-hand basin or hot water, because, they said, "You see this is only a miner's house." I have just left my own town of Barrhead, in Scotland, where my intimate friends are practically all engaged in the work of sanitary engineering, making wash-hand basins, baths, water-

[1] Reported in *The Times* of 28th January 1931.

closets and so on. At the present time they are all working short time, and they are just going back to work after the extended Christmas holidays, anxious to make baths, wash-hand basins, and other sanitary equipment. They are also very anxious to get coals for their fires. I leave Barrhead, where my friends are unemployed, because there is no demand for baths and wash-hand basins, and I go to South Wales where I find the miners want wash-hand basins and sanitary equipment, and they are unable to get them. These miners are unemployed, because my engineering friends in Barrhead are unable to buy coal.'

And then there would be the voice of Sir Richard Hopkins, Controller of Finance and Supply Services at the Treasury, telling (on 29th January 1931) the Royal Commission on Unemployment Insurance that the extent to which the Unemployment Fund has to borrow in order to pay unemployment benefit is 'coming to represent in effect State borrowing to relieve current State obligations at the expense of the future, and this is the ordinary and well-recognized sign of an unbalanced budget.' In other words, instead of paying off debt, we are borrowing to pay our way; and Sir Richard further observed we have been critical of foreign countries in the past, and must expect similar criticisms from abroad now – a matter that needs bearing in mind in view of our wide international connexions.

And finally (for the present) he would hear the stern warning of the Chancellor of the Exchequer given to the House of Commons on 11th February 1931 – 'I say with all the seriousness I can command,' were Mr.

Snowden's words, 'that the national position is so grave that drastic and disagreeable measures will have to be taken if Budget equilibrium is to be maintained and if industrial progress is to be made.'

Moreover, sweeping the overseas horizon, he would see Signor Mussolini making a general cut in wages, salaries and fees of workers, government employees, and company directors, retail prices, goods rates on railways, house rents and hotel charges;[1] Germany cutting her Budget by £75,000,000, Japan hers by £30,000,000; America on the other hand faced by a deficit amounting to £180,000,000, and nevertheless passing an Act enabling war veterans to borrow (on the security of the compensation certificates that have been given to them as a reward for services) to an extent that may oblige the Treasury to find £200,000,000.[2]

With these examples before him, how would he feel inclined to act?

Wage reductions he might regard as the last thing to be tackled if they can possibly be avoided. But he would be bothered by that awkward question, whether it is possible for a nation to maintain a standard higher than that of its neighbours, when it has to compete with those neighbours in the markets of the world.

It is clear that a country like Australia, with big debts owed abroad and an income derived largely from the sale abroad of wheat and wool, the price of which depends on the demands of foreign customers, cannot decide for itself how well it is able to live, but, except

---

[1] *The Times* (City article), 5th January 1931.
[2] *Economist*, 4th April 1931, p. 727.

at times when it is able to borrow, has to divide what it gets.

To what extent are we in the same condition? We owe, on balance, no foreign debt, but own a large net holding of foreign debts, obligations and investments. That is one big difference; and though it seems to be in our favour, it has this disadvantage, that it gives us a cushion on which we might sit comfortably for some years and then find that it was wearing very thin and that our seat was not so comfortable. Moreover this cushion does not look as solid as it did with the debtor countries terribly weakened by the fall in prices and threatened with the possibility of a further catastrophe. And the rather precarious position of our shipping industry, which has hitherto brought us an income from foreign customers of £120,000,000 to £150,000,000, has already been noted.[1]

It seems therefore to be clear that if we wish to feel secure about the maintenance of our standard of life, it must not be allowed to prevent our being able to sell goods abroad to a value not far from sufficient to provide us with the food and raw materials that we require to maintain it. In 1930 according to the Annual Commercial Review, published with the *Economist* of 14th February 1931, our retained imports (that is imports that were not re-exported) of food, drink, tobacco, raw materials and articles mainly unmanufactured, had a value of £664,000,000, against £795,000,000 in 1929 and £865,000,000 in 1928, the fall in values being largely due to the fall in prices.

It may be true that if we organized our agriculture,

[1] See *ante*, p. 209.

or could induce our farmers to organize themselves on more businesslike lines, we could grow a larger proportion of our food at home. 'British agriculture,' said Lord Weir in the letter quoted in Chapter III,[1] 'appears to me as a gigantic derelict engineering plant, and to attack it as a whole is impossible and too risky, but to fail to experiment on a substantial scale seems inexcusable. Let me take a typical agricultural area in England, covering, say, 10,000 acres, and view it as a food-production facility or business, the potential products being beef, dairy produce, and pig products. At present it is divided into, say, 40 farms of 250 acres each. What degree of efficiency can be expected from such an organization involving forty managing directors with forty different policies, forty sets of overlapping functions and facilities and no sales or distribution organization? Imagine asking for the safeguarding of such an organization! A demonstration area is urgently required to provide the data for fuller development.' Evidently, here are great possibilities that will need a long time before they can be made into anything else; and the proposals lately put forward by the Government to assist their realization have been bitterly opposed by agricultural interests. In the meantime, to the extent of the food and raw materials that we have to import we are in the same position as Australia and cannot maintain a standard unless we can earn it in the markets of the world in competition with those who are prepared to work harder for less reward (partly, it is suggested, because their wives spend their money for them to better purpose).[2]

---

[1] See *ante*, p. 54.   [2] See *ante*, p. 150.

And quite apart from this dependence, in our case and Australia's, on selling abroad in competition, can any country maintain a high standard in any other way except by successful work, not necessarily for long hours at low pay, but work that is whole-heartedly directed to producing the goods that are wanted? For a time, perhaps, it may keep the general standard high by eating the capital of the very rich. But doubts were expressed, in Chapter XI, as to the real efficiency of this process, and even if it works, it could not work long.

America has lately presented the world with the spectacle of seven or eight years of unexampled prosperity, with high wages and high profits that only failed to produce high contentment because everybody was always wanting more. How was it produced?

It was produced in just the same way as we in England produced our amazing effort during the war, when we sent the best of our manhood to the front or into training and nevertheless not only provided them with equipment and munitions, but (until the U-boats became too effective) gave our general population a higher scale of living than they had ever enjoyed before. We were able to do this because we all, or nearly all, worked as hard and well as we could, and, above all, because we gave machinery a fair chance to work for us, instead of allowing it to be checked by stuffy employers who thought the old ways of doing business were best, and by obstructive trade unionists who thought that more machinery used, meant fewer hands wanted.

America not only gave machinery a chance but encouraged it to work as hard as it could; and the consequence was an immense increase in production, which is the only way in which we can all be made better off. How far the efficiency of the machine inflicted hardship on the human hands that were superseded by it we shall never know exactly; because America had no unemployment insurance and practically no unemployment records. We have to be content with general statements to the effect that the growth of new industries and wants gave a chance to every one who lost a job to get a new one.

There, then, in those prosperous years the problem of creating wealth and consuming it (though not, perhaps, of enjoying it, which is quite another matter) seemed to have been solved by high wages and the utmost possible use of machinery. A New Era had dawned and there was to be no end to progress along these lines. And then the beautiful dawn was swallowed in the earthquake of 1929.

Why did this happen? Because it had been financed in the wrong way – through a Stock Exchange boom. When production increases, it is necessary, unless it is to bring with it all the inconveniences that result from falling prices,[1] that the increase should be accompanied by a roughly corresponding increase in the amount of money available to buy the goods with.[2] That this happened in America appears to be proved by the steadiness of prices there during the years of prosperity. In these years the banks, by advancing and investing, as described in Chapter V, increased the volume of bank deposits, which, as we know, are money on which

[1] See *ante*, p. 284 *et seq.*
[2] See *ante*, p. 80, on the Quantity Theory of Money.

their customers can draw cheques, by more than $19,000,000,000, or £3,800,000,000 – from $34,845,000,000 in 1921,[1] to $53,852,000,000 in 1929.[2] And a great deal of this new money found its way into the pockets of the public through speculating profits made on the Stock Exchanges of the country. Between September 1921 and 1929, the Standard Statistics Company's price index of common stocks spread from 53·18 to 225·3;[3] and as this huge and steady advance went on, all classes in the country were joining in it and making money out of it, as an ever new set of buyers came in to buy stocks at higher prices, in a rise that began to be regarded as part of the scheme of the universe, and as certain as the rising of the sun. These speculative profits were looked on as a regular source of income and were spent as such. And the extent to which the public mind and attention were absorbed in Wall Street's movements can hardly be believed. A friend of mine who visited America at the time when the boom was at its height, went to a rest-cure place somewhere in the South, to look for a business acquaintance whom he had hoped to find in New York, but whom the doctor had ordered to take a change of air. He and the other inmates of the so-called rest-cure were found spending most of their time sitting in luxurious fauteuils before a screen, on which were thrown the latest New York prices.

Financed by the above-mentioned expansion of banking credit, this speculative orgy provided a stream

[1] Statistical Abstract of the U.S., 1928.
[2] Federal Reserve Bulletin, February 1931.
[3] Dept. of Overseas Trade Report on Economic Conditions in the U.S.A., March 1931. Stationery Office.

of fresh buying power, with which and with the development of the system of instalment purchases, the public took the goods as fast as they were turned out and all went well as long as the boom lasted.

But the worst of booms is that they cannot stay beyond a certain point. There comes a day when people begin to wonder whether prices of shares based on profits that are going to be earned some day may not be too high, and when the speculation is as enormous and as nation-wide as it was in America, the consequent revulsion of feeling brings about a fearful crash, followed by long-drawn depression. (As we now see, though I must admit that I believed, at the time, that America's confidence in herself and her future would have enabled her to recover much sooner than she did.) Moreover, this boom had upset the rest of the world by sucking money that was badly wanted elsewhere into America to finance it, and so causing that drying up of the international capital market that has hurt us all so much; and we have also seen that when the crash came, and the boom-fed buying power was cut off, reduced American consumption was an important cause of the fall in commodity prices.

So we must hope that when America sets to work to revive that prosperity of hers, as she surely will, she will base it on some sounder foundation than a stock market gamble. One thing that a wise ruler there – or anywhere else – might do with advantage is to make speculation dear and difficult, and make investment easy, cheap and safe. Because Stock Exchange speculation, though beneficial in some ways,[1] is, in normal

[1] See *ante*, pp 114, 115.

times, emphatically not a pastime for those who cannot afford it; and when they indulge in it they do themselves and everybody else more harm than good.

But because the New Era in America had this fault in its foundation, which toppled it over with a crash which shook the world, it does not follow that it could not have continued happily if more soundly financed – if, for example, the great increase in buying power, necessary to absorb the increasing flow of goods and distribute prosperity, had been provided through credits granted to enterprise of all kinds at home and abroad on more old-fashioned lines – if there had been less blowing out of the balloon of share values and more increase of world prosperity by the continuance and increase of foreign lending, especially if accompanied by a reduction in American import duties or, at least, by a pause in their advance. If America, acting on the principle laid down by Thomas Jefferson, that a creditor must not by tariffs and prohibitions deprive its debtors of the means of payment,[1] had set this example of freer trade to the rest of the world, she might easily have furthered its adoption by stipulations obliging all countries that borrowed from her to make gradual reductions (or at least no further increase) in their tariffs. In this policy American finance would have had the hearty support of the British financial authorities; and these two leaders with their joint power as the chief foreign lenders, might have stayed the process by which international trade was being hampered; and so, of two of the chief evils that have caused the present crisis – growing tariffs and a dried-

---

[1] *Wall Street and Lombard Street*, by F. W. Hirst, p. 160, note.

up flow of international lending – one would have been lessened and the other would never have happened; and the New Era, with a less hectic flush on its cheek and a less bloated flabbiness in its thews and sinews, might have gone from strength to strength, at a slower but surer pace.

CHAPTER XXIV

WHAT A REAL RULER MIGHT DO

Giving Machinery a Chance – Convincing the Wage-earners –
Encouraging Employers – A Revenue Tariff – With Rebate on
Exports – Protecting the Consumer – Abolishing Dole Abuses –
Other Economies – Relief of Direct Taxation – A Sounder
Financial System – Development Schemes – Dealing with Combines – Public Boards.

PONDERING this American example, our British ruler might well feel that there is a good deal to be said for the view expressed by Labour leaders, that cutting wages is a stupid way of curing a crisis due to glut, and would probably only be followed by similar cuts abroad, foiling England's effort and lowering the Continental standard still further; and remembering what he had heard from Mr. Keynes and Sir Walter Layton about the strength and vigour of England's business body, he might agree with Sir Oswald Mosley's contention that 'these suggestions to put the nation in bed on a starvation diet are the suggestions of an old woman in a fright,' and that 'what is needed is a policy of manhood which takes the nation out into the field and builds up its muscles and its constitution in effort.'[1]

But he would also be convinced that high wages can only be paid if they are earned, and that they can

[1] Parliamentary Debates, House of Commons, 12th February 1931.

394

only be earned if, as in America, machinery is given every encouragement to assist man-power and cheapen production, so that the employer and the manager are given a chance of earning a profit for themselves and for shareholders. Wage-earners who want wages as usual and better than usual but will not allow machinery to earn them,[1] are preventing the fulfilment of their own reasonable demand.

To make them see this, they have to be acquainted with the facts, shown the working of cause and effect, and above all be convinced by practical results that they will benefit by abandoning the policy of obstructing machinery. To carry out this missionary work their own leaders are evidently the right apostles, and they might be ready enough to do it if once they were convinced that the object of the ruler was first and foremost the improvement of the wage-earners' lot. The broad aspect of the nation's business needs would be put before us in the periodical messages thereon that he would publish as advised by his committee of economists if he could induce it to give an agreed and comprehensible opinion; the needs and problems of any particular industry would be dealt with by its trade-union leaders, after consultation with the employers and managers, and supplied by the Economic Committee with any theoretical powder and shot that was wanted and relevant facts about conditions in competing countries and so on. This is a boon that the country very seriously needs – information about its business problems expressed in plain language and given on authority that is above all suspicion of political

[1] See *ante*, pp. 60, 61.

or class bias. As it is it is deafened by conflicting clamours.

But the proof of the pudding would be in the eating, and it would have to be shown by practical experience that any hands displaced by machinery would either be wanted elsewhere or at least would not be prevented, owing to displacement, from getting a full share of the increasing wealth that machinery was providing.

Here we have the core of the problem that mankind has to solve, which is, how to adapt itself to a fundamental change in its business arrangements. Hitherto it has provided its material needs by the use of human hands assisted by machinery. Henceforward it will do this job more and more by means of machinery guided by human hands. This change ought to make the job much easier and accomplish it much more successfully. But it is held up and made difficult by the fact that all the ease and success, as things are, tend to be secured by those who own the machinery and direct its use – the employers, managers and shareholders.

A boot factory that doubles its output of boots and halves the number of employees by installing machinery provides – or can provide – the public with cheaper boots and increases the dividends of the shareholders and the commissions paid to managers. What of the men displaced? They may be wanted for the new factory that will be set up by the same or some other management, because the cheapening of boots will make it easier for all of us to have a new pair oftener and so there will be an immense increase in demand. This is an excellent result as long as it lasts. But when everybody has new boots as often as they need them, what next? After that, those displaced from boot-making will have to move on into some other industry, which the variation and growth of human wants will have called into being. There will be the less difficulty about this because whereas in the old days of hand work the skill of a cobbler was wasted when he was asked to become a blacksmith or a weaver, in the days of machinery the skill of machine tending is much more easily transferred from one industry to another, owing to the family likeness that exists between all machines. But this power to move from one job to another has to be accompanied by equal readiness to do so, and here again much missionary work would be necessary before our ruler can secure the necessary spirit in England.

But if we like to look still further ahead and foresee a time when all the material wants of all can be supplied with less human effort, the obvious and very pleasant solution is that all wage-earners will work shorter hours, or fewer days a week; and here again the question of foreign competition will arise and it may not be possible for a nation that has to sell abroad to bring in a change that will, or may, have the effect of raising the cost of production; because the machine can only do its best if it is kept going, as far as possible, continually.

Plenty of solutions of this difficulty will suggest themselves – an obvious one is that the wage-earners should spread the work among themselves by a system of part-time working such as the present crisis has developed. As production increases, with machinery encouraged to work instead of checked, the wage-paying power that its increases involves will not only give the wage-earners more leisure but more money to spend in it, and so incidentally increase the demand for goods or services; because it is while we are amusing our leisure that we need other people to work for us.

In the meantime, and in so far as the pleasant solutions here suggested are made impossible by the stress of foreign competition, there are plenty of jobs into which displaced wage-earners could be shifted. These jobs want doing but are not tackled by industry, as now organized, because they do not appear to be directly profitable to anyone who undertakes them. Such schemes are among the planks of two of our political parties but are held up by lack of money and the alleged opposition of the City. No one can go outside his own door or look out of his window without seeing things that want doing or removing or improving. We are always crowing about our roads and saying that they are the best in the world; but it is difficult to drive or walk far without coming to a railway level crossing or a bad corner or something else that needs abolishing.

We are told that immense efforts have been and are being made, and now and then one sees evidences of patching or even a by-pass under construction or reconstruction. But the amount of effort is pitiful in relation to the number of things that need doing; and besides our bad roads there are items such as water supply in country villages that could keep many heads and hands busy with advantage to the community. Of course there are difficulties – difficulties about housing the workers where they are wanted, perhaps only for a time, and providing their other needs; but these difficulties all mean that work is wanted to be done in order that work may be done. They were solved during the war and they could be solved now if a ruler who meant to do it could call out of the country half the readiness to get things done that it showed when it knew that it was fighting for its life.

In order to do so he has to create the necessary willingness to meet the position not only in the minds of the wage-earners but also in those of the employers and financiers.

As to the employers it is to the bad specimens among them in the past that most of England's industrial difficulties, that are usually attributed to the obstinacy and shortsightedness of trade unions and their leaders, are due. In favour of this view one may cite the evidence, already quoted, of Mr. Stanley Baldwin, whose family, as he has said himself, has been engaged in nearly every branch of the iron trade since the days of one John Baldwin 'of the forge' in the reign of Charles the Second. In a speech to the Engineering and Allied Employers' Association, Mr. Baldwin observed that 'had the employers of past generations all of them dealt fairly with their men there would have been no unions.'[1]

As to the present, we have the evidence of the Balfour Committee presided over by a distinguished and successful industrial leader. On page 298 of its final report it says that '*pari passu* with the enlargement of the business unit and the reconditioning of plant and equipment it is essential that there should be at least an equivalent improvement in the quality of high

[1] *The Times*, 15th January 1931.

399

control. This involves a great change in the attitude of the average business man towards new ideas, and in particular towards the results of scientific research and of higher education.'

This change is rapidly being made, thanks to the pressure of adversity, and the larger rewards now offered by industry than by the professions, which attract into business young men of ability and education who in old times would have gone to the Bar or into the services. Cambridge gives year by year an education in business fact and theory to men who will succeed to posts in industry, well qualified in knowledge and human sympathy to fill them; and the late Lord Melchett's work for co-operation between employer and employed must have helped the growing recognition among the former of the need for a more reasonable attitude towards the ambitions of the workers. Nevertheless progress can be terribly retarded by the inert opposition of the still unenlightened minority; and our ruler's task in securing that improvement in the higher control of industry, demanded by the Balfour Committee, will need all the ingenuity and determination that he can command.

At the same time he can offer certain inducements which would have an immense effect on the atmosphere and state of mind among both the employers and managers of industry, and the financiers and investors who have to provide the necessary capital for reconstruction and development. The first thing that he has to do is to show industry a fair chance of earning a profit by relieving it from some of the disadvantages under which it at present competes with its foreign rivals. These are high wages, trade union restrictions, high taxation, an unprotected home market, and governmental interference of the wrong kind.

If our ruler, as for the present we are supposing, considers that wage reductions and what Sir Oswald Mosley calls a 'starvation diet' are remedies that he will only try when all else has failed, how otherwise can he relieve British industry from its disabilities?

Measures have already been mentioned by which he might overcome trade union opposition to the free use of machinery when once their leaders are convinced that the machines will work for the benefit of the workers. As to the other disadvantages, industry has already been relieved by the late Conservative Government through its Derating Act of 1929 of the unfair incidence of local rates which weighed most heavily on those trades and those districts that were not depressed; but this sound and long overdue reform (marred, when it came, by the blundering way in which relief was given to the overfed as well as to the hungry) has had no chance of showing its good effects, which were smothered under the bad ones of the world crisis.

But in the matter of Imperial taxation, the programme of Protection long advocated by the Conservatives and now admitted to be desirable by many members of the other parties, might evidently be used to put heart and courage into the British industrialist – exposed to every blast of adversity from every quarter – and at the same time to lighten the direct taxation that depletes his reserves, as shown by Sir Robert Horne and 'Tantallon.'[1] Whatever may be thought

---

[1] See *ante*, pp. 383 and 348.

about the theoretical and practical objections to Protection, there can be no doubt that some measure of it, especially if the revenue derived from it were used to relieve direct taxation, and if the interests of the export traders were duly safeguarded, would create a quite different atmosphere in industry and also in the City, as was shown by a short-lived demand for British industrial shares in the autumn of 1930, when City gossip created, and for a few hours believed in, a Coalition Government that was going to make Protection a plank in its programme.

One advantage in a change in fiscal policy designed at once to give some Protection and relieve direct taxation would be that it would have to provide as much revenue as possible, and consequently the duties imposed would have to be both low and general. This would make for simplicity and also would have the inestimable advantage of relieving us from the fear of all the log-rolling and wire-pulling that are involved, when different industries get special treatment, and so all are competing for a specially juicy 'slice of tariff pie.' It would also avoid the formidable complications of the proposal made by Sir Oswald Mosley and the others who signed his manifesto of 6th December 1930. The terrific amount of bureaucratic machinery, and the capricious uncertainties of the kind of Protection proposed by Sir Oswald and his colleagues, were lucidly exposed in an article by Sir Herbert Samuel in the *Nation and Athenæum* of 20th December 1930, as follows:

' "A manufacturer who is given the protection of a tariff," says Sir Oswald, "should submit to a private costing process to ensure that he is not raising prices unduly to the consumer, and also might be asked to give satisfaction that the maximum efficiency was being maintained in the industry." Imagine this idea embodied in an Act of Parliament and applied in practice. There are in Great Britain a quarter of a million separate factories and workshops, producing tens of thousands of articles of every variety of character and of quality. There is to be "a private costing process" to determine the efficiency of the prices that are charged. According to the result of such inquiries the tariffs on foreign imports are to be imposed or removed, raised or lowered. It is unnecessary to discuss this proposal. It is only necessary to state it. The utter impossibility of applying it in practice is obvious.

'There are also to be "Commodity Boards," representing producers from the great industries and consumers of their products. "Your Commodity Board," Sir Oswald says, "would have the power to advise the Minister, under licence, to let in foreign products free in the event of the industry not undertaking proper reorganization to meet the competition at the foreign prices." Here, again, picture the Board in session. Imagine its discussions with regard, not to half a dozen standardized articles, but to hundreds or thousands of separate commodities, the prices probably fluctuating month by month. The duty laid upon it of granting or refusing import licences to foreign producers according as "the industry" did or did not undertake "proper reorganization," would be quite impossible of performance.'

All the schemes in which Protection, in order to

prevent its sheltering inefficiency, is made subject to tests applied before it is granted, seem to be quite unworkable. Who is to judge whether the test has been passed? How long will it take to get a judgment? And what will be the condition of the industry while the question is under debate? And similar objections lie in the way of the suggested bargains, so likely to lead to international and inter-Imperial friction, by which goods from certain countries, that agree to take a certain quantity of British goods, should come in on special terms.[1] If we are to have Protection let us keep it simple and keep it clean.

This can best be done by making it universal on all imports of every kind that come in with a slightly lower level of duties, if that be thought desirable, on British Empire goods. A scheme at once simple and ingenious has lately been mooted by which 10 per cent. should be charged on all goods entering the country with a corresponding bonus of 10 per cent. on all exports, to compensate the export trades for any possible rise in the price of materials, due to the import duty. On the figures of 1930, on the assumption that no imports would be stopped by such a duty, and that the 10 per cent. is in addition to any existing duties, a revenue of £104,000,000 would be derived and a rebate of £66,000,000 would have to be paid to exporters, leaving a balance for tax reductions of £38,000,000. But it seems fairly certain that some goods would be kept out; though the increasing prosperity of the country, if the ruler's other measures were successful in applying the necessary ginger to

---

[1] See above, p. 274.

industry, might have the effect of increasing imports, especially of food and materials; and it is also reasonable to expect that the stimulus given to exports by the rebate would increase their amount and consequently the cost of the rebate.

But it is also evident that to give exporters a 10 per cent. rebate is much more than is necessary to protect them from any possible rise in the price of materials and food owing to the 10 per cent. import duty; because the cost of the material is seldom more than half of the cost of producing any kind of manufactured article. A scheme advocated by Mr. Rupert Trouton in a pamphlet entitled *Unemployment, Its Causes and their Remedies*,[1] seems more sensible from this point of view. He was in favour of a 15 per cent. all-round import duty and a $7\frac{1}{2}$ per cent. rebate on exports, and a bonus to shipping which, according to his estimate, was to cost £5,000,000. By this device, which was blessed by Mr. Keynes in a Foreword, he anticipated, after allowing for administration costs, contraction of imports and expansion of exports, a net revenue of over £85,000,000.

His proposed bonus to shipping was necessitated, according to his argument, because, owing to the bonus on exports, British ships sold abroad could be sold cheaper than those sold to British shipowners. The large net revenue derived from the plan arises, first, from the higher duty imposed on imports as compared with the bonus granted on exports; and secondly, from the fact that, as we saw in examining England's trade balance, our imports are regularly considerably higher in value than our exports of goods.[2]

[1] Published by Messrs. Faber and Faber.   [2] See above, pp. 208 and 209.

Thus the Treasury would continually receive a larger sum in import duties than it would have to pay out on the export bonus to the industries that sell goods abroad.

Against these suggestions it may be argued that anything like a bonus or subsidy on British exports would have a very bad effect abroad, exacerbating the bitterness due to the abandonment of free trade by the proposed imposition of import duties.

How far should our ruler be swayed by this objection? He would recognize that the goodwill of our foreign customers is a valuable asset, but he would also consider that they are on the whole reasonable people, and that they have had plenty of warning, at Geneva and elsewhere, that the tendency of nearly all other nations to raise tariffs against British goods has made it increasingly difficult for England to maintain the open market that served her and them so well in the past, when conditions were different. Since a change in fiscal policy had been forced, as he might fairly contend, on England by the action of other countries, they could have no reasonable ground for criticizing the details of the new system. A world message, explaining and justifying his action in the matter, could make a very strong case, by setting forth the services that England has rendered to the rest of the world in the past by supplying young countries with capital, machinery and immigrants, and by showing that the measures proposed would be likely to make her a better market than ever for foreign goods by increasing her prosperity and purchasing power.

But if the objections to this particular form of stimulating exports were thought to be too strong, it might be replaced by some system of reducing income tax on profits earned by means of exports. Foreign countries which habitually help their exporters by special transport rates and other devices, could make little objection to relief given in this way.

If Protection in this or some other form were adopted, it would be well for any Government that introduced it to see that it did not lead to the exploitation of the poorer consumers by any undue rise in the necessaries of life, such as bread, bacon, tea and sugar. Owing to the relatively high retail prices of these articles a moderate import duty should not necessarily cause any rise in their cost to the consumer; ('the eightpenny loaf,' says Mr. Christopher Turnor in the *Spectator* of 7th February 1931, 'is based upon wheat at 65s. per quarter; to-day wheat is under 30s.') But our ruler would need the help of some measure like the Consumers' Council Bill brought in in 1930 and again in 1931 giving power to the proposed body to inquire into the reason for the high cost of living at a time of low wholesale prices and to take measures, if necessary, to reduce it. The Bill was bitterly opposed by the Conservatives on the ground that it was inquisitorial and would inflict an intolerable nuisance on honest traders; but if its operation were confined to a few of the chief and most necessary articles of consumption, it would allay fears of dear food and show that exploitation of the many was not to be a result of import duties in England. A threat of the possible establishment of governmental or municipal shops, to supply the public with any necessary articles about which private enterprise was proved to be too greedy, might be more efficacious than the proposal, originally part of the scheme, to give the Council power to fix prices, and private enterprise would only have itself to thank, if by its greed it invited such bureaucratic developments, with all their obvious drawbacks. More light on all this question of retail prices is very much wanted. If, as seems likely, shopkeepers are unjustly suspected of rapacity by the public, it is to their interest that the facts should be made known. At a Conference of the National Chamber of Trade, held in May 1931, the Presidential Address referred with regret to statements that had been made, by chairmen of industrial companies and banks, implying that there had been an unnecessary and avoidable delay in the fall of retail prices. 'We cannot,' said the President, 'too strongly emphasize throughout our organization that there is no machinery for the regulation and maintenance of prices.' He admitted that there might be in certain sections of the distributive trade some general understanding as to what should be the current price of certain commodities, but he contended that this did not invalidate the active working of that competition which was one of the most conspicuous features throughout retail distribution. 'The public should remember,' he continued, 'that there were many commodities which the retailer had to handle, the prices of which were fixed by the manufacturers.'[1]

Just so. But surely it is only fair to shopkeepers that we should know more about these arrangements which the public so easily misunderstands; and it is only fair

[1] *The Times*, 5th May 1931.

to the public that in these days of price-holding rings, some public authority should always be watching the interests of consumers and prepared to act, if necessary, on their behalf.

By means of moderate fiscal measures, more or less on the lines indicated by Mr. Trouton, our ruler would find himself with a considerable balance in hand for the relief of taxation and for other purposes; and this balance he could increase by putting a full stop to the abuses of the dole, as enumerated by Sir Alfred Watson, the Government Actuary, in his evidence before the Royal Commission on Unemployment Insurance. The relief of the genuine unemployed, thrown out of work by causes for which they are not remotely responsible, is a form of Government expenditure of which every reasonable tax-payer must heartily approve; but we do not want to subsidize the incomes of women who have left employment in order to marry and gone to live in a place where there is no work of the only kind for which they are qualified (even if they were available for it); or of coal trimmers who work regularly and for very long hours on two or three days in each week during which they earn from £5 to £7 a day; or of professional football players who are paid £6, 10s. a week and are 'unemployed' for four days a week; or of girls and women who have 'a standing job as week-end assistants in stores and have probably been deterred from entering domestic service by the attractiveness of such employment combined with unemployment benefit for the rest of the week'[1] – the inclusion of examples such as these, given by Sir Alfred, not only

[1] *The Times*, 30th January 1931.

costs industry and the contributing workers and the State, money that none of them can afford, but also adds to the general feeling of depression by swelling the unemployment total by the inclusion of people who are no more unemployed than I am.

The saving that would be effected by getting rid of these abuses has been stated by the Chairman of the Commission to be officially estimated at £10,000,000.[1]

Other economies in public administration such as those about to be discovered by a Committee promised by the Government in 1931 would evidently be more easily secured by a ruler (if we could find him) who was not obliged to consider the question of votes, and made it clear to the country that what he meant to do was to give industry a better chance of earning the profits out of which wages, taxation and everybody's income from fees and services ultimately have to come.

With this object in view he would give the first relief that his increased income and diminished outgo made possible to industry by modifying the regulations which govern the payment of income tax by firms and companies on sums allocated to depreciation. Sir Arthur Salter in the second of a pair of interesting articles in *The Times* on what he called our 'frozen trade system,' observed that the present method of assessing income tax makes the scrapping and replacing of plant out of earnings dependent largely upon rules of the taxation authorities as to wear and tear or the minimum life of plant before it may be regarded as obsolete. 'All such rules,' he added, 'tend naturally to lag behind competitive conditions,' and he made the suggestion that a

[1] *The Times*, 27th March 1931.

simple reform, if it were possible, would be to assess income tax not on calculated profits, but on dividends paid.[1]

Relief in this direction is clearly the first thing to be done in any reform of the incidence of income tax, the disastrous effects of which as at present administered were shown by Sir Robert Horne in his speech quoted on page 383.

But more than that has to be done. There can be no doubt that Mr. Snowden's well-meant effort in his Budget of 1930 to put the whole weight of the £47,000,000 of fresh taxation then imposed on the shoulders of the wealthier tax-payers has had a bad effect at home and abroad – an effect which is worse for industry and the wage-earners than for the rich people whom it directly affects. The personal comfort of the latter is hardly affected; but the economies that they have to effect – by closing houses in town and country and so on – increase unemployment; and their diminished saving power helps still further to dry up the capital fund which had already diminished to a trickle. The impression was produced abroad (partly by the too vigorous protests of the Conservative press) that Mr. Snowden was deliberately penalizing capital. What he was trying to do, as he said in his Budget speech, was to lay the burden on the shoulders best able to bear it. But the burden did not stay there. It forced the rich tax-payers either to spend less or invest less and, whichever they did, so to increase unemployment; and it frightened foreigners who had balances in England, causing them to withdraw them and so increase a drain

[1] *The Times*, 9th December 1930.

of gold which affected the City's nerves, depressed the price of securities and deepened the atmosphere of gloom, mistrust and bad temper, which is fatal to the filling of the pool of wealth.

To secure us from it our ruler would see that we have to put our whole scheme of Government finance on a new basis, in one all-important matter. Hitherto it has been the custom for a Government to consider how much it wants to spend and to decide how best – or, more often, how with least offence to the multitude of voters – it can raise the money. When the national expenditure was a comparatively small part of the aggregate income of the nation, the system did little harm, though if practised by any business it would evidently very soon have led to disaster. Now that expenditure is so high, and is met in such a way that the very rich tax-payers have less than nothing to live on by the time they have paid income tax and surtax and insured against death duties,[1] it is high time to revise our system.

Robin Hood legislation,[2] so excellent in its effects within due limits, as shown by Mr. Tawney's admirable exposition of its benefits in his book on *Equality*, has overreached itself. It is eating into the big incomes and big estates which are so important as revenue producers; it is eating into the capital fund of industry so impairing its power to re-equip itself and go ahead; and it is eating into the hearts and courage of the organizers because they believe themselves to be unfairly treated. These facts were practically recog-

[1] See *ante*, p. 344.
[2] See *ante*, p. 346.

nized by Mr. Snowden in his 1931 Budget, which laid no further burdens on the wealthiest tax-payers.

Moreover, our present system produces chronic uncertainty in the months before the Budget whether the prospect is of surplus or of deficit. Who will be relieved? Or who will be hit? are almost equally unsettling questions when the business community has to make guesses about the answer. We want a system that will, in the first place, cut the coat according to the cloth; and in the second, give us more stability in fiscal expectations.

To this end our ruler would set on foot a short and searching examination of this question of the tax-paying power of the nation as reorganized on the lines suggested above. If he found, for example, that the limit of income tax, surtax and death duties, as they stood before Mr. Snowden screwed them all up in 1930, was as much as could safely be imposed without hurting the real interests of the nation and of the wage-earners, he would stabilize them at that point. But whatever might be the details of his new scheme, he would lay it down as the scheme of taxation that was to be followed for the next five or ten years. On the revenue derived from it he would base his expenditure. If, as may fairly be expected, the revenue increased, not 'by leaps and bounds' but steadily and rapidly, under the encouragement given to industry, he would expand expenditure on the social services and the thousands of desirable objects on which public money can be spent, part of the surplus being devoted either to increasing the pace of debt redemption, or to accumulating a national capital fund to be used in times of emergency such as the present. If the revenue did not suffice to meet the current rate of expenditure, expenditure would have to be reduced.

In the meantime what would be the attitude of our ruler towards the schemes of national development lately urged on the Government for utilizing the labour of the workless? Pledged, as we saw him at the outset, to see that any hands set free by the full use of machinery were amply provided for, would he want them to stand about idle, or to do some of the countless things that want doing and are not done, because industry does not see its way to making a profit out of them, and public bodies have not the courage or the power to set about them, and so everybody talks and waits and nothing is done?

The case for such schemes was admirably put by Sir Herbert Samuel in his speech on Unemployment in the House of Commons on 12th February 1931. He told us that 'in the last ten years the nation has spent upon the unemployed . . . apart from the expenditure from the Poor Law, the sum of £545,000,000, and we have, to show for that £545,000,000, not a mile of road, not a single cottage, and not an acre of woodland. If this is economy, what is waste? That sum would have given us a million houses and more. It would have paid for the whole of our road programme, the whole of our electricity programme, docks, harbours and forests over and over again. We have nothing whatever to show for it.'

But, of course, there are objections to Sir Herbert's contention that the Government should set about doing things needed for the improvement of the national equipment, the cost to be met by public loans to be subscribed from the capital resources now awaiting investment (which he showed to be plentiful); the service of these loans to be met partly out of economies in national expenditure, partly out of the Road Fund, and partly by a tax on the increased land values to be created by these schemes.

One objection is the argument put forward in a Treasury White Paper,[1] to the effect that any capital raised for these purposes would necessarily reduce the fund of capital available for industry and so would make unemployment as fast as it would check it. The Treasury is staffed by a very clever and brilliant set of gentlemen, whose only bias is a wholesome one against spending a penny of public money if it can be saved; and in normal times, when industry is active and confident, their argument is doubtless true. In 1929 there may have been a good deal of truth in it; but ever since then, as our leading industries were smothered under a deeper and deeper cloud, and vast amounts of capital are lying idle because industry offers no profitable outlet, it has become, as its authors would probably now acknowledge, increasingly fallacious.

There is also the alleged opposition of the City, which roused Mr. Lloyd George to keen invective in the course of the same debate. Certainly the City shivers, in the present state of markets, when grandiose suggestions of a £200,000,000 or £250,000,000 loan are put before it. But City opinion, as far as I gauge it in periodical visits, is by no means opposed to action of this kind on

---

[1] Memoranda on Certain Proposals relating to Unemployment, May 1929. (Cmd. 3331.)

a moderate scale. One of the shrewdest men at work there lately pointed out to me how much wanted doing, and how necessary it was that some body could be created which would act instead of waiting for the chatter to stop, which it never does. He mentioned Liverpool Street Station as clamouring to be put underground, so creating an exceedingly valuable site. Another City friend of mine wondered why, with 180,000 men unemployed in the building trade, little or nothing was done about slum clearances. Here, as he truly observed, there was no question of putting men into jobs to which they were not accustomed. And how many more years are we to have useless cackle, and nothing done, about Charing Cross Bridge and all the reconstruction there necessary?

Works of this kind, that would give employment to wage-earners and profits to contractors, but might not produce direct monetary benefit to those who paid for them, would evidently best be financed out of any surplus revenue provided by the reformed system of taxation suggested above. But there is no reason why something should not be done in this direction by loans raised by public bodies that would benefit by the rate-paying capacity of improved areas, or by Government loans if the schemes were on a national scale.

In fact there is a good deal of misunderstanding about this matter of public debt and the burden of it, and the dangers of increasing it. We are constantly terrified by being told that the debt charge costs nearly a million a day. So it does, but we collect it from ourselves and pay it back to ourselves (bating the small amount that goes to foreign holders, which is a fleabite compared with the sums that we collect from foreign debtors). This collection and distribution is a tiresome nuisance which we owe chiefly to the bad finance with which the war was paid for – or borrowed for – by Messrs. Lloyd George and Bonar Law;[1] and it warps the distribution of the national wealth in a way that has bad effects; but it does not reduce the national wealth, and moderate additions to debt, in times of emergency, have to be considered carefully, but not rejected as necessarily disastrous.

Along these lines, by securing a chance for machinery to work for us as it did during the war, and by adopting the tariff policy of the Conservatives, the maintenance of wages desired by Labour and the national schemes advocated by the Liberals (or some of them) our ruler might secure a great reduction in cost of production and a more confident spirit in industry and in the City.

It is not suggested that by means of Protection he could tax the nation into prosperity. But by a reduction of direct taxation and a moderate import duty, he could shift the fiscal burden in a way that would increase the funds available for investment and would allow industry to feel that at last it had something like a fair chance.

If, on the other hand, he decided that he had to follow the example of Germany, Italy and Japan and make all-round reductions, he would, we may hope, carry them out as impartially as Signor Mussolini has done, imposing them on all classes of the community, perhaps even including debt-holders and *rentiers* – all who receive fixed incomes and so get an advantage from

[1] See my book on *Bankers and Credit*, pp. 51, 52.

the lowered cost of living, as suggested by Sir Arthur Salter in the article already cited on page 410. (Sir Arthur only suggested special taxation on 'high' unearned incomes of this kind, but if all wage and salary earners are to be mulcted, why not all *rentiers*? — especially if the cut is to be tempered, as it should be, by retail price reductions.)

Any Government that gave the nation the right lead and put the facts of the position clearly before it would get a fine response from all classes and especially from the wage-earners. Witness Mr. Snowden in his speech at Colne Valley on 21st February, who said that since he had spoken in the House of Commons of the grave national emergency he had had thousands of letters, most of them from working-men. 'One was from a working-man at Birmingham who said he was greatly troubled about the position of the country and was only a poor man, but he wanted to do his bit and was sending a golden sovereign which he had kept since before the war and which he wished to be put to the national revenue.'[1]

If wholesale prices continue to fall some general readjustment of this kind will be forced upon us and upon all the rest of the commercial world. All the more reason for clear thinking on the measures involved by it and for clear explanation of the why and how to those whom it will affect.

Having thus given industry a chance to recover its confidence, and machinery a chance to shower a growing quantity of goods upon us, and the wage-earners and other consumers a chance to buy and

[1] *The Times*, 23rd February 1931.

enjoy them, our ruler would, I think, be inclined to leave industry free to develop itself under the guidance of the better spirit which the explanations of his experts would have helped to foster and extend. To this *laisser-faire* attitude he would be impelled by the results, for example, of the well-meant efforts of Governments to control the price of wheat[1] and of the Coal Mines Act of 1930, designed with the best intentions and followed by results which are not only disastrous but absurd. It was criticized during its passage through the House of Commons as involving Protection for foreign coal-using competitors by giving them cheap British fuel, and penalizing British industry by giving it dear coal. As to the working of the quota system, by which the output of different districts was regulated, we have the expert testimony of Sir Richard Redmayne expressed in a letter printed in *The Times* of 12th February 1931. 'The Act,' he writes, 'became operative at the beginning of the present year, and already some of its disastrous consequences are apparent, especially in the coal-exporting districts of Northumberland, Durham, and the East Coast of Scotland. At one colliery in Northumberland with which I am acquainted, situated in an isolated district, the demand which the colliery can meet is considerably in excess of the quota of production allotted to the colliery; consequently the consumers have to go far afield and pay a much higher price for their coal. A possible alternative – seeing the district is near to a port – would be for the larger users to import cheap Polish coal.

---

[1] See *ante*, p. 324.

'Another colliery had, under a well-conceived scheme of development spread over a long period, at last attained to an economic output and was worked at a profit: its quota killed that. Another profitable colliery has had to reduce its staff of workmen to the extent of one thousand owing to its enforced reduction of output. At yet another colliery the owners have determined to raise only the large coal, leaving the small coal below ground, a forced necessity which is definitely not in the national interest. The effect of the enforced reduction of output is clearly jeopardizing the colliery developments in Kent, which were so promising. And further instances might be given of the devastating effects resulting from this ill-conceived measure.

'The Coal Mines Bill of 1930 was nicknamed the Dear Coal Bill; it might, with equal relevance, have been designated the Unemployment Promotion Bill. Already suggestions are being made in certain quarters as to the advisability of repealing the provisions as to the quota. It is to be hoped, for the good of the industry, that these suggestions will become insistent, urgent, and widespread.'

Such examples of the effects of well-meant efforts by Governments to assist industry would encourage a wise ruler to incline to the old-fashioned view of the function of Government on matters touching enterprise – namely that it furthers the general interest best by leaving enterprise a free hand, while at the same time keeping a watchful eye on it in the interests of those parties to it which are weakened by numbers and by want of association. Formerly the wage-earners were most conspicuous by these weaknesses and though the power of the trade unions has enormously strengthened their position, no Government that desires to maintain the strength of the nation could afford to relax its vigilance concerning their interests. But in these days of amalgamations and combines and agreements among the managers of enterprise to restrict output and control prices, the interests of the consumer also need very careful watching.

Having for some time amused myself by bothering my friends by asking them what they would do if they were set to rule the country, I have been surprised to find how many of them have answered, 'Break the rings and combines that tyrannize over the shopkeepers and fleece the public,' or words to that effect. Other critics attack the huge amalgamations that have grown up in industry on the ground that they are now so bloated and top heavy that they have lost all elasticity and are more bureaucratic than a Government office.

Would a well-advised ruler set out to destroy them, or would he remember Mr. Pierpoint Morgan's saying that 'you cannot unscramble scrambled eggs,' and accept combines as things which, if well managed, promote economies and serve the public well? He might well consider that all that is wanted is clearer light on the processes that make the goods that we buy so often look monstrously dear as compared with the price of the materials that compose them. With this object he would use the powers of the Consumers' Council referred to on page 407, intimating to the organizers of the combines that if they were found to be persisting in fleecing the consumer he would take measures to hand over their business to municipal or public enterprise, or to bodies such as the Electricity Board or the London Transport Authority.

It has long been a commonplace among those who try to peer into the future that industry, by giving up competition and working for monopoly, is doing more to promote Socialism than the arguments of the Socialists. In the old sense of State Socialism, with all enterprise to be managed by public officials, Socialism is in these days somewhat out of fashion. We have the evidence of that keen but candid Socialist, Mr. G. D. H. Cole, cited on page 94, that 'the Civil Service method of administration is too rigid and slow in its working to fit the needs of a big modern business.' And the fashionable tendency among those to whom the alleged greed and wastefulness of private enterprise are too disgusting to be borne, is in the direction of these public boards working, on the lines that have been tried and tested by private enterprise, to provide the public with necessary services. London's transport problem is handed by a Socialist Government not to the Ministry of Transport or the London County Council but to a statutory board which is to be composed of persons who have wide experience, who have shown capacity in industry, commerce (including transport) or finance, or in the conduct of public affairs.[1] How these boards will work remains to be seen. If they succeed they may prove to be an excellent compromise between bureaucratic and private control of industry, especially in certain lines of service that have an assured market and do not need the nimble-

---

[1] Mr. H. Morrison on the London Traffic Bill. *The Times*, 24th March 1931.

ness of the individual working for his own profit. But there is plenty of room for all forms and kinds of enterprise. If only we can keep our tempers and be moderately reasonable and sensible, production is going to be so vast and the satisfactions and enjoyments of men and women are going to be so many and so varied that there will be work for State Socialism, public boards, international cartels mapping out the world into markets and reducing tariffs to waste-paper, combines turning out standardized stuff on mass production lines, small firms and companies specializing on finer products – and we shall even be able to afford to revive the craftsman, working for us with his own hands on choice and beautiful things. We need not be afraid of mechanization or of being mechanized, for if we make the right use of machinery it will give us so much wealth and leisure that we can bring back the handicrafts and even, if we are so inclined, be craftsmen ourselves.

CHAPTER XXV

WHAT WE CAN DO OURSELVES

Recognizing the Point of View of Others – Working Well – Economic Freedom – 'Disinclination to Work' – Good Sense Behind the Feeling – Justified by Better Work while we are at it – Our Recent Slackness – Is Saving a Mistake? – Need for Capital – Wealth and Contentment.

How can we all of us help to bring all these pleasant things about?

First of all by being good tempered and reasonable and seeing that other people, whose interests appear to be opposed to ours, have a point of view that we have to consider, and that we can only get what we all want, which is a pleasant and happy life and plenty of material comfort, if we all work together for it.

If we are capitalists and employers we have to remember that the claims of those who do the hard, dull work, to a better share of the good things produced, is eminently reasonable, and that the granting of this claim in ever-increasing measure will be good for us and for business in general, because it means increased buying power and a steady consumers' market; and further, that if the wage- and salary-earners sometimes seem in too much of a hurry to press their claim, that is largely owing to mistakes made by our predecessors in the past.

If we are wage- and salary- and fee-earners, belonging to that great mass that has to make its own way in life with no inherited advantage behind us, we may, perhaps, think that we do not get a fair start in life or a fair share of the good things produced and that those who are born better off have unfair advantages which enable them to exploit us. But that is no reason for regarding them as wicked and tyrannical blood-suckers. They are, in fact, just the sort of people that we should have been if we had been born and bred as they have been. They have been taught to believe that property and the rights of property are a necessary part of the scheme of life as it has been developed by our civilization, and that the world could not be fed and clothed and made comfortable – as it has been with growing success during the past century – without them; and that until a new system has been evolved which will do the work better they are fully entitled to believe that the preservation of their rights is essential to the prosperity of all. Even if we think this reasoning wrong, we need not accuse those who employ of being wicked or selfish, because in fact most of them are quite ordinary human beings and no more wicked or selfish than any of us.

If we are born to great wealth, or with gifts or with luck that bring us great wealth easily, we have to remember that we could not have inherited or won or fluked our way to wealth, if the rest of the community had not been there to provide it. However great our gifts it is our fellows who enable them to fructify – a fact that we should never forget when enjoying their rewards.

Having made this reformation in our attitude of mind towards all the other people who are claimants to a share in the flow of wealth, we shall find that we have changed the whole atmosphere in which the business of the world is conducted. It is no longer one of bitterness in which everybody is trying to defend himself against somebody else's unjust aggression, but one in which we are all making a fair and reasonable effort to better our position. And when once this is recognized it becomes clear that the great increase in the general power to produce the things that everybody is wanting becomes a blessing instead of a curse, because it enables us to achieve our reasonable ambition by dividing a constantly growing supply of material comfort.

If we only try to increase our share by taking a bit of somebody else's, the consequent friction prevents growth of the general product. The essential thing is to increase the general product first and then do our best to see that our proportion of the general dividend is as good as we can claim, with due consideration for the claims of others.

In order to help the general increase in the product each one of us can do something by doing his or her job well according to the old copy-book virtues of punctuality and honesty and so on, recognizing that each of us puts a tiny trickle of service into the great pool, out of which, owing to the work of all the others, we can help ourselves to a great and growing diversity of benefits.

But this great pool is only fed by the multiplicity of these millions of trickles, and if everybody thinks only of what he or she takes out and tries to put as little as possible in, the pool instead of being full to the brim of pleasant contents is filled with muddy coagulations which cannot get distributed because of what is called maladjustment.

Coming down from the general to the particular, we have to recognize that the great majority of us, who are blessed with average intelligence and gifts, have to do some work that other people want. It is only the genius who is justified in deciding that he knows what work he wants to do and will not do any other. 'Economic freedom' is a claim that is often put forward as the birthright of every man and woman born in a civilized country, as it surely is. But what does it mean? It cannot be freedom to work on what interests and amuses us and to refuse to work on anything else; for if we all did that, the contents of the pool would be varied rather than useful and might be uncomfortably scanty. However high the level of civilization under which we live may be, we are still, just like our primitive ancestors, obliged to make some effort, of a kind that is probably in some ways irksome, if we are to make the best material use of our span of life. The freedom that civilization gives us is the right to work on any work that we can do that is wanted by other members of the community; to be kept alive by our fellows if we fail; and to enjoy an immense range of benefits if we succeed or even if we fail.

Some day, if we can all leave off quarrelling and give machinery a fair chance to work for us, wealth may grow so fast that the Anarchist conception of society may be realized, under which, as Mr. Bertrand Russell tells us, 'all the commoner commodities will be available to every one without stint, in the kind of way in which water is available at present,' and there would be what he calls a 'vagabond's wage,' sufficient for existence but not for luxury.[1] But we have not yet reached that point, and in fact we still have to pay water rates for the water that he believes to be available without stint.

If we bear these platitudes in mind and remember that all work under modern conditions brings us into association with our fellows and that this association is one of the pleasantest things in life if it has good temper behind it, and that good temper is bound to be behind it if we supply enough of it ourselves, work becomes a pastime instead of a nuisance – as indeed many of us find when we are bored on holidays because we have not learnt the very necessary art of amusing ourselves.

'I venture to suggest,' said a chairman at a meeting in February 1931, 'that the disinclination to work, which appears to have affected all classes in England, lies at the root of our trouble.' This attitude towards work on the part of the citizens of this country, though highly inopportune at the present crisis, has a certain sound sense behind it. To turn oneself into a working machine with no other interests in life apart from our job is to renounce the chance of being a human being in the fullest sense of the phrase. Work is a means to enjoyment and if we can get a certain amount of enjoyment out of it, so much the better; as we can if we are good tempered about it and work with good-

[1] *Roads to Freedom*, pp. 108 and 179.

tempered people. But we waste our lives if we make work our one object as the typical American as portrayed by Mr. Garet Garrett is alleged to do – 'he does not know what to do with idleness. He does not understand it. Generally it kills him.'[1] But leisure, if we know how to use it, is not idleness at all, but the time in which we are most active and alive.

Compared with this ideal of life, which turns men into beings working as tirelessly as bees or ants, there is much to be said for the English preference for short hours and long week-ends in the upper ranks of the business army, for the demand of the wage-earners to 'do little work and to receive Imperial wages which the Continental worker does not claim,' as described by an Italian critic quoted in an earlier chapter,[2] and for the refusal of our women, as M. Siegfried tells us,[3] to delight in economy as they do in France – haggling for half an hour over a ha'porth of greenstuff is not really an ennobling pastime.

Rightly used, the greater opportunities for leisure claimed by our business leaders and those whom they organize, may make them do their work all the better while they are about it; and they certainly, if not insisted on beyond a point that the country's industry can afford, give those who indulge in them a chance of leaving behind them a more civilized race. It may be that England, having shown the world how to industrialize itself, and supplied it with much of the capital and equipment and many of the hands needed for the task, has now to teach it how to make reasonable use

[1] Quoted by Mr. Truslow Adams, in *A Searchlight on America*.
[2] See *ante*, p. 57.   [3] *England's Crisis*, p. 72.

of the leisure that science and machinery are to provide, but which few people know how to enjoy.

But if we are disinclined to work and have in normal times a good deal of common sense behind this prejudice that is all the more reason for putting quality into our work, and doing it quickly and well instead of scamping it, either because we are lazy or because we believe that if we leave some of it undone there will be all the more for others to do. When it takes two to do a job that ought to be done by one the cost of the article produced is raised, the consumer is charged too much, and cannot buy so freely, the shareholder or whoever it may be that provides the capital gets a lower profit, and so there is less inducement to capital to expand enterprise and want more hands and machinery, so that more good things may be turned out to supply the public with more material comfort.

At a time of crisis such as the present when the cheapening of manufactured articles, so as to bring back equilibrium between their price and that of food and materials, is essential to the recovery of world trade on which all countries depend more or less for prosperity, we can all help this great cause by working well and intelligently while we are about it, and getting the best reward that we can for our work, with due consideration of the other parties – those who provide the machinery and equipment, those who organize the manufacture and distribution, and those who buy the article that is finally delivered.

If England is to maintain her relatively high scale of wages, and the social expenditure in which she has set the world so fine an example, blotted as usual by blunders and bungling, this improvement in the quality of the work in all the ranks of her industrial army is evidently required. The Balfour Committee's insistence on the need for 'at least an equivalent improvement in the quality of the higher control, accompanying technical and physical reorganization,'[1] has already been quoted as also its observations on the attitude of labour in England as compared with America, concerning the free and full use of machinery[2] and the slackness of British industry in looking for trade openings and applying the necessary salesmanship is a commonplace that hits one's eye almost every time that one opens a newspaper. To-day's example is to be found in *The Times* of 25th February 1931, which summarizes a report of the Sheffield Industrial Mission to South America. The two main points dealt with in the report are, why Sheffield has lost trade in South American markets, and the steps necessary to increase trade. On the first point the report states that 'the falling off is due primarily to two factors – the war, which gave competitors in North America a priceless opportunity to establish their position, and our serious neglect of the South American market. Many well-known Sheffield firms appear to have no representation in the whole Continent or representation in a few areas only. Visits of managing directors, sales managers, etc., from the factories are infrequent.

'As a result, firms of old-established connexions and well-known brands have been losing ground through lack of personal contact and not keeping *au fait* with the changes of requirements, market conditions, and prices.'

[1] See *ante*, p. 399.   [2] See *ante*, p. 61.

It is clear that we have been over-indulging that disinclination to work which is so sensible within due limits. As a nation we have been running on too rich a mixture – paying our debts while our neighbours have been repudiating all or most of theirs, raising the standard of our wage-earners' lives in a period of world crisis, lending more than we could afford while others have been hoarding, spending while others have been scraping and stinting, and at the same time working on slipshod methods and generally treating life as a game (which it ought to be), when it was really rather serious. This mistake, if we correct it, gives us a useful card up our sleeves as compared with our rivals who have been working their hardest while we have been wanting too much and doing too little. If we do not correct this mistake our finer conception of what business life should be, runs risk of bankruptcy.

And when we have done our work better what should we do with the reward – spend every shilling that we earn, or save a proportion of it, to provide for our old age and for any dependents that we may leave? The old-fashioned idea was that by saving we not only gave ourselves a comfortable feeling of security but supplied industry with capital, without which it cannot expand or even maintain its activity in providing the wants of all of us. Nowadays, many people believe that saving is a mistake and quote in favour of this view the high authority of Mr. Keynes, who told the listening millions in the course of a broadcast address, that according to the best guess he could make, 'whenever you save five shillings, you put a man out of work for a day.'[1]

[1] The *Listener*, 14th January 1931.

Taken by itself this sentence seems to encourage us all to indulge in any form of extravagance that we fancy and it was so interpreted by *Punch*, which next week depicted a lady buying, as a matter of duty, a hat which, as she admitted, she did not need, because somebody had said that every five shillings saved put some poor dear thing out of work. But the worst of these great economists is, that they contradict one another nearly always and themselves very often. A minute before, Mr. Keynes had mentioned as mistaken, those who believe that the most useful thing that they can do to mend the situation is to 'save more than usual.' Which did he mean – that saving more than usual is wrong, or that all saving is wrong?

It is very puzzling; and so was another of his observations – that 'the object of saving is to release labour for employment on producing capital goods such as houses, factories, roads, machines and the like. But if there is a large unemployed surplus already available for such purposes, then the effect of saving is merely to add to this surplus, and therefore to increase the number of unemployed.' But is it not also the object of saving to provide the money for those who would like to employ it, and, with it, all the human hands that capital expenditure sets busy on enterprise at home and abroad?

Further on in the same address Mr. Keynes tells us, in an eloquent and noble passage, that he would like to 'pull down the whole of South London from Westminster to Greenwich and make a good job of it – housing on that convenient area near to their work a much greater population than at present in far better buildings with all the conveniences of modern life, yet at the same time providing hundreds of acres of squares and avenues, parks and public spaces, having, when it was finished, something magnificent to the eye, yet useful and convenient to human life as a monument to our age. Would that' – he asked triumphantly – 'employ men? Why, of course it would!'

And, of course, 'so say all of us.' But how is it to be done if nobody saves the necessary money? Perhaps Mr. Keynes means that there is also a large unemployed surplus of capital, and that public bodies that asked for it would find no difficulty in supplying themselves, which is quite true – at a price. But if more were saved and invested the price would be lower, and borrowers would be encouraged to do the kind of work that he has so attractively described. And all over the world there are openings for capital, if more saving made it more plentiful and less shy. Mr. Graham, President of the Board of Trade, told us some time ago that over a large part of the world we have only scratched the surface of economic development and that there are countries in Europe 'which, rightly guided, could carry three or four times their present population.'[1] To-day China, having apparently finished her civil war, offers immense possibilities of development and of demand for machinery, railways, and all other kinds of industrial equipment; and Mr. Keynes, as already quoted on page 323, has told us that 'the whole course of international trade and finance depends on the steady flow of lending'; and though he also expressed the view that England should sit back until someone else takes up the

---

[1] *The Times*, 23rd October 1929.

running in the lending business, he also said that
'someone must lend if a catastrophe is to be avoided.'
And the stimulus given by foreign lending to the
export trade, now so generally depressed, was noted on
page 105. But we cannot lend if we do not save.

But all these puzzling counsels appear to be meant to
apply to the present crisis. In the broadcast address
which made saving appear to be a wicked folly, Mr.
Keynes, if I have not misunderstood him, admitted that
in certain circumstances it would be quite right for us
not only to save but to save more than usual; and by
acting as chairman of a Life Insurance Company he
evidently lends his high authority to that valuable form
of saving, which is not indulged nearly as freely as it
ought to be.[1] So that on the whole we may conclude
that saving is certainly good for ourselves and can
make out a fair case for being good, both now and at
all times – until the whole capitalist system has been
reconstructed so that private savings are no longer
necessary – for England and for the rest of the world.

Finally, we have to remember that all efforts made,
whether by nations or by individuals, to increase their
wealth and their command of material comfort are
useless and worse if they do not bring us contentment;
that nothing will bring us contentment unless we make
it for ourselves; and that if we have contentment we
can snap our fingers at the tricks of fortune. If we are
always going to think that we are poor because Jones
round the corner has more money to spend, there can

[1] The Chairman of the Prudential Assurance Company stated, at its
meeting held on 5th March 1931, that the approximate sums assured per
head of the population in the United Kingdom is £53 compared with £164
in the United States, £137 in Canada, and £79 in Australia.

be no end to struggle and dissatisfaction. Real wealth is merely well-being, and that we can make for ourselves very easily by taking a cheerful view about our position, comparing it with that of our predecessors of a hundred years ago who had just about a quarter of our material comforts and none at all of many other advantages that we now enjoy, and remembering that a small income well used gives much more happiness than a big one that is wasted on ostentation, emulation and vulgarity.

If we take this view we can make life what it ought to be, an amusing game that we play, not to win a heap of counters, but for the fun of playing the game like good sportsmen.

THE
QUICKSANDS
OF THE CITY

and a Way Through
for Investors

HARTLEY WITHERS
Author of *The Meaning of Money*

'In *The Quicksands of the City*, Mr. Hartley Withers has added one more to the series of eminently readable books which he has already written on economic subjects. The object of the present work is to help investors to avoid the numerous pitfalls that beset them. . . . It will be more acceptable to the general public because the author has the great gift of using language, even when dealing with the more abstruse branches of economics, that is as understandable to the layman as it is to the trained economist.'

The Daily Telegraph

'An excellent book has been written by Mr. Hartley Withers, the distinguished economist, and a man of very sane views on financial questions.'

Sir George A. Touche Bt. speaking at the ordinary general meeting of the Industrial and General Trust Ltd.

6s. net

JONATHAN CAPE · BEDFORD SQUARE · LONDON

INDEX

INDEX

INDEX

INDEX